Evidence

Evidence
Essential Terms and Concepts

Mark Reutlinger
Seattle University School of Law

ASPEN LAW & BUSINESS
A Division of Aspen Publishers, Inc.

This publication is designed to provide accurate and authoritative information in regard to the subject matter covered. It is sold with the understanding that the publisher is not engaged in rendering legal, accounting, or other professional services. If legal advice or other professional assistance is required, the services of a competent professional person should be sought.

—From a *Declaration of Principles* jointly adopted by a Committee of the American Bar Association and Committee of Publishers and Associations

1 2 3 4 5

To my parents and to Analee and Eliana

Summary of Contents

Contents

Contents

Chapter 4.   Scientific and Probabilistic Evidence   49

Contents

Contents

Chapter 6.   Real and Demonstrative Evidence — 121

Contents

Chapter 8. Testimonial Evidence 147

Contents

Chapter 9. Opinion Evidence 181

Contents

Contents

Contents

Acknowledgments

My thanks to Seattle University School of Law and Dean Jim Bond for their continuing support of my publications. I am grateful as well to my secretary Nancy Ammons for her usual flawless work on the manuscript; to my colleagues George Nock and John Mitchell for their helpful comments; to the editorial staff at Little, Brown, including Carolyn O'Sullivan, Joan Horan, Amy Novit, and Vanessa Corzano; and, as always, to my students, for all I have learned in the course of teaching them.

Introduction

This book is the second I have written in this series. The first dealt with the subjects of estates and trusts. This book, on the subject of evidence, has the same format, structure, and underlying philosophy as the former one. It too seeks to combine the benefits of a quick reference work with those of a short treatise, using simple language, concise discussions, and clear examples. There are also numerous diagrams and charts to illustrate some of the more complex or esoteric concepts: Just as mysteries like the rule against perpetuities were clarified by diagram in the first book, so are concepts such as hearsay and presumptions diagrammed here.

Because, then, the books are identical in all but subject matter, I reproduce below the introduction to my first book, suitably modified and containing additional information relevant only to the present book. If you have already used the estates book, you are familiar with my methods and can begin with section 3, on style.

1. Functions of this Book: When and Why to Use It

One of the most difficult aspects of a student's attempts to master a legal subject is the new, esoteric language that each subject employs. As a student you encounter not only unknown words but also unfamiliar concepts requiring more explanation than a dictionary definition can provide. Moreover, you do not necessarily encounter these terms and concepts in the order in which they will be taken up in class; they appear all along the way, since it is difficult or impossible to cover early materials (and edit early cases) without referring to concepts that will be more fully discussed later.

Of course, you can look up individual words in a law dictionary; there they are briefly defined and scattered throughout the book, with no immediate connection to one another. At the other extreme, you can turn to a full treatise, look for the term or concept in the index, and if you are fortunate and the index contains what you are seeking, you can read a lengthy discussion that at some point and in some manner relates to the term or concept in question. Most often, however, the index either is insufficiently detailed and lacks the particular term in question or contains the term but leads to a much broader discussion than you want or, at this stage, need.

Just as early materials cannot be presented without some reference to what will appear later, later materials usually must refer back to earlier terms and concepts that you may no longer recall. And when studying for exams, you will often need to review a forgotten term or the essence of a fuzzy concept. Here again neither a dictionary nor a treatise fully serves. What you need for all these related purposes is a quick reference text geared to specific terms and concepts.

This is that book. It is a short textual analysis of specific topics in evidence. You can peruse these discussions before or after their coverage in class to prepare yourself for, or confirm your understanding of, the primary course materials. Many entries include detailed examples that supplement those in your casebook or class notes.

This book, then, is neither a legal dictionary nor a treatise. It goes beyond mere definition of terms and concepts but does not purport to cover all their legal implications and permutations. Rather, it is intended to be used as a companion to your casebook or text. As such it has been organized for use in the two principal ways just discussed:

(1) As a quick-reference glossary of definitions and explanations of individual terms or concepts in the law of evidence. In this mode, it is a resource for the times when, in reading an assignment, you encounter a term or concept that has not yet been covered in the course or whose meaning you cannot immediately recall. Even if a term or concept is vaguely or generally recalled, reference to it in these pages will offer another definition, often with explanatory illustrations, that may solidify your understanding of it.

(2) As a brief overview of a given area of the law of evidence. While not intended as a comprehensive text (and containing few of the case or statute references of a research volume), this book is structured by topic so that it can be read as a unified discussion by moving through a chapter from one entry to the next. At the beginning of each topic and subtopic, a brief introduction sets out the general content and organization of the material that follows. This topical format can serve several related purposes: It can be used to survey briefly an area of the law prior to its detailed treatment in the course, familiarizing you with the meaning of the major terms and concepts before they are encountered—and puzzled over—in the assigned materials. This should make your subsequent reading of the cases and other materials easier and more productive. And because related terms and concepts are placed together in logical order, you are encouraged to read beyond the initial entry that you looked up to learn about related concepts, thus

putting the discussion into context and resulting in a better understanding of the relevant area of law.

2. Format of the Book: How to Use It

As indicated, terms and concepts in this book are set out in logical, not alphabetical, order. To find an item alphabetically, simply look it up in the Master Word List in the back of the book, where you will find the page on which it is principally discussed. To look up an item according to its topical placement, turn to the beginning of any chapter and review its word list, where each term or concept is set out in the order in which it is found in that chapter.

Principal terms and concepts are set out in **bold type** prior to their discussion. Within any entry, other terms or concepts that are primarily explained at that point are similarly set out in **bold type.** (If you look up such a term or concept in the Master Word List, it will refer you back to the present discussion.) If a term or concept is primarily defined or discussed elsewhere in the book, it is in normal type. If you wish to find that principal discussion, simply look up the word in the Master Word List. By using cross-references, you can obtain a more comprehensive understanding of the concept that you first looked up. However, each entry is intended to be self-contained and generally should not require reference to any other.

3. Notes on Style

You will note the frequent use in this book of terms such as "general" and "usual." Because it is not the purpose of the book to set out all of the law in an area, but only to familiarize you with the general meaning and application of a term or concept, in most instances no attempt is made to account for all possible variations of a definition or doctrine that states might have developed. Thus reference is made to the "general" rule, what is "usually" done, or what "most" statutes provide. If you are concerned with the law or practice in a specific jurisdiction, you should be sure to seek this information in an appropriate text or statute, and you should not assume that the general statement set out here necessarily applies to your state.

An exception to the above is the Federal Rules of Evidence. Whenever a term or concept has a Federal Rules counterpart, that Rule is set out in **bold type** and any substantial differences from the general concept are explained. (The Federal Rules of Evidence List will refer you to these bold-type references, for easy access to specific Rules.) In addition, where the Federal Rules are silent or there are important state variations on a concept, reference may be made to the Uniform Rules of Evidence (URE) or the California Evidence Code (CEC). I have chosen California's code based on its significant departures from the Federal Rules, its place as a pioneering evidence code that was an important precursor to the Federal Rules, and the practical fact that many evidence courses and course materials use it as an example of a "non-Federal Rules" approach to evidence.

The terms "state," "jurisdiction," and "statute" (as in "some states' [jurisdictions] [statutes] require . . .") are usually used synonymously and interchangeably for stylistic variety, not to connote different concepts or legal entities.

The definition or explanation of a term or concept in this book relates specifically to the subject of evidence, although there may be other meanings or usages of the term outside these fields. The term "relevant," for example, is defined here according to its use as a term of art in the law of evidence, although it may have a somewhat different meaning or connotation in general usage.

Although I have included detailed reference to the Federal Rules of Evidence, I have kept citation to cases to a minimum. The cases supporting the rules discussed in this book are all found in any standard evidence casebook. As this text is intended primarily as a supplement to other course materials, it does not attempt to duplicate their coverage or function. When, however, a case is so important to, or so identified with, a topic or concept that it should not be omitted, it is indeed mentioned, with citation. There is also occasional reference to the treatises of the great evidence scholars of this and previous generations, such as Thayer, McCormick, and, of course, Wigmore.

Finally, gender-specific references have been avoided whenever possible and when an alternative would not be awkward.

4. Topical Organization: An Overview

Because the organization of this book is similar to that of many evidence casebooks (although there is wide variation in this regard), you should be able to follow in it the progress of the course. It is divided into chapters representing the major topics in the course and in the law of evidence. Within a chapter, terms and concepts are set out and discussed individually in a logical, unified order. Subheadings are used to indicate a logical breakdown of subtopics within a chapter, and each chapter and subheading begins with a brief overview of the material to follow.

Here is a synopsis of the topics covered. (You may want to look up any of the terms you do not recognize, as they are all explained in the chapters that follow.)

Introduction

Chapter 1 contains concepts that form the general "language" of evidence. It covers everything from the term "evidence" itself, evidence codes, and the order of presentation of evidence in a common-law trial to the concepts of admission, foundation, and objection. Chapter 2 concerns relevance, the *sina qua non* for the admission of any form of evidence. It distinguishes direct from circumstantial evidence and describes, with diagrams, the operation and function of an inference. Chapter 3 explores a particular aspect of relevance, the use of character evidence. It discusses the types of character evidence that are and are not admissible, as well as the form in which such evidence, when admissible, may be presented. The subject of Chapter 4 is the use of scientific evidence (also an aspect of relevancy). The *Frye* and *Daubert* formulas are explained, and a separate section is devoted to the increasingly important field of probability theory.

Chapter 5, the longest in the book, examines the subject to which most evidence courses devote the most time, hearsay. It explains, with numerous examples and diagrams, the definition of hearsay and how to distinguish hearsay from non-hearsay uses of evidence. It then covers each of the traditional hearsay exceptions, as well as the newer, "nontraditional" ones found in modern evidence codes like the Federal Rules.

Chapter 6 is as brief as the previous chapter is lengthy. It discusses real and demonstrative evidence, that is, the various objects that are introduced into evidence, from a murder weapon found at the scene, to a diagram of the scene sketched on a pad, to a computerized re-creation of the crime itself. Chapter 7 also concerns tangible evidence, in this case, writings. Both authentication and the effect of the Best Evidence (or original document) Rule are discussed. Chapter 8 covers the broad topic of testimonial evidence. It is divided into sections describing the presentation of testimonial evidence (including witness qualification and examination) and the challenges to testimony by such devices as cross-examination and the introduction of impeaching evidence.

Opinion evidence is the subject of Chapter 9. Both lay and expert opinion, and the areas in which they overlap, are explained and illustrated. Chapter 10 then covers the substantial topic of privilege. The chapter begins with a description of privileges in general and proceeds to an examination of specific privileges, such as marital and attorney-client privilege. For each such privilege, there is a summary description of the major elements as well as a more detailed discussion (with examples) of its operation.

Chapter 11 discusses burdens of proof and presumptions. There are numerous diagrams illustrating the sometimes mysterious operation of these basic procedural devices. Finally, Chapter 12 is about the often neglected but nevertheless important topic of judicial notice, an "evidence substitute" that can greatly simplify the proof process. The chapter discusses taking notice of both adjudicative and legislative facts.

This is the logical order (or at least *a* logical order) in which these topics arise. But the book is meant to be used in any order, topic by topic or term by term. Turn to it often and let it help you around and through both the basic and the more esoteric concepts in the law of Evidence.

Evidence

1

General Principles and Terminology

A. Sources of the Law
  Common Law
  Federal Rules of Evidence
  Uniform Rules of Evidence
  Evidence Codes
B. Basic Concepts and Procedural Terminology
  Evidence
  Adversary System
    Inquisitorial System
  Trier of Fact
    Bench (Court) Trial
    Stipulation
  Exhibit
    Marked for Identification
  Foundation
    Preliminary Questions
    Predicate
  Admissibility
    Weight
    Trial Tactics
  Limited Admissibility
    Multiple Admissibility
    Limiting Instruction
    Cautionary Instruction
  Curative Instruction
  Authentication (In General)
    Identification
  Self-Authentication (In General)
  Corroboration
  Objection
    Specific Objection
    General Objection
    Continuing Objection
    Sustained
    Overruled
    Plain Error

1

Introduction and Overview of Chapter

Chapter 1 introduces the basic terms and concepts that underlie all of evidence law. It begins with an explanation of the various statutory and non-statutory sources in which the law of evidence is (or has been) found. It then defines evidence itself and explains the procedural mechanisms by which evidence is offered to the court and evaluated for admissibility.

In other words, this chapter contains the means by which to apply all of the rules of evidence that make up the balance of this book.

A. SOURCES OF THE LAW

Common Law

The Anglo-American legal system; also, the law of a jurisdiction developed by its courts, rather than set out in its statutes. The term is generally capitalized in the former usage, but not in the latter.

Most state and federal law is based on the English Common Law. In contrast, the legal system of Louisiana is based on the **civil law** system, derived from Roman law and prevalent in most of continental Europe. (In this work, when a comparison is made between the Federal Rules of Evidence (FRE) and the pre-existing "common law," the lower case will be used, although state common law often is identical with the Common Law as originally received from England.)

All states have or had a body of common law of evidence, but most have now codified their evidence law in whole or in part. (See *Evidence Codes*.) The federal court system operates largely under the FRE, and many states have adopted these rules as their own. Even the federal courts, however, must turn to federal common law for the determination of certain evidentiary issues, such as privilege.

Federal Rules of Evidence

The rules of evidence that govern trials in federal courts, both civil and criminal.

The Federal Rules of Evidence were promulgated in 1975, after a long and tortuous journey. In 1942, the American Law Institute created a uniform code of evidence that could be adopted by both federal and state jurisdictions. No state, however, adopted this Model Code of Evidence. In 1953, the National Conference of Commissioners on Uniform State Laws (the sponsors of such widely adopted uniform rules as the Uniform Commercial Code) promulgated Uniform Rules of Evidence (URE), but only a few states adopted them or codes based on them.

In 1965, Chief Justice Warren appointed an Advisory Committee on Rules of Evidence, as had been proposed by the Judicial Conference of the United States. (This is the "Advisory Committee" whose notes appear in most annotated versions of the Rules.) The Supreme Court approved a final version in 1972, after seven years of drafting and comments from bench, bar, and public. Due to special legislation, however, the FRE still required specific approval of both houses of Congress. Hearings were held by the House and Senate Committees on the Judiciary, many amendments were made (some quite significant and a few after heated political debate), and finally, in January of 1975, the Federal Rules of Evidence were signed into law by President Ford.

Current status. To date, about three-quarters of the states (plus Guam, Puerto Rico, and the Armed Forces) have adopted or modelled their own evidence rules on limited or substantial parts of the FRE, making them and their interpretive cases the most important single body of evidence law in the United States. It must be emphasized, however, that none of the states has adopted all of the Federal Rules; moreover, the 14 states that do not follow the FRE include California, New York, Illinois, Virginia, Pennsylvania, and Massachusetts, representing nearly half of the country's population. Even if your state has adopted a substantial portion of the Federal Rules, you should not assume that the FRE represent the only, or necessarily the best, solution to any given evidence problem.

It is also important to remember that evidence rules existed in every jurisdiction long before the FRE were promulgated, and for the most part the FRE were themselves a codification and refinement of those existing rules. Therefore, even if your evidence course covers only the FRE, the meaning, intent, and rationale behind this modern codification are found in its common law roots and their development over the several centuries prior to 1975.

Uniform Rules of Evidence

A body of evidence rules intended as a model for adoption, in whole or in part, by individual states.

The URE were first propounded in 1953, by the National Conference of Commissioners on Uniform State Laws.

While not as widely adopted as the Federal Rules of Evidence, the URE were very influential in the drafting of several state evidence codes and of the FRE themselves. They often provided a significant variation on, or contrast to, positions taken by the FRE.

In 1974 the Uniform Rules were substantially rewritten, and as revised they closely follow the Federal Rules, with some significant variations. Unless otherwise indicated, references in this book to the URE are to these revised Rules.

Evidence Codes

Bodies of evidence rules compiled and codified by state legislatures, to fit the needs and inclinations of their particular trial court systems.

The California Evidence Code, one of the earliest and most thorough codifications, influenced the drafting of the Federal Rules of Evidence, which in turn serve as the model for the majority of current state codes. Occasional reference is made in this book to the California code (CEC) as an example of a "non-Federal Rules" codification.

A state's evidence code often will combine features common to all or most state evidence law (such as the basic hearsay rule) with some that are unique to that state (such as a state's "rape shield" statute or rules regarding privilege or impeachment of witnesses). Even those evidence codes that largely adopt the Federal Rules of Evidence will have at least some different or modified provisions; therefore, it is important always to consult the evidence code of the state in whose trial court an evidentiary issue arises.

Not every state has codified its evidence law. In some, most or all evidence rules are still found in decisional law (state common law), with reliance on stare decisis to assure uniformity of application.

B. BASIC CONCEPTS AND PROCEDURAL TERMINOLOGY

Evidence

That body of material which proves, or is offered to prove, a matter in issue. The law of evidence is a set of rules that determines which parts of that body of material may be presented to and considered by a court or other tribunal.

Categorizing evidence. There are several ways in which evidence can be categorized, all of which are discussed in this book. The major distinctions and some typical examples of them are as follows:

Types of Evidence

- Testimonial (a live witness) vs. Physical (a tangible object).
- Within physical evidence, Documentary (a letter, deed, or contract) vs. Real (the alleged murder weapon) vs. Demonstrative (a diagram of where the murder weapon was found).
- Direct ("I saw him do it") vs. Hearsay ("He told me he did it").

Uses of Evidence

- Direct ("I saw him commit the crime") vs. Circumstantial ("I saw him near the scene of the crime").
- Substantive (testimony by W that defendant committed the crime) vs. Impeachment (proof that W couldn't have seen defendant committing the crime).

Evidence and admissibility. Evidence must be distinguished from admissible evidence. (See *Admissibility.*) A fact may, in the abstract, prove or tend to prove another fact and yet not be admissible as evidence of that fact in a trial. Thus evidence, in a legal sense, is always a relative term: The question is not whether the smoking pistol is evidence of the defendant's guilt, but whether it is admissible evidence of his guilt. And inevitably, the answer will be, "it depends." As the discussions on "relevance," "materiality," and "prejudice" will explore, it may depend on whether the fact in issue (to be proved) is possessing a weapon or murder; murder by poisoning or by shooting; shooting by pistol or by shotgun; whether the defendant has conceded the act or contested it; and to what extent the proof would be cumulative, time-consuming, or unduly prejudicial.

Adversary System

The method of formal adjudication, or settling of disputes, used in Common Law jurisdictions, that relies on the opposing parties ("adversaries") to present and defend their respective positions before an impartial and largely passive tribunal. (The term "adversarial system" is often used, but in this context "adversary system" is technically correct.)

In an adversary system, evidence is gathered and presented by the parties or their advocates (attorneys). In contrast, most countries of continental Europe (Civil Law countries) employ the **inquisitorial system** of adjudication, under which primary responsibility for gathering and presenting evidence is placed on the judge.

Although the term "inquisitorial" has a bad image because of its association with the Spanish Inquisition, the Grand Inquisitor, et al., it refers to nothing more sinister than proceeding by inquiry, and as it is a system that is employed by a substantial part of the world's population, a word should be said on its behalf. Those who favor an inquisitorial system contrast its emphasis on a search for the truth with the adversary system's resemblance to a game or contest, in which victory depends more on being a good "player" than on being in the right. Because the adversary system does place great emphasis on procedural fairness and individual procedural rights, even at the expense of objective truth, it has been said that, given a choice, most criminal defendants who are guilty would prefer to be tried under the adversary system, while those who are innocent would prefer the inquisitorial.

The pattern of an adversarial trial. An adversarial trial has a definite pattern, based on the theory that the plaintiff/prosecution, as the moving party and the one with the burden of proof (see Chapter 11), should first make its case to the trier of fact, with the defending party answering. The parts of this pattern are discussed in various entries in this and subsequent chapters. Very briefly (and omitting some of the more technical details), the pattern in a typical Common Law jury trial is as follows:

After such preliminary proceedings as pretrial discovery, jury selection, and the resolution of any pretrial motions, the parties' attorneys make opening statements to the jury, with the plaintiff going first. Next comes the plaintiff's case in chief, evidence intended to prove the plaintiff's case. The evidence may be of any type but will usually include the direct examination of witnesses. The plaintiff's witnesses are first questioned ("interrogated") by the plaintiff's counsel and then cross-examined by the defendant's, with the possibility of further questioning on re-direct, re-cross, and so forth. (See *Order of Examination; Cross-Examination.*)

After the plaintiff rests, the defendant may move for a directed verdict or nonsuit, to end the trial at that point. (Either party may do the same at the end of the defendant's case.) If this is unsuccessful, the defendant repeats the process of presentation of evidence in its case in defense, both to counter the plaintiff's case and to prove any affirmative defenses. The defense counsel examines witnesses and plaintiff's counsel cross-examines the defendant's witnesses. Next may come the plaintiff's rebuttal (answering the defendant's evidence) and, less often, the defendant's rejoinder. When both parties have closed, and following closing arguments (plaintiff again first), the case goes to the jury, with instructions from the judge (usually as proposed by the parties) as to the law they must apply.

As each stage of a trial closes, it may be possible for either party to seek summary relief, cutting short the trial at that point. A motion for a directed verdict, mentioned above, for example, asks the judge to take the case away from the jury because no reasonable jury could find for the opposing party. A motion for summary judgment makes a similar request because there is no triable issue of fact. If these motions fail, the trial continues. Similar post-trial motions are available, such as for a judgment notwithstanding the verdict (j.n.o.v., or judgment as a matter of law) following an adverse jury verdict. And after all of this has been done, there may come one or more appeals to courts of higher jurisdiction, on disputed questions of law.

The adversarial process, then, can be short and simple or long and complex. The rules of evidence pervade it all. This is because in order to facilitate the presentation of evidence to the court and the assessment of that evidence by the neutral factfinder (especially a jury), the adversary system requires an elaborate set of rules of procedure for the admission and exclusion of particular items of evidence. It is these rules that are the subject of the course in evidence and of this book.

Trier of Fact

The person or persons who, after hearing the evidence presented by the parties at trial, decide from that evidence matters of disputed fact. In other words, the trier of fact decides "what happened," to the extent the parties cannot agree. In a jury trial the jury usually tries (decides) the facts, and of course in a nonjury (**bench** or **court**) **trial,** the judge decides.

In either a bench or jury trial, the judge decides the law, perhaps after seeking guidance from the parties by way of briefs or memoranda of law. In a jury trial the jury then applies the facts it has found to the law it has been given by the judge to reach its conclusions regarding the ultimate outcome of the dispute.

If the parties enter into a **stipulation** as to particular matters of fact, they have in effect agreed on those facts and have removed them from dispute. Such stipulated facts are no longer before the trier of fact to decide, and evidence may not be introduced if it relates merely to the proof of those facts. See *Materiality.*

Exhibit

A tangible thing (including a document, chart, or item of real evidence such as the alleged murder weapon) that has been introduced in evidence, so it may be viewed and considered by the court or jury.

Generally an exhibit must first be **marked for identification.** This is just what it sounds like, marking or labeling the item (with a number or letter) in whatever way is practical, to aid the court and attorneys in making reference to it. The party producing it then "lays a foundation" for its admission, seeking to demonstrate that it is what it purports to be (for example, a letter signed by the defendant, a chart showing the plaintiff's potential annual earnings, or a gun found at the scene of the crime). (See *Foundation*.) This is the process of "authentication," discussed below.

After the foundation is laid, the exhibit is usually shown to opposing counsel, and then it can be introduced into evidence. It thus becomes a part of the case, entered in the record and usable by court or jury in making their decision. It usually can also be taken by the jurors into the jury room during their deliberations, although there are some instances (such as items that are too unwieldy) in which this is not permitted.

Foundation

Preliminary matters that must be proven before an item of evidence can be admitted. The term may also be used more broadly to include the prerequisites for invoking any rule of evidence, whether of admission or exclusion.

The Federal Rules do not use the term "foundation," but they refer instead to **preliminary questions** concerning witness qualification, privilege, or admissibility.

In its narrower sense of the prerequisites for admission (rather than exclusion) of evidence, the foundation is sometimes called the **predicate** for the evidence. But "foundation" is more descriptive: most items of evidence cannot stand on their own, and unless their proponent lays a foundation on which they can stand, they will not be permitted in the case. Nor can exclusionary rules such as privileges be invoked in the absence of a supporting foundation.

There are two general types of foundational matters: those that are required by some technical rule of evidence (such as the qualification for a person to be a witness), and those that are required in order to render the proffered evidence relevant, or sufficiently probative of a matter in issue. These are sometimes called questions of competency and conditional relevance, respectively. (See *Conditional Relevance*.)

Generally, facts that determine the application of technical rules of admission of an item of evidence are decided by the court, whereas those that determine only its logical relevance are decided by the jury. This distinction is embodied in **FRE 104(a)** (preliminary questions of admissibility are for the judge) and **FRE 104(b)** (conditional relevance is for the jury). Even when the jury is to decide, however, the judge determines whether there is *sufficient* evidence submitted for the jury reasonably to decide that the foundational fact has or has not been established. (This screening function is the same as that performed by the judge in deciding whether there is sufficient evidence of the ultimate facts for the case to be submitted to the jury for decision. See Chapter 11.)

Example 1.1: Don is on trial for the murder of Vic. Before his death, Vic was heard to say, "I knew Don would try something like this!" The prosecution offers Vic's statement, which is hearsay, as a dying declaration, an exception to the hearsay rule. A dying declaration must have been made by a declarant (Vic) who believed that his death was imminent. This fact, without which the statement cannot be admitted, is one of several that form the foundation for its admission. It is a preliminary matter the judge must determine. If, for example, there is evidence that Vic had asked for the last rites from a priest, the judge would evaluate that evidence in deciding whether Vic believed he was dying, and therefore whether (if the other prerequisites were present) the exception was properly invoked.

Example 1.2: Same facts as Example 1.1. To prove motive, the prosecution calls Wendy, Don's wife, to testify that Don had falsely accused Wendy of having an affair with one of her "friends from the office." A marital privilege prevents Wendy from testifying to any statements of Don made to her in confidence during their marriage. Confidentiality thus is part of the foundation for, or a question preliminary to, invoking the privilege. It is, like the hearsay foundation in Example 1.1, a factual question allocated by the common law and FRE to the judge for final decision. If the prosecution calls bystander Bea to testify that she was present at the time of Don's statement, so it was not confidential, the judge will decide if Bea is telling the truth and, if so, whether under the circumstances the statement was confidential. See FRE 104(a).

When foundation also ultimate issue. An exception to the allocation of functions just described is usually made when the technical matter of admissibility, which the judge would usually decide, is also an ultimate issue in the case, which the jury would usually decide. In order to avoid letting the judge determine an important issue that ordinarily is the province of the jury, the jury may be permitted to make the decision on the foundational question. **FRE 1008** embodies one such instance, in which the foundation fact for avoiding the requirement of offering only original documents (such as "the original never existed") may also be an ultimate issue in the case. (See *Original Document Rule*.) On the other hand, the Supreme Court has held that the existence of a conspiracy, as a question preliminary to invoking the co-conspirator exception to the hearsay rule, is one for the judge under FRE 104(a), even if it is also a substantive issue in the case, a position some common law courts had also taken.

Not bound by evidence rules. In deciding preliminary facts such as those in Example 1.1 and 1.2, generally and under the FRE, the judge is not bound by the usual rules of evidence, other than the rules of privilege. We trust the judge more than the jury to recognize the limitations and proper use of potentially unfair evidence; and in any event, often it is impossible to decide whether evidence satisfies one or another foundational requirement without considering that evidence itself, although it has not yet been shown to be admissible. Thus, if Bea's testimony is that she *was told* that someone else was present when Don spoke to Wendy, it would be available for the judge's consideration in determining the preliminary question of confidentiality, although for other purposes it would usually be excluded as hearsay.

Conditional relevance compared. Even if, however, Wendy is free to testify about Don's statement to her, it is only *relevant* (logically probative of whether Don murdered Vic) if Vic was (or Don thought he was) one of Wendy's "friends from the office." This is not because of some technical rule of evidence, but because of common sense: Don's jealousy aimed at one group of persons has no logical bearing on whether he murdered someone who was not a member of that group; its relevance is conditional upon whether Vic was considered by Don to be one of Wendy's friends from the office. This preliminary decision is for the jury (see FRE 104(b)).

Example 1.3: Evidence is presented that Vic was one of Wendy's co-workers. If the judge considers this evidence sufficient to warrant the jury's finding that Vic was a "friend from the office" of whom Don might have been jealous, the jury will be permitted to decide that preliminary, foundational question of fact. If the jury believes that Vic was such a person, then Don's statement to Wendy is relevant, and the jury will be permitted to use that statement in its ultimate determination of guilt or innocence. See *Conditional Relevance*.

Connecting up. Although preliminary matters generally must be established before an item of evidence can be admitted, sometimes the court will permit the evidence to come in subject to later demonstration of the foundation (failing which it would be subject to a later motion to strike). In effect, the attorney offering the evidence promises to lay its foundation later if allowed to submit the item of evidence now. In Example 1.1, to avoid interrupting the flow of Wendy's testimony the state might offer to "connect it up" (by showing that Vic worked with Wendy) later.

Admissibility

Qualification for receipt by the court in evidence.

Admissible evidence has passed muster under applicable rules of evidence and may be made known to and considered by the trier of fact in reaching its decision.

Admissibility and weight.   Admissibility is generally contrasted with **weight,** or the importance of the evidence in reaching a decision. If a certain type of evidence is of questionable value, it may be excluded entirely or it may be admitted on the assumption that the trier of fact will be able to take its deficiencies into account in weighing its importance. Of course, it is the job of opposing counsel to bring out such deficiencies as might not be obvious and to call the jury's attention to the deficiencies in argument.

Example 1.4:   Pam sues Denny, and Pam herself is called to testify in her own behalf. At common law parties were not permitted (were "incompetent") to testify, because it was assumed their interest would cause them to lie. Under modern procedures (such as **FRE 601**) Pam would be competent and her testimony would be *admissible* evidence; it would be left to the jury (with the help of Denny's counsel) to take into account her obvious interest and decide how much, if any, *weight* to give to her testimony. In other words, interest now goes to weight, not admissibility.

Admissibility and trial tactics.   Admissibility should be distinguished from questions of **trial tactics.** Admissibility is a question only of whether particular evidence *could* be put before the trier of fact. It must be considered separately from the tactical question of what evidence *should* be offered in the best interests of the case. An attorney operating within our adversary system must be concerned with both questions, all of the time. As only one example, evidence of a criminal defendant's good character is generally admissible (see Chapter 3); but because presenting such evidence "opens the door" to rebuttal evidence of the defendant's bad character, its use may be poor trial tactics and a disservice to one's client.

A trial, then, is in this sense like a game of chess: The rules tell us when and how the various playing pieces may move; but the player who looks only for permissible moves and does not think ahead to the consequences of each will soon face a check-mate, the chess equivalent of an adverse verdict.

Limited Admissibility

The availability to the trier of fact of an item of evidence for a limited purpose only. This limitation might extend to certain parties, to certain issues, or to both. It is sometimes called **multiple admissibility.**

Example 1.5:   John and Joanne are co-defendants in a murder trial, accused of conspiring to kill Vi. In an unrelated case, John and Joanne were convicted some years before of conspiring to commit fraud. John testifies for the defense, while Joanne does not. Evidence of

John's prior conviction may be admissible for the *limited* purpose of impeaching John's testimony (showing he is a person of bad character unworthy of belief), but not for the purpose of showing that, because he committed a crime in the past, he is more likely to have committed the present one. (See *Propensity Evidence*.) It will also be limited to use against John only; since Joanne did not testify, her character for truthfulness is not in issue and the prior crime is thus completely inadmissible against her.

Limiting instructions. Note that in Example 1.5, on request by defense counsel the jury will be given a **limiting instruction** that admonishes them to consider the evidence for only the allowable purpose (impeachment, not propensity to commit crime), and only against the proper defendant, John. **FRE 105.** In addition, if possible any reference to Joanne will be excised to avoid inadvertent misuse against her (see *Redact*). But if in a given situation the court believes that, despite an instruction, the jury is too likely to misuse an item of evidence, so that its potential unfair use ("prejudicial effect") outweighs the benefits of its proper use ("probative value"), the evidence may be excluded entirely. **FRE 403**; see *Prejudice*.

In some situations a limiting instruction is constitutionally insufficient. If a defendant's confession that is admissible only against that defendant also implicates a co-defendant by name or clear reference (John claims that "Joanne and I did it together"), admission of the confession might violate the co-defendant's constitutional rights despite the giving of a limiting instruction. (See *Bruton v. United States.*[1]) Admission is permissible, however, if the reference is deleted or the confessing defendant takes the stand.

Limiting instructions should be contrasted with **cautionary instructions,** which do not forbid the jury from a particular use of evidence but which might advise them to be careful in using the evidence because of its questionable trustworthiness.

Curative Instruction

Any attempt to cure an error through an instruction to the jury.

Examples of curative instructions are limiting instructions, which attempt to limit the use that the jury makes of an item of evidence; instructions to disregard evidence entirely as if it had not been offered; and explanatory or cautionary instructions, which (naturally enough) explain or warn against, but do not forbid any use of evidence.

There is much debate over a jury's ability to follow either of the first

---

1. 391 U.S. 123 (1968).

two kinds of instruction. Using a prior inconsistent statement, for example, to discredit present testimony while avoiding reliance on its truth is a difficult feat of mental gymnastics, but one that juries are asked to do regularly. Disregarding entirely evidence that has been presented in error is even more doubtful and has been likened to ignoring a skunk thrown into the jury box or trying to "unring the bell."

Compare *Curative Admissibility*, another means of preventing prejudicial error.

Authentication (In General)

The process of establishing that an item of nontestimonial evidence is what it purports to be — that is, proving its authenticity. The term applies to both objects and writings, although it is more commonly used with respect to the latter. If the process involves proof of the voice on a telephone or the like, it may be referred to as **identification.**

Authentication establishes some connection between the item of evidence and the case in which it is offered. It is an aspect of basic relevance, a part of the foundation that must be laid before evidence is admitted, since evidence that is not what it purports to be has no probative value (at least not in that capacity).

Authentication (or identification) is covered by **FRE 901(a),** with examples of how to authenticate specific items of evidence in **FRE 901(b).** It is, like other aspects of conditional relevance, a matter for the jury's decision, so long as the judge finds that sufficient evidence of authenticity has been submitted. **FRE 104(b);** see *Foundation.*

Note that while authentication demonstrates an item of evidence is what it purports to be, it does not prove anything else about the evidence, such as the part it supposedly played in the litigated facts or whether it satisfies other foundational requirements for admission.

Example 1.6: Nanette is accused of theft of a valuable diamond ring owned by Melinda. At trial the prosecution offers two items of evidence: the stolen ring purportedly found in Nanette's house and an accusatory letter purportedly written and signed by eyewitness Nancy. Before either can be admitted, a foundation for each must be laid, including its authentication. The ring would be authenticated by evidence showing that it is indeed the ring belonging to Melinda, such as testimony by the owner herself. The letter would be authenticated by proof (such as handwriting comparison) that it was, as alleged, written by Nancy. None of the following purported facts, however, is part of the authentication process, although each may eventually have to be proven: that the ring was stolen, rather than borrowed or given to Nanette; that the ring is a diamond, of a certain value; that Nancy wrote the letter under circumstances that satisfy some exception to the hearsay rule; that Nancy was in fact an eyewitness; or that the statements in the letter are true.

As Example 1.6 illustrates, to be authentic is not necessarily to be relevant, or if relevant, admissible. Even a genuine diamond ring will not support a theft conviction if it was only borrowed; and even an "authentic" accusatory letter may be untrue, and even if true, if it does not satisfy the hearsay rule, it may be worthless as evidence.

Self-Authentication (In General)

Establishing authenticity (that an item of evidence is what it purports to be) without resort to extrinsic evidence, that is, by reference only to the item itself. Such items "prove themselves."

Example 1.7: Bill is suing the Hitrite Hammer Co. for an injury to his hand when the Hitrite hammer he was using broke in two. He has the offending hammer, with the familiar "Hitrite" label, and wishes to introduce it into evidence. He need not prove, through testimony or otherwise, that it is in fact a genuine Hitrite hammer. Under **FRE 902(7)** and its equivalents, labels and other trade inscriptions are self-authenticating. Bill still must prove, however, that it is the hammer that he was using and that it broke in the manner that he alleges.

Not conclusive. Self-authentication is not conclusive, but only prima facie. It "gets the evidence in" without the usual need for its proponent to offer any proof of its identity or genuineness (See *Authentication (In General)*), but the opposing side may still dispute its authenticity. In Example 1.7, Hitrite may try to prove the hammer is an imitation made to look like their product, if it truly believes such an unlikely thing has occurred. In effect, then, self-authentication shifts the initial burden of proving authenticity or nonauthenticity to the item's opponent.

Self-authentication is most common for certain types of writings, such as certified copies of public records (see *Self-Authentication (Writings)*) and newspapers or periodicals. The rationale for most instances is simply the unlikelihood that they are not genuine, often combined with the practical difficulty of proving their authenticity.

A few types of documents were self-authenticating at common law, and statutes in most states continue their status. **FRE 902** contains a much more extensive list of self-authenticating documents.

Corroboration

Production of additional evidence that supports or tends to verify evidence already before the court.

The modern Common Law, breaking away from the civil and canon law maxim *testis unum testis nullis* ("the testimony of one is the testimony of none"), has generally considered the evidence of one witness sufficient, but there are exceptions. Traditionally there were particular classes of evidence (such as the unsworn testimony of a child) that were not considered sufficiently reliable to prove some disputed fact unless they were supported by other evidence. Additionally, there were classes of cases (such as prosecutions for perjury) that could not be decided upon the testimony of one uncorroborated witness.

Many of these requirements of corroboration no longer exist, but some (such as that for perjury) have continued in some states and a few others have been added. For example, **FRE 804(b)(3)** requires that a confession of an unavailable third party offered to exculpate the accused ("It was me that pulled the job; Lefty had nothin' t'do with it") is inadmissible "unless corroborating circumstances clearly indicate" its trustworthiness. Such statements are viewed with great suspicion, and traditionally they were not admissible at all. See *Statement Against Interest.*

Although corroboration usually takes the form of an additional witness, nontestimonial corroborating evidence generally will suffice (a prominent exception being the rule that conviction of treason required two eyewitnesses to the act). There are or were also rules of practice that merely require the judge to warn the trier of fact of the danger of acting upon uncorroborated evidence. A common example is conviction upon the testimony of an accomplice.

Objection

A challenge to the admission of an item of evidence.

In most instances, an objection at the soonest possible time is a prerequisite to any later attempt to have the evidence excluded or to remedy its consequences. In effect, "no objection, no appeal." To avoid such a waiver, an objection must be both timely and specific. See **FRE 103(a)(1).**

A **specific objection** ("I object: counsel is leading the witness") indicates clearly what rule of evidence is being violated. This enables the trial judge to assess its merits, opposing counsel to correct any defects, and an appellate court to review the trial court's ruling. In contrast, a **general objection** ("I object, your honor") is almost totally uninformative and usually will not preserve the objection on appeal. (Perry Mason's favorite "incompetent, irrelevant, and immaterial," although technically stating the grounds of irrelevance and immateriality, has become a meaningless litany that will usually be taken as a mere general objection.)

Sometimes evidence unsuccessfully objected to, or evidence of a similar nature, is offered again later in the trial. Instead of fully renewing the objection each time, a **continuing objection** can be made. Then with no or only brief further mention, the error will be preserved while saving time and the patience of the jury.

An objection is **sustained** if the judge agrees with it and rules accordingly to exclude the evidence. It is **overruled** if the judge disagrees and admits the evidence.

Plain error.   Lack of a timely and specific objection is excused in the case of so-called **plain error.** This is a violation of the rules that is (or should be) so obvious to court and counsel that no objection should have been necessary to bring it to their attention, and so substantial in effect that it warrants consideration despite opposing counsel's silence. Courts will not, however, often find plain errors, and they must in any event be both very obvious and very prejudicial — in the language of **FRE 103(d),** "plain errors affecting substantial rights."

Plain error can be compared to "harmless error," discussed separately below. Both are real errors of the court in admitting or excluding evidence, but plain error is so obvious and substantial that it can be addressed even in the absence of an objection, while harmless error is so insubstantial that it cannot be remedied despite the presence of an objection. More common, however, is a garden-variety **prejudicial** (or **reversible**) **error,** which does warrant a remedy but also requires a timely objection to preserve.

Motions before or after the fact.   If an objection cannot be made in time to prevent admission of the evidence, perhaps because the witness has answered too quickly or the answer was unresponsive to the question, a **motion to strike** the evidence (sometimes called an "after-objection") is appropriate. Generally, if the motion is granted the jury will be instructed to disregard the offending evidence. On the other hand, if an objection can be anticipated, and especially if it is one counsel would rather not make before the jury, a **motion in limine** ("at the outset") can be made outside the presence of the jury before the evidence is introduced or even before trial. If overruled before trial, the objection can (and usually should) be renewed at trial. Certain constitutional objections to evidence may be required to be made in a pretrial motion to suppress.

Offer of Proof

A presentation to the court of the nature and purpose of an item of evidence that has been objected to or that the court has ruled inadmissible. It is sometimes called an "avowal."

An offer of proof has the dual function of aiding the judge in ruling on the objection, perhaps even causing opposing counsel to withdraw the objection once the true nature of the offer has been clarified, and of apprising the appellate court of what the evidence would have been had the judge permitted it to be presented. Without an offer of proof, a party may be found to have waived an appeal of the court's exclusion of the evidence. See **FRE 103(a)(2).**

Example 1.8: Perry has sued Della for negligence following an automobile accident. Perry has called witness Wilton to the stand and asks Wilton whether he heard bystander Barry make a statement at the time of the accident. Della's counsel objects that the question "calls for hearsay." Either before the judge rules or after the objection is sustained, Perry (out of the hearing of the jury) states on the record that Wilton intends to testify that Barry, an eyewitness, made the statement to Wilton under circumstances that satisfy an exception to the hearsay rule.

In the alternative, the judge in Example 1.8 might simply excuse the jury and have Wilton testify, the parties then being permitted to argue the hearsay point. If the ruling is not changed, the point has at least been preserved on the record for appeal.

Like the objection itself, the offer of proof must be sufficiently specific to perform its functions properly. An offer of proof may be unnecessary, however, if the nature and purpose of the proffered evidence is or should be apparent to counsel and the court.

Harmless Error

An erroneous ruling of the court that is too trivial or insubstantial to warrant relief on appeal.

In the language of basketball, harmless error is the equivalent of "no harm, no foul." In the language of **FRE 103(a),** an error must affect "a substantial right of the party." Thus, the emphasis is not on how grievous the mistake might be in the abstract, but on what, if any, effect it had on the rights of the affected party. Calling a ruling on evidence "harmless" does not in any way mean it was correct or excusable, but simply that under the circumstances it caused little or no harm. Evidence that looms large in one context may appear merely cumulative and trivial in another.

Example 1.9: Doreen is convicted of murder. At trial she objected to admission of the hearsay statement of an eyewitness which named her as the perpetrator. The statement was in fact hearsay and no exception exists for its admission. If it was the only substantial evidence against Doreen, an appellate court would doubtless reverse Doreen's conviction. But if several other eyewitnesses testified in person to the same fact, it would probably be harmless error.

The opposite of harmless error — the type that will result in action by an appellate court — is often called reversible error. See also *Plain Error* (with which reversible error should not be confused).

With a very few exceptions, a **constitutional error** — an error that violates a party's constitutional rights — can nevertheless be found to be harmless. In a criminal trial, however, harmlessness must be found beyond a reasonable doubt. See *Chapman v. California*.[2]

Invited Error

An error that is considered "harmless" because the affected party's own improper actions were responsible for it.

If a party's own questions of a witness fairly elicit a response to which the party could otherwise have objected, the party cannot complain that the response was prejudicial error. ("*Fairly* elicit," because if a witness's improper response is volunteered or not responsive to the questioning, it will not be considered "invited.") Likewise, if the party's questioning of a witness brings out matters to which the opposing party is forced to respond with otherwise improper evidence, that response will be considered to have been invited and harmless error.

Example 1.10: Dana is on trial for murder. Her counsel asks a defense witness a question that fairly elicits a response demeaning the character of the murder victim, evidence that under the circumstances would not be admissible. The prosecution probably will be permitted to rebut this evidence with proof of the victim's good character, which would also have been inadmissible and possibly prejudicial error were it not invited by the defense.

Invited error can be contrasted with so-called **door opening.** When a party deliberately chooses to offer evidence that, while perfectly proper, permits the opposing party to rebut it with evidence that otherwise would have been inadmissible, the first party has "opened the door" to that rebuttal evidence. Door opening, then, is a proper and deliberate (though sometimes ill-advised) invitation to the introduction of otherwise inadmissible evidence; invited error is an improper introduction of evidence which, in fairness, cannot itself be deemed reversible error or permits a similarly improper response by the opposition.

2. 386 U.S. 18 (1967).

Example 1.11:   Same facts as Example 1.10, except that Dana's counsel elicits direct testimony regarding Dana's nonviolent character. This is perfectly proper evidence (see FRE 404(a)), but it opens the door to the prosecution's rebuttal evidence of Dana's bad character traits, evidence that otherwise would have been inadmissible. (See Chapter 3.)

The term **curative admissibility** is sometimes used to mean the same as invited error. It merely refers to admitting evidence as a means of "curing" what would otherwise have been a reversible error. (See also *Curative Instruction.*)

The rule of completeness (see Chapter 7), which permits an opposing party to introduce immediately other relevant parts of a document or statement that the offering party has introduced or referred to only in part, is actually a form of door opening. It provides for the introduction of evidence that would not otherwise be admissible, either at that time or at all. See **FRE 106.** It also allows the picture to be completed immediately, rather than later, during the opposing party's case, which may be too late to avoid a misleading first impression.

The Federal Rule of completeness is limited to "writings or recorded statements." Federal courts are divided as to whether Rule 106 permits the opposing party to introduce evidence that, even during the opposing party's case, would not otherwise be admissible. As door-opening evidence in other contexts regularly permits the introduction of otherwise inadmissible evidence, however, it seems appropriate that when fairness requires it, the rule of completeness do the same.

All of these terms, because they have related meanings, may be used interchangeably (if not always accurately) to mean any device that permits or makes admissible, or renders harmless evidence that would otherwise be excluded or, if admitted, would constitute reversible error.

Exception

A challenge to a ruling of the court.

An exception differs from an objection (with which it should not be confused) in that an exception is taken after an adverse ruling, not before it. It is thus intended to urge the judge to change or withdraw the ruling, and failing that, to preserve the error on appeal. The practice of requiring an exception in addition to an initial objection is diminishing, and it is not required by the Federal Rules.

Bill of Exceptions

A statement or list, usually signed by the judge, of the objections and exceptions taken to the rulings or other actions of the court, drawn up following trial and for purposes of appeal. Like the exception itself, it is not generally required in modern procedure.

Redact

To edit so as to delete certain material from an item of evidence.

If oral or written evidence contains material that is admissible and also material that is not, the court may order that it be redacted, that is, that the inadmissible parts be edited out and only the admissible parts be put before the trier of fact.

Sidebar Conference

A discussion among trial counsel and the judge held outside the hearing of the jury, usually at the side of the judge's bench.

A sidebar conference (sometimes just called a "sidebar," and sometimes spelled "side-bar") may or may not be recorded.

The origin of the term is in English practice: There was once an actual "sidebar" or divider in Westminster Hall, from within which motions were argued by counsel.

2 Relevance

Introduction and Overview of Chapter

This chapter examines relevance, the relationship to the case that every item of evidence must have in order to be admissible. We are familiar with this term in everyday discourse, but the law gives it a very particular meaning that may or may not coincide with its colloquial or nonlegal usage.

The requirement of relevance is fairly straightforward, once its technical meaning is understood. What occupies most of the law of evidence is the concept of excluding evidence despite its relevance, usually because its relevance is outweighed by more important considerations. The general rules for weighing and excluding otherwise relevant evidence are covered in this chapter; the more specific classes of exclusion (such as character evidence and privileges) are covered in subsequent chapters.

Also discussed is the concept of circumstantial evidence, which by its nature depends for its relevance on the validity of one or more inferences from the fact in evidence to the fact to be proved. The nature of an inference is revealed through exposure of the syllogisms, with their often unstated major premises, that lie (sometimes surprisingly) behind the purported relevance of an item of circumstantial evidence.

The special relevance problems of scientific evidence are omitted here and discussed in detail in Chapter 4.

Relevance

The logical relationship of an item of evidence to a matter in issue.

Relevance is the fundamental requirement for all admissible evidence. Although (as we shall see) not all relevant evidence is admissible, *all admissible evidence must be relevant.*[1]

Probativeness and materiality. Modern codes such as the Federal Rules define relevance as, in effect, logically probative of a fact in issue. See **FRE 401.** Thus defined, relevance combines two related concepts which at common law were treated (and may still be treated) separately: relevance and **materiality.** In its narrower, traditional sense, evidence is relevant if it is logically probative of the proposition for which it is offered, regardless of whether that proposition is pertinent to the case at hand; whereas the evidence is material if that proposition for which it is offered is in issue in the case, or in the language of **FRE 401** "of consequence to the determination of the action." (The Federal Rules do not actually use the term "material.") What is in issue is in turn determined by the substantive law and the rules of pleading. Put another way, relevance is a relationship between the evidence and some fact to be proved, while materiality is a relationship between the fact to be proved and the case. While this work will generally conform to the modern, inclusive usage of the term "relevance," it is extremely important to remember that relevance in this broader sense is a two-step process: probativeness and pertinence.

Relevant to what? As is true of almost every rule of evidence, one cannot decide whether evidence is relevant without knowing the facts or issues which it is offered to prove. Relevance does not exist in the abstract.

Example 2.1: Paul sues Don for battery, alleging that Don struck Paul and caused him serious injuries. In order to prove that Don hit him,

---

1. You will see the term "relevancy" used either in place of or randomly intermixed with "relevance." While "relevancy" is an older form often now considered a secondary usage, its use in the FRE, Uniform Rules, and some state codes has kept it current. If used, it should be reserved for the more general concept defined above, and not in reference to particular instances. Thus: "Relevancy is a requirement of all admissible evidence. The relevance of that testimony, however, is open to question." For consistency, this work will employ only the term "relevance."

Paul calls Wendy as a witness. She testifies that, although she arrived at the scene after the fight had already started, she saw Don hit Paul with his fist. Wendy's testimony is logically probative of the fact that Don hit Paul; it thus passes the first test of relevance. And since harmful or offensive contact is an element of the tort of battery, it is logically probative of a matter in issue, passing the second test.

Example 2.2:   Same facts as Example 2.1, but Don has conceded in his pleadings that he struck Paul, alleging in defense that Paul hit him first. Although Wendy's testimony is still logically probative of the fact that Don struck Paul, Don's concession has taken that fact out of the case and rendered it immaterial: it is no longer in issue, or of consequence to the determination of the action. Unless Wendy's testimony is relevant to some other, material issue (such as the severity of Paul's injuries), it will be inadmissible.

Note that in Example 2.2 the substantive law would have made Wendy's testimony material, but the pleadings then rendered it immaterial. If harmful contact were not an element of the tort of battery, however, Wendy's testimony in Example 2.1 would also have been immaterial, logically probative of a fact (harmful contact) that under the substantive law was of no consequence to the action.

Any probative value sufficient.   If evidence must be logically probative of a matter in issue, just how probative need it be? The answer is: not very. Any particular item of evidence need not prove a matter in issue, nor even make that matter more probable than not. In fact, under modern doctrine, evidence is relevant if it adds *in any way* to the determination of an issue. In the words of FRE 401, it need only "have any tendency" to make a fact of consequence "more probable or less probable than it would be without the evidence." Wigmore referred to the need for it to have some "plus value"; McCormick, however, best illustrated the concept with the phrase, "a brick is not a wall." Ultimately the attorney must construct a wall of proof, but each item of evidence need only be a single brick in the edifice.

Sufficiency distinguished.   The requirement of relevance, then, is in contrast to that of **sufficiency.** Evidence may be relevant even if it is not by itself sufficient to meet the standard of proof necessary to convict of a crime (beyond a reasonable doubt) or render a civil verdict (more probable than not). Combined with other evidence, the cumulative effect may or may not be sufficient to meet the standard. Using McCormick's metaphor, the requirement for relevance is a brick; that for sufficiency is the wall.

Example 2.3:   Diane is on trial for the murder of Vicki. The prosecution introduces the testimony of witness William that he saw Diane and

Vicki arguing some hours before Vicki was killed. This evidence is relevant because it logically establishes a motive for Diane to kill Vicki, and (unless removed by some pleading or procedural device such as an admission) motive is "of consequence" (material) to the ultimate issue of Diane's guilt. But motive is not alone sufficient to convict Diane; only if combined with other evidence (perhaps Diane's fingerprints at the scene, her ownership of the murder weapon, and so forth) would a conviction be possible. On the other hand, were William to testify that he actually saw Diane kill Vicki, if believed, William's evidence should be both relevant and sufficient by itself to convict.

Exclusion of Relevant Evidence (In General)

Exclusion of an item of evidence despite its logical connection to a matter of consequence in the case, for some reason of practicality or policy.

If relevance is a necessary (in fact, the fundamental) requirement for the admission of evidence — because all evidence must be relevant to be admissible — it is nevertheless not always a sufficient basis for admission.

Since lawyers seldom offer evidence that is totally without logical relation to a disputed issue, most of the law of evidence is concerned with the many exceptions to the basic rule that "relevant evidence is admissible." For one reason or another, we are afraid that it would be unwise, unhelpful, or even dangerous to expose the trier of fact, and especially a lay jury, to that evidence. Thayer put the point best in his Preliminary Treatise: "It is . . . the rejection on one or another practical ground, of what is really probative . . . which is the characteristic thing in the law of evidence, stamping it as the child of the jury system."

The relationship between relevance and admissibility can be illustrated either mathematically:

$$
\begin{array}{l}
 \text{Relevant evidence} \\
-\ \underline{\text{Exclusionary rules}} \\
=\ \text{Admissible evidence}
\end{array}
$$

or graphically by the figure on the following page.

Specific and general exclusionary rules. These exceptions, or bases for exclusion of relevant evidence, generally take the form of categories such as hearsay, privilege, character evidence, lay opinion, and so forth, all of which are discussed in subsequent chapters. There is, however, a less specific ground for exclusion at common law that is carried over into modern codes: the so-called "trial judge's friend." This rule states that evidence can be excluded in the discretion of the judge if its probative value would be out-

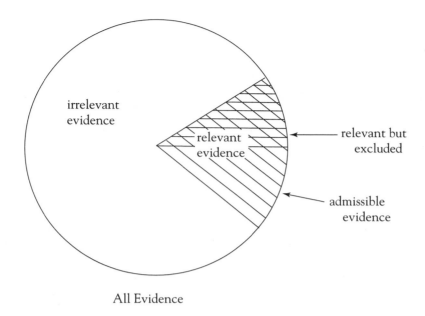

All Evidence

weighed by its likelihood to create unfair prejudice, waste the court's time, confuse the issues, mislead the jury, or (in some jurisdictions) cause unfair surprise. **FRE 403,** based on California's CEC 352, codifies this rule, sometimes referred to as the test of **legal** (as opposed to logical or technical) **relevance.**

Rule 403 and its counterparts contemplate, in effect, a cost-benefit analysis of evidence: If the cost of the evidence to the integrity of the trial process is sufficiently great in comparison to its benefit in terms of proving a material issue, the evidence should be excluded.

It is the first-mentioned danger, that of unfair (or "undue") prejudice, that is the most common basis for exclusion under this rule, although there is much overlap; for example, unfair prejudice can be due to a tendency to mislead or confuse the jury. See generally *Unfair (Undue) Prejudice*.

Unfair (Undue) Prejudice

Prejudice to which the opposing party ought not in fairness be subjected because of its tendency to detract from the rational factfinding process. See **FRE 403.**

As indicated above (see *Exclusion of Relevant Evidence (In General)*), Rule 403 and similar rules require the judge to weigh the "costs and benefits" of admitting an item of evidence, with the most prominent cost generally being unfair prejudice. It is impossible to list or even suggest all of the possible ways evidence might be unfairly prejudicial to a party. The most likely would be a jury's misuse of the evidence (deciding the case on an improper basis) or according to it undue weight or significance.

Unfair prejudice must outweigh probativeness. Whatever the nature of the supposed prejudice, the emphasis must be on the term "unfair." It is no objection to evidence that it will prejudice (that is, adversely affect) the party against whom it is offered; if it did not, there would be little point in offering it. And even if there is found to be a possibility of unfair prejudice, this does not necessarily lead to exclusion of the evidence. It still must be weighed against probative value to determine if its benefits outweigh its dangers.

Example 2.4:   Daryl is on trial for the murder of Jose. The prosecution introduces color photographs of the gruesome murder scene. The photographs are relevant, in that they logically tend to prove several disputed facts, including the fact and manner of Jose's death, the degree of violence used in killing him, and so forth. On the other hand, the jurors might be so emotionally overwhelmed by the photos that they lose their impartiality and become determined to "make someone pay" for such a crime, with Daryl being the only person available to convict. Decisions based on emotion rather than reason are contrary to our notions of justice and in that sense would be "unfair" to Daryl. Whether the danger of such unfair prejudice is sufficient, however, to outweigh the probative value of the photos may depend upon such factors as whether the fact or manner of death are sharply disputed issues or merely preliminary matters generally conceded, and whether the photos show only the detail necessary to make their point or are gratuitously and unnecessarily gruesome. Also important is whether a limiting instruction is likely to dispel or at least lessen the prejudicial effect in the minds of the jurors.

Example 2.5:   Same facts as in Example 2.4, except the evidence in question is testimony that Jose had once come home from visiting Daryl looking like he'd been the loser in a fight. This is circumstantial evidence of Daryl's guilt, and although it is relevant (it has some probative value), its relevance depends on several inferences (for example, that Daryl and Jose had a fight, and that one who fights later murders: see *Circumstantial Evidence*). Here it is the relative weakness of the evidence, when weighed against the possible prejudice of painting Daryl as a violent person, that might lead to its exclusion.

This weighing process is subjective, and appellate courts give trial judges broad discretion in applying it. This in turn means that some inconsistency of results can be expected.

Standards for weighing. There also are variations in the weighing formula used. For example, at common law, exclusion required merely that probative value be outweighed by prejudicial effect. FRE 403, reflecting a strong preference for admission of otherwise relevant evidence, requires for exclusion that probative value be substantially outweighed by the danger of unfair prejudice; whereas the California variant (CEC 352) goes even further and requires probative value be substantially outweighed by a probability of a substantial danger of prejudice. As will be seen in Chapter 8, **FRE 609** contains three different weighing formulas for the exclusion of evidence of prior convictions used to impeach a witness.

Conditional Relevance

Relevance of an item of evidence that depends on the existence of some other fact or condition, in the absence of which the evidence would be irrelevant.

To be relevant, evidence must be logically probative of (make more or less likely) a fact in issue. Sometimes one cannot tell whether this is true without first knowing some other fact; if so, the relevance of the evidence is conditional upon that other fact.

Example 2.6: Tess's will is contested by Carla. Carla contends that Tess was incompetent at the time she executed the will, and as proof she offers evidence that Tess made a gift of her car to uncle Ulrich, who is legally blind and hasn't owned or driven a car for years. This would seem to be logically probative (though perhaps not conclusive) of the issue of competence, *provided that Tess was aware of Ulrich's condition at the time of execution.* If she did not know of Ulrich's condition, it was perfectly reasonable for her to make the mistake of giving him her car, and the evidence of the gift makes the fact of Tess's competence no more or less likely than it was without the evidence. The relevance of the fact of the gift, therefore, is conditional on the existence of the fact of knowledge.

It generally would be up to the judge in Example 2.6 to decide whether Carla must demonstrate the fact of knowledge before being allowed to introduce evidence of the gift, or whether the evidence can be admitted subject to being "connected up" by proof of knowledge later. Usually if Carla produces evidence sufficient to permit the jury to find (or infer) knowledge, it will be left to the jury to decide whether knowledge has in fact been proven. If it has not, the jury should disregard the evidence of the gift as irrelevant. See *Foundation;* FRE 104(b).

It is easy to assume that conditioning facts exist or to fail to recognize that they are necessary to the relevance of the evidence.

> <u>Rule of Thumb</u>: Ask yourself whether you really know enough facts to make the evidence in question relevant, or whether there are unstated factual assumptions that you are taking for granted. If so, you probably have a case of conditional relevance.

Circumstantial Evidence

Evidence that tends to prove a fact not directly, but by proof of some intermediate fact, from which the fact ultimately to be proved can be inferred. **Direct evidence,** in contrast, is evidence that tends to show the existence of a fact without the intervention of proof of any other facts, or the need to draw any inferences from such intermediate facts. Circumstantial evidence is sometimes simply called **indirect evidence.**

Example 2.7: Danny is on trial for the murder of Maria. The murder weapon was a six-inch knife. The prosecution introduces Danny's admission that he owns the knife in question. The fact that Danny is the owner of that knife, if established, would be circumstantial evidence that Danny killed Maria, because it does not, in and of itself, constitute evidence of the killing; it merely may permit an inference that since Danny was the knife's owner, he was the one who used it to kill Maria. On the other hand, testimony by Winston, an eyewitness, that he saw Danny stab Maria with the knife is direct evidence of Danny's guilt: if Winston is believed, no inference is necessary to establish Danny's guilt.

Danny's ownership of the knife in Example 2.7 may be called an **evidentiary fact** and the proposition it helps to establish, Danny's killing of Maria, an **ultimate fact.** (The equivalent terms favored by Wigmore are good examples of arcane Legal Latin: **factum probans** and **factum probandum,** respectively.)

Determined by use. Note <u>carefully that whether an item of evidence</u> is <u>direct or circumstantial is a matter of how it is used and depends</u> entirely on <u>the proposition for which it is offered.</u> In Example 2.7, although the evidence of Danny's ownership of the knife is circumstantial evidence of Danny's killing of Maria, it is direct evidence of that ownership. If Danny were on trial for unlawful ownership of a deadly weapon, rather than murder, no further inference would be required to establish the fact in issue, and ownership would be direct evidence of Danny's guilt. Similarly, if the issue in the case were not murder but whether Danny liked Maria, Winston's eyewitness testimony, although direct evidence of murder, would be only circumstantial evidence of Danny's feelings toward Maria.

what is offered to prove?

2. Relevance

Circumstantial requires inferences. As seen in the following figure, circumstantial evidence consists of a chain of inferences, from evidentiary facts to other evidentiary facts or to facts in issue. It usually is a combination of such items of evidence, perhaps together with one or more items of direct evidence, that constitutes sufficient evidence to render a verdict (in McCormick's metaphor, sufficient bricks to build a wall).

Example 2.8:   As in Example 2.7, Danny is on trial for killing Maria, and the murder weapon was a six-inch knife. Here, however, the evidence of Danny's ownership of the knife consists of a witness's testimony that she often saw Danny carrying a knife just like the one that killed Maria. An eyewitness to the killing was 100 feet away at the time. In addition, the prosecution submits evidence of Danny's fingerprints on the knife and testimony that Danny was jealous of Maria. The four items of evidence might be diagrammed as follows ("i" means "inference"):

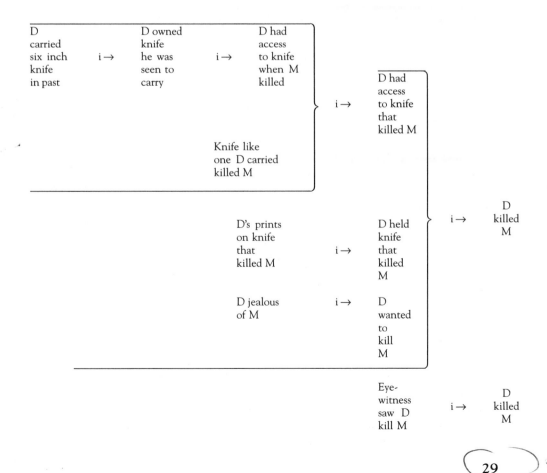

You can see in Example 2.8 that all of the items of evidence and inferences from them may, alone or together, add up to sufficient evidence to conclude that Danny killed Maria; and that each item of evidence requires one or more inferences in order to reach that conclusion except for the eyewitness to the killing. The latter is direct evidence which, if believed, leads to the conclusion that Danny killed Maria without the intervention of any other facts or the need for any inferences. For a more detailed discussion of the importance and operation of the reasoning process behind the use of circumstantial evidence, see *Inference (Circumstantial Evidence)*.

Inference (Circumstantial Evidence)

The process of reasoning in a logical manner from one fact to another that follows from it. Generally, an inference is a conclusion the trier of fact is permitted, but not required, to draw from a given fact (see Chapter 11, *Inference (Permissible)*).

Circumstantial evidence depends upon the process of inference for its relevance. An item of circumstantial evidence is relevant to a fact in issue only if that fact, or another intermediate ("evidentiary") fact, can be inferred from it. (See *Circumstantial Evidence*.) The probative value of the circumstantial evidence thus is a function of the strength of the inferences underlying it.

Process of deduction. Although we seldom think about just how we draw inferences, the process can be broken down to reveal the actual strength of a given item of circumstantial evidence. At its heart, most circumstantial evidence relies on a process of **deduction,** reasoning from the general to the specific. Once one recognizes the general proposition behind a given process of deduction, it is possible to evaluate the strength and validity of that process.

Example 2.9: As in Example 2.8, Danny is on trial for killing Maria. Among the items of evidence offered against Danny is the fact that he was jealous of Maria. If jealousy is indeed circumstantial evidence of (a motive for) murder, it is only because we believe that, in general, those who are jealous of others are more likely to act violently against the objects of their jealousy than are those who have no such feelings. Given that general belief, if we learn that in this particular case Danny was jealous of Maria, we can infer from this fact that Danny is (or at least might be) the one who murdered Maria.

Example 2.10: Same as Example 2.9, except that the evidence offered is that Danny has blue eyes. Since we do not believe (I hope) that in general blue-eyed people have a greater tendency to commit murder than do those with other eye colors, circumstantial evidence of Danny's blue eye color does not permit an inference that Danny is more likely to have murdered Maria; the evidence is therefore irrelevant. If, however, there is independent evidence that Maria was murdered by someone with brown eyes, Danny's eye color does become relevant because of the validity of the general proposition that, *in this case*, eye color is logically linked to the identity of Maria's assailant.

The underlying syllogism. Even better for understanding inference is a diagram of the process. Specifically, when drawing inferences one utilizes, consciously or subconsciously, a series of syllogisms. A **syllogism** is merely a series of three propositions: a general statement about the world or about the case (the major premise), a statement of the particular facts offered in evidence (the minor premise), and a statement of the conclusion that supposedly follows from the first two. If the major premise is valid and the minor premise is established, then the conclusion should be valid as well. It is the validity and degree of certainty of the major premise that holds the key to the strength of the inference, and thus the strength and relevance of the item of circumstantial evidence.

The hidden major premise. Usually the major premise of a syllogism is not stated; only the minor premise (the fact offered in evidence) and the conclusion (the fact it is offered to prove) are articulated — that is, we appear to reason inductively from the item of evidence, not deductively from a general proposition. We may not even realize we are taking the major premise for granted. Therefore it is often surprising when we examine just what assumptions we must make to draw a particular inference.

The syllogisms for the inferences in Example 2.8 can be set out as follows (note that major premises are in capital letters and only Inference 1 is annotated).

Inference 1: "Danny was jealous of Maria; therefore Danny likely murdered Maria."
Syllogism:

[1] THOSE WHO ARE JEALOUS OF ANOTHER ARE [A LITTLE, MUCH] MORE LIKELY TO MURDER THE OTHER THAN THOSE WHO ARE NOT JEALOUS (that is, than those about whom we do not know such a fact). [Major premise: general proposition]

[2] Danny was jealous of Maria. [Minor premise: specific item of evidence being offered]

[3] *Therefore*, it is [a little, very] likely that Danny murdered Maria (that is, a little or much more likely than if we did not know this about Danny). [Conclusion: inference drawn]

Inference 2: "Danny has blue eyes; therefore Danny likely murdered Maria." Syllogism:

[1] THOSE WHO HAVE BLUE EYES ARE LIKELY TO COMMIT MURDER.
[2] Danny has blue eyes.
[3] *Therefore*, Danny likely murdered Maria.

Inference 3: "Danny has blue eyes; therefore Danny did not murder Maria." Syllogism:

[1] A PERSON WITH BROWN EYES MURDERED MARIA.
[2] Danny has blue eyes.
[3] *Therefore*, Danny did not murder Maria.

Several things should become obvious from these syllogisms. First, as indicated above, the validity of each conclusion depends upon the validity of the major premise. If having blue eyes does not cause people to commit murders at all, the evidence of Danny's blue eyes is simply irrelevant.

Second, even if the major premise is valid, one must decide just what degree of certainty can be attributed to it. If jealous people always murder those of whom they are jealous, we can infer that Danny certainly did. If murder is only probable, so is Danny's guilt; and so forth. Again, the likelihood need only be greater than without the evidence to pass the test of relevancy.

Third, not only the major premise, but also the minor premise must be valid. In other words, it is only on the assumption that Danny in fact was jealous of Maria, or has blue eyes, that we can ascribe any validity to the conclusion.

Validity of major premise. How do we decide whether the major premise is valid? That will depend upon its form. Often the validity of the major premise is a matter of common knowledge or human experience: jealousy leads to violence, blue eyes do not. Sometimes, however, we may need scientific or other evidence to determine whether an inference is warranted. In Inference 3 above, the major premise is actually based upon another item of evidence, presumably direct evidence such as an eyewitness (no pun intended) account. The validity of the conclusion drawn from it depends on the strength of that original evidence of the color of the perpetrator's eyes, as well as the strength of the evidence that Danny has blue eyes.

Try this method with the other inferences in Example 2.8. It will quickly become clear which circumstantial evidence is strong and which relies upon weak or questionable premises.

3

Character Evidence

Introduction and Overview of Chapter

Chapter 2 discussed relevance and the process of excluding even relevant evidence if its probative value is outweighed by its potential prejudicial effect. This chapter highlights one important type of evidence that, as a class, is judged to be overly prejudicial and thus is excluded without case-by-case weighing. First the chapter will cover character evidence in general and then it will proceed to a detailed discussion of the rules governing specific types and uses of character evidence that are presumptively admitted or excluded, together with the inevitable exceptions to each category.

Character evidence also relates to Chapter 2 in another respect: The most common use of character evidence is as circumstantial evidence, to draw an inference of some action by the person in question. It is seldom (but can be on occasion) direct evidence of a fact in issue.

Character evidence is relevant as well to the credibility of a witness, and the rules relating to its use in that context are discussed in Chapter 8.

Character Evidence (In General)

Evidence that relies for its relevance on a person's character traits, such as honesty or aggressiveness.

Example 3.1: Deidre is on trial for fraud. The prosecution offers evidence that she has committed fraud three times in the past; in two of those instances she was convicted and served time in jail. This is character evidence, offered to prove Deidre's disposition to commit fraud, and thus (circumstantially) her likelihood to have committed the fraud for which she is on trial.

Whether character evidence is admissible depends on both its use and its type. Following is a general outline of the rules governing its admissibility, all of which are discussed more fully in specific entries.

Propensity use excluded; exceptions. Generally, evidence of a character trait cannot be used to prove, by inference, action in conformity with that trait. There are, however, recognized exceptions to the propensity rule under which a criminal defendant can prove pertinent good character traits and either the defendant or, under some circumstances, the prosecution can prove pertinent traits of a victim of crime. See **FRE 404(a)(1), 404(a)(2).** See generally *Propensity Evidence.*

Types of character evidence. Character can be demonstrated by three types of evidence. In Example 3.1, the likelihood that Deidre would commit fraud was demonstrated by evidence of prior similar acts. See *Prior Crimes/ Acts Evidence.* But it might also have been shown by evidence of her reputation in the community or by someone's personal opinion about her.

Example 3.2: As in Example 3.1, Deidre is on trial for fraud. The prosecution offers the testimony of Fred, who lives in Deidre's neighborhood, that Deidre has a reputation in the community for dishonesty, and the testimony of Ginger, a business acquaintance of Deidre, that in her opinion, Deidre is a person who would lie or cheat. The testimony of both Fred and Ginger, like the evidence of her prior acts, is intended to demonstrate Deidre's propensity to be dishonest, and therefore the likelihood that she committed fraud on the occasion in question.

See generally *Reputation and Opinion Evidence.*

Use determines type. The use of the character evidence will determine which, if any, of these modes of proof are either required or permitted. See

FRE 405. For example, most propensity uses of character evidence, when permitted at all, are limited to proof of reputation or opinion, whereas evidence of specific acts is permitted for non-propensity uses and when character is itself in issue. See *Prior Crimes/Acts Evidence*; *Character In Issue*.

Impeachment use of character. The credibility of witnesses is always a relevant issue, and character evidence is a common means by which credibility is assessed. Because it is pertinent only in the limited area of testimonial evidence, however, and because the rules for its use tend to differ from those for its substantive use, the topic of impeachment use of character evidence is covered in detail with testimonial evidence in Chapter 8.

Weighing against prejudice. Even if a use of character evidence is within one of the numerous categories of permissible use, its probative value in a particular case still can be outweighed by its prejudicial effect, at least when it is bad character that is being proved. (See *Exclusion of Relevant Evidence (In General)*; FRE 403.) Whatever the purpose of introducing evidence of character (such as through prior bad acts), it still carries a significant danger of misuse by the jury (for example, to convict for the prior crimes rather than the present one). Such evidence therefore still may be excluded if this danger of prejudice sufficiently outweighs the strength and importance of its non-propensity use.

Three tests of character evidence. Character evidence, then, must pass three tests, which are exemplified by the three applicable federal rules: (1) there must be a proper use of character evidence (FRE 404), that is, either a non-propensity use or a propensity use that comes within a recognized exception to the general prohibition; (2) there must be the proper type of character evidence (FRE 405), that is, reputation, opinion, or specific acts; and (3) the evidence must be sufficiently probative not to be overcome by its inherent prejudice (FRE 403).

> <u>Rule of Thumb</u>: When dealing with character evidence, look for proper use, proper type, and probative value.

Propensity Evidence

Evidence of a tendency or disposition to act in accordance with a particular character trait, used circumstantially to prove action in conformity with that trait.

As a (very) general rule, propensity evidence may not be used to imply that a party acted in conformity with that propensity on a given occasion (as in Example 3.1). For example, the prosecution in a criminal case cannot use evidence of the defendant's propensity to commit crimes to prove the likelihood the defendant committed the crime charged; the plaintiff in a civil case cannot use evidence of a propensity to be negligent to prove the defendant's negligence on the occasion in question; and a civil defendant cannot use "good character" evidence to establish the defendant's own propensity to be careful, honest, or the like. See **FRE 404(a).**

Rationale for exclusion.   Propensity evidence is excluded because it is considered substantially more prejudicial than probative. This is partly because the inference from propensity to action often tends to be fairly weak (even dishonest people do not always lie, and many violent acts have been committed by otherwise peaceable citizens); and because evidence of other acts raises numerous side issues. (Did the defendant actually commit the alleged other acts? If so, were there extenuating circumstances?) But in criminal cases the primary reason for exclusion is the danger that a jury might misuse the evidence. Jurors might become prejudiced against the defendant and convict not for the crime charged, but for those other crimes and bad acts.

Exception for criminal defendant's good character.   Partly because there is no such danger of prejudice, and partly because of our desire to give a defendant every opportunity to raise a reasonable doubt of guilt, a criminal defendant is permitted to prove a propensity for good traits such as honesty. This exception is sometimes called the "mercy rule," for obvious reasons. Tactically, however, this is a somewhat risky thing for the defendant's attorney to do, because it opens the door to rebuttal evidence by the prosecution in the form of the defendant's bad traits, such as dishonesty (thus the common reference to door-opening evidence). See **FRE 404(a)(1).**

Example 3.3:   Darren is on trial for fraud. The prosecution has evidence that Darren is a dishonest person, but as its use would merely prove Darren's propensity toward dishonesty, it is inadmissible. Darren, however, in his defense offers evidence that he is an honest, law-abiding person (that is, that he has a propensity to act honestly and lawfully). This evidence is admissible as an exception to the general prohibition against propensity evidence. Now, however, the prosecution is permitted to rebut Darren's evidence with the very evidence of his dishonest and lawless character that it was prohibited from using earlier. Darren's evidence of his good traits has "opened the door" to the evidence of his bad ones.

To be admissible, evidence of the defendant's good character must always be pertinent to the crime charged: If Darren is charged with fraud, evidence he is peaceable would not be relevant. Likewise, the prosecution could not rebut Darren's evidence of honesty with proof of his violent nature. A general trait like lawfulness (and lawlessness in rebuttal), on the other hand, is pertinent to most criminal charges. Note that the more good traits the defendant puts into issue, the more bad traits the prosecution will be permitted to prove in response, another important tactical consideration. In other words, the defendant may be able to choose how widely to open the door.

Character of victim. A similar exception exists for evidence of the character of a victim of crime. The defendant generally can offer evidence of a pertinent trait of the victim, such as aggressiveness, when self-defense is alleged; again the prosecution can rebut with opposing character evidence. In some circumstances the prosecution can offer evidence of the victim's character without waiting for the defendant to open the door, although this may be limited, as in **FRE 404(a)(2),** to the character of a homicide victim for peacefulness, to rebut evidence that the victim was the aggressor.

Character of sex offense defendant. FRE 413-415 create significant and controversial new exceptions to the prohibition against propensity evidence. Under **FRE 413,** if a defendant is charged with sexual assault (as very broadly defined in Rule 413(d)), evidence of the defendant's commission of other offenses of sexual assault "is admissible . . . for its bearing on any matter to which it is relevant." There is no limitation to convictions or indication of the type of evidence that is admissible to prove the other offenses; nor is it clear whether the judge has any discretion to exclude the evidence under Rule 403. No mention is made of rebuttal evidence by the defendant. **FRE 414** and **415** provide similarly in, respectively, criminal cases of alleged child molestation and civil cases predicated on the commission of either sexual assault or child molestation.

These new rules were motivated by the same general policies as FRE 412 (see *Rape Shield Statutes*), which is why they are found adjacent to that Rule rather than within Rule 404, where they logically seem to belong. The Judicial Conference recommended against adoption of these rules (and proposed in the alternative a more moderate amendment of Rules 404 and 405). Because, however, Congress failed to reject the proposed rules, they took effect by default in 1995. There has been considerable doubt expressed about their constitutionality, but as of this time both their practical and their constitutional implications have yet to be tested.

Distinguishing propensity evidence. It is sometimes difficult to differentiate a propensity use of character evidence from a non-propensity use. In most instances, however, they can be distinguished as follows:

> Rule of Thumb: If the reasoning from the character evidence to the fact in issue for which it is offered requires as an intermediate step consideration of a character trait from which action in conformity is inferred, it probably is a propensity use; if it does not require such a step, it probably is not.[1]

Example 3.4:   Denny is on trial for the burglary of Vern's house and the theft of certain securities. The burglar apparently had a key to a locked room in Vern's house where the stolen securities had been stored. The prosecution offers evidence that, some weeks earlier, Denny had stolen from Vern's pocket some personal belongings, including the key to the locked room containing Vern's securities. This evidence is relevant, of course, because it shows that Denny had access to the key that was used in the later burglary (and thus had the opportunity to commit the later crime). The reasoning requires three steps, from the prior act of theft to opportunity by access to the key to the later burglary. If diagrammed, the reasoning would look like this:

Theft of key———→Opportunity———→Burglary

The internal step (opportunity) is not a character trait of Denny. Therefore this is not propensity evidence, and if it meets all other prerequisites it will be admitted.

Example 3.5:   As in Example 3.4, Denny is on trial for the burglary of Vern's house and theft of securities. The prosecution offers evidence that on a prior occasion, Denny stole some personal belongings from Albert. It is not alleged that anything was taken from Albert that was used in the later burglary of Vern's house. The only possible relevance of the evidence is to demonstrate that Denny is a thief, that is, has a propensity to steal, and therefore it can be inferred Denny is more likely to have committed the theft charged. Diagrammed, there are again three steps necessary in the use of this evidence:

Theft from A———→D is a thief———→Theft from V

The middle step here is Denny's character trait (thievery), from which is inferred action in conformity with that character (theft). This is typical propensity evidence, and generally it is inadmissible.

---

1. Suggested in Saltzburg & Redden, Federal Rules of Evidence Manual 183 n.1 (4th ed. 1986).

Example 3.6: Denny has sued Georgena for defamation because Georgena called Denny a "thief." Georgena's defense is truth, that is, she alleges that Denny is in fact a thief. Georgena offers evidence that at some time in the past, Denny stole some personal belongings from Vern. The evidence is relevant, of course, because if Denny stole from Vern, Denny is in fact a thief. This reasoning requires only two steps from evidence to fact in issue, with no intermediate inference from a character trait:

character in issue.

P stole from A ⟶ P is a thief

Therefore this is not propensity evidence and is admissible.

Note that in Example 3.6, the second step is Denny's character as a thief (his propensity to steal); but because in this case Denny's character is itself an issue in the case, and there is no attempt to reason from his propensity to action in conformity with it, the character evidence is admissible. Put in terms of the above Rule of Thumb, Denny's character trait of thievery *is* the fact in issue; it is not simply an intermediate step from which we can infer, by assuming he acted in conformity with that trait, the fact in issue (theft). See *Character in Issue*.

In addition to the several exceptions to the general rule excluding propensity evidence, some uses that appear to be propensity uses in fact, upon closer analysis, are not. The most important are discussed below.

Prior Crimes/Acts Evidence *Similar Act Similar happening)*

A type of character evidence consisting of the introduction of a person's prior acts (criminal or otherwise) as the basis for proving that the person committed the act presently alleged.

Like character evidence generally, prior acts evidence is neither admissible nor inadmissible per se; its admissibility depends on the use for which it is offered.

English and other Commonwealth courts use the term **similar fact** (or **similar happening**) **evidence** for any evidence of a party's prior acts, whether actually similar or not. In the United States it is usually employed only with reference to civil cases and non-criminal acts, as in Example 3.7 below. The more common use of such evidence, however, is in criminal cases. Here the law may distinguish between **prior convictions** of crime and other prior acts, including crimes of which the actor was not convicted.

In federal practice, the general rules respecting substantive use of prior acts (which are similar to the common law and most codes) are found in FRE 404. Those that concern only the use of prior acts to impeach witnesses are primarily in FRE 608(b) (conduct other than convictions) and FRE 609 (convictions), both of which are discussed in detail in Chapter 8.

Propensity use. Evidence of prior acts is generally prohibited when it is merely propensity evidence, that is, when it depends for its relevance on the premise that one tends to act in conformity with one's characteristics, and that by inference the person in question did so on this occasion. Non-propensity uses are usually permissible. See **FRE 404(b).** See generally *Propensity Evidence.*

Example 3.7: Dr. Hertz is sued by patient Polly for operating on Polly's arm in a negligent manner. Specifically, Hertz is alleged to have sterilized her instruments improperly, causing Polly's arm to become infected. Polly attempts to prove that on two other occasions in the past year, Hertz had failed to sterilize her instruments, because of which two other patients suffered infections. Polly is asserting, in effect, that the prior instances show that Hertz has a *propensity* to act in this negligent manner, from which it can be inferred that she (more likely) did so when she operated on Polly. This use of prior acts would be inadmissible.

Note that Polly's attempted use of the prior incidents in Example 3.7 is an instance of the use of circumstantial evidence, and that its validity depends upon the validity of the major premise that "Those who have been negligent [generally or in a certain way] in the past are more likely to have been negligent [generally or in that way] at a later time." See *Circumstantial Evidence.*

Non-propensity uses. It is usually permissible to use evidence of prior acts for any reason other than to show propensity. This is not so much an exception as a corollary to the propensity rule. These permissible uses may sometimes be exclusionary, confined to a specific list; but modern rules, like FRE 404(b), are usually inclusionary, worded to include as admissible all "other purposes." Most of these non-propensity uses are not attempts to use the person's character as evidence at all, but merely to use evidence that, although directed at some other fact, incidentally does reveal a person's character trait.

Example 3.8: Same facts as Example 3.7 (Polly sues Dr. Hertz for negligence), except that Hertz concedes that she sterilizes her instruments in the manner alleged by Polly. Her defense is that it is perfectly safe to do so. Polly now introduces the evidence of the two prior instances not to prove that Hertz has a propensity to sterilize her instruments in a certain way and therefore probably followed the same (allegedly negligent) practice on the present occasion, which is admitted, but only to prove that sterilizing instruments in the manner she did can indeed cause harm to a patient, as it did on the two prior occasions. In other words, the evidence is introduced not to demonstrate a character trait or propensity to act negligently, but to prove causation, a causal link between an admitted practice and a harmful result. For this purpose, Polly's evidence is admissible.

Causation is one of the common permissible (non-propensity) uses of evidence of past acts. Some others are: motive (prior fight as motive for later attack); plan (prior theft of guns as part of plan for later holdup); opportunity (prior theft of guns to provide weapons later used in holdup); **modus operandi** ("method of operation"), also called **signature** (prior crimes committed by defendant in same unique manner as present one was committed, thus identifying defendant with present crime); knowledge (prior safecracking as proof of ability to crack safes); and lack of mistake (prior deliberate misrepresentations negating likelihood that present one was unintentional). There is also what sometimes is called the **doctrine of chances,** of which the "Brides in the Bath" case (*Rex v. Smith*[2]) is the most famous (other drownings of wives in bath render unlikely claim that present wife's drowning was accidental).

Reputation and Opinion Evidence

The opinion of a person's character that is held — or at least expressed — by the public or a segment of the public (reputation); and a witness's own beliefs and conclusions about a person's character (opinion). "The defendant is held in high esteem by his colleagues and friends" would be reputation; "I believe the defendant to be honest and peaceable" would be opinion.

There are three possible ways to prove one's character: by one's reputation in the community, by the opinion of individual witnesses, or through specific acts one has committed. Specific acts are probably the most reliable indicator, reputation the least reliable. Yet at common law, in those limited instances in which evidence of a person's character was admissible as circumstantial evidence, it could be proved only by reputation evidence. This was probably because although less reliable, reputation was less likely than specific acts (and to some extent opinion) to prejudice the jury unfairly against a party and less likely to introduce confusing side issues. In some jurisdictions this rule continues today, although most modern codes and **FRE 405** permit evidence of both reputation and opinion, excluding only specific acts.

2. [1915] All E.R. 262.

Specific acts to impeach a character witness. Inquiry about specific acts may be permitted on cross-examination of a character witness (one who has testified to a party's character), to test the basis for the witness's opinion or purported knowledge of the party's reputation. Thus a reputation witness, it is said, may be asked on cross-examination "*Have you heard* [that the defendant robbed a bank, etc.]." An opinion witness, on the other hand, may be asked "*Do you know* [that the defendant was arrested, etc.]." This is because (and illustrates that) reputation is concerned only with what the community at large is saying about a person, and opinion with what a particular individual (the witness) believes about that person. While as a practical matter we can only test the existence, not the basis, of the community's opinion about a person, we can test the basis for an individual witness's opinion. Therefore it is relevant to inquire into what the reputation witness has heard about a person (has the witness really heard everything the community is saying?), and what the opinion witness knows about the person (does the witness really know what the person is like?). Since these uses are limited to testing the character witness's knowledge, any use of the evidence as proof of the party's actual character would be improper, and if requested the judge should give a limiting instruction to this effect.

Specific acts may also be proved when a trait of a party's character is itself in issue (see *Character In Issue*).

Character In Issue

Evidence of character as an element of a claim or defense, and not as circumstantial evidence of some other fact in issue.

Most attempts to use evidence of a person's character traits are as circumstantial evidence implying that the person committed some act in conformity with that trait. In most such instances, the evidence is not admissible (see *Character Evidence (In General)*). In those circumstances in which it is permitted, character may be proved only by evidence of reputation, or reputation and opinion, but not specific acts (see *Reputation and Opinion Evidence*). If, however, a person's character or trait is itself in issue (or in the language of **FRE 405(b)** if it is an "*essential element*" of a charge, claim, or defense"), generally that trait may be proved by any of the three types of evidence. (A few courts permit only specific act evidence, and not reputation or opinion, when character is in issue.) Contrast the following:

Example 3.9: Percy sues Diana for the tort of defamation, alleging that Diana called Percy a "violent thug." Diana asserts the defense of truth and offers evidence that Percy was twice convicted of violent assault. Because in this lawsuit one of the issues (an "essential element of [Diana's] . . . defense") is whether or not Percy is in fact a

put in outline

violent person, specific acts of assault may be used to prove that trait.

Example 3.10:   Del is on trial for assaulting Patty. Del's defense is that he was provoked by Patty and acted in self-defense. Del offers evidence that Patty was twice convicted of violent assault, from which he wishes the jury to infer that Patty, as an aggressive and violent person, is likely to have provoked Del. Patty's aggressive or peaceful nature is not an essential element of either the crime of assault or the defense of self-defense, but it is merely circumstantial evidence that Patty was the aggressor. Therefore the prior convictions, as specific acts, are inadmissible for this purpose. Evidence of Patty's reputation for violence, however, and in modern rules evidence of an individual's opinion to that effect, would be admissible to prove Patty's violent nature, which could imply provocation in this case.

Admissibility distinguished.   Be very careful not to assume that just because a character trait is admissible (as in Example 3.10), it is "in issue" or an "essential element" of the case. Thus, in that example, Del will be convicted of assault if he was not acting in self-defense, regardless of whether Patty is by nature a peaceable or violent person; and Del will be acquitted if he was acting in self-defense, regardless again of Patty's nature. Patty's character trait, to the extent relevant and admissible, is only an item of circumstantial evidence in the proof of, and not itself, one of the essential elements of the case, the need for self-defense. In Example 3.9, on the other hand, Diana's defense of truth requires that Percy have a violent nature; it is not just evidence of an essential element, it *is* an essential element.

In most cases, then, whether admissible evidence of character is also an instance of character in issue can be determined using this

> Rule of Thumb: If the issue for which the character evidence is offered requires some form of proof of character, and no other evidence will suffice, character is in issue. But if the issue could just as easily be proved using other, noncharacter evidence (assuming it was available), then character is not in issue.

See also *Propensity Evidence* and the Rule of Thumb for distinguishing propensity from nonpropensity evidence.

Habit

A recurring response to specific circumstances, such that the response may be considered virtually automatic. Unlike more generalized character traits, habits are admissible in most jurisdictions to prove action in conformity with them on the occasion in question. See **FRE 406.**

Propensity evidence distinguished. Habit is a character trait, but it is distinguished from mere propensity evidence by its specificity, frequency, and regularity.

Example 3.11: David is accused of driving while intoxicated. The incident took place on a Friday night. A witness asserts that she saw David drinking whiskey on the night in question, but David denies it. The prosecution introduces evidence both of David's frequent public drunkenness and of his regular Friday night drinking routine. Drunkenness is "character"; having six double whiskies at the Spar Tavern every Friday night for the past ten years is "habit." The latter is admissible to help prove that David was drinking on the Friday night in question; the former is not.

If, in Example 3.11, having those six double whiskies had occurred only once or twice in the past ten years, or had occurred every Friday night but for only two or three weeks, it would not be evidence of habit. Where in between these extremes habit falls must be decided case-by-case.

Example 3.12: Pamela is injured when her car is struck by Daisy's car. Pamela sues Daisy, who alleges Pamela's injuries were partly her own fault because she wasn't wearing a seat belt. Several witnesses testify for Pamela that they have driven with her and that she invariably buckles her seat belt before she starts the engine. This evidence of Pamela's habit would be admissible as tending to prove she buckled her seat belt on the occasion in question.

It is significant that the seat belt habit in Example 3.12, unlike David's drunkenness in Example 3.11, is more than just a frequent routine: It is a reflexive, semi-automatic motion performed largely without thinking. This sort of habit, being the most likely to be followed, is the most likely to be admissible.

Older rules, largely but not entirely superseded, would either reject habit evidence entirely or permit it only if corroborated or if eyewitness testimony were unavailable. FRE 406 expressly rejects these limitations.

Similar to habit (but more universally accepted) is evidence of a regular **business routine.** Again it requires specificity, frequency, and regularity.

Example 3.13: Delivery Corp. is sued for permitting its truck to leave the shop without a proper brake inspection, resulting in an inability of the truck to avoid a collision with Yvette. There is no direct evidence that the truck was actually inspected on the occasion in question, as no such records are kept. However, evidence that over the past several years Delivery Corp. has routinely inspected the brakes on every truck passing through its shop would be admissible to prove that it inspected the brakes on this truck as well.

Note that, as with habit, evidence in Example 3.13 that Delivery Corp. was always careful, or that it had frequently inspected brakes, or that it had done so on the two other trucks it inspected that day, would lack sufficient specificity, regularity, or frequency to be admissible evidence of business routine.

A traditional limitation now seldom applied is that business routine, particularly the mailing of a letter, is admissible only if there is specific proof that part of the routine (placing the letter in the "out" box, for example) was followed on the occasion in question.

Similarity of circumstances. Finally, habit or routine evidence is only relevant if the circumstances under which the regular act occurred are virtually identical to those in issue, at least in all important respects. Thus if the accident in Example 3.11 had occurred on a Thursday afternoon, or that in Example 3.13 had involved the truck's steering gear rather than its brakes, the evidence would indeed be of a habit or routine, but in the context of this case it would nevertheless be inadmissible as indicating, at best, a general tendency to drink or to be careful. As such it would be mere propensity evidence.

All of the above can best be remembered by keeping in mind the following:

> <u>Rule of Thumb</u>: To distinguish habit or business routine from general character, look for evidence of *specificity*, *regularity*, *frequency*, and *similarity*.

Rape Shield Statutes

Statutes that exclude evidence of the prior sexual history of the victim/complainant in a criminal prosecution or civil proceeding in which the defendant is accused of rape or sexual assault. See **FRE 412.**

Example 3.14: Dean is charged with the rape of Victoria in an incident that occurred in his car after Dean took Victoria to a party. Dean's defense is that Victoria consented to intercourse, and she only later charged him with rape when her parents found out about the incident. Dean introduces evidence that Victoria consented to intercourse, under virtually identical circumstances, with several other men during the three months preceding the alleged rape. He also introduces evidence that Victoria has a widespread reputation for being an "easy" person with whom to have intercourse. All of this evidence of Victoria's prior sexual activity or reputation would be inadmissible under a typical rape shield statute.

Variations. Although popularly called *rape* shield statutes, these laws vary in the type of case they cover and are not necessarily confined to the technical crime of rape. They also vary in how completely they prohibit the admission of prior sexual experience. Many, for example, ban such evidence only in a criminal prosecution and when used to prove that the victim consented to the charged sexual activity (see URE 412), while others cover virtually any purpose, in any type of proceeding. Some, like FRE 412, are outright prohibitions on use; others merely require the judge to screen the evidence to avoid undue prejudice to the victim. Some, again including the federal rule, distinguish among the three types of character evidence (reputation, opinion, and acts), banning the first two outright but providing some exceptions for prior acts.

Exceptions. Typically there are exceptions that permit use of prior sexual history either for all purposes except proving consent, or for certain specific purposes. Perhaps the most common of these are proof of a prior sexual relationship between the victim and the accused, and proof that another person is the source of physical traces (such as semen) or injury. Most statutes also permit uses such as proving a motive to falsify the charge (for example, that the complainant has a lover who would be jealous if he believed she had consented to intercourse with the defendant) or a history of making false allegations of similar crimes.

Constitutional concerns. FRE 412, although it lacks the two exceptions just mentioned, does contain a general (and superfluous) exception for any use that is constitutionally compelled. It is superfluous because even without it, an unconstitutional restriction could not be sustained. The major constitutional provisions with which a rape shield statute, and especially one as restrictive as FRE 412, might conflict are a defendant's rights to present a defense under the Due Process clause and to confront and cross-examine witnesses under the Sixth Amendment's Confrontation Clause. See generally *Confrontation Clause*, Chapter 5.

Compare non-sexual cases. Rape shield laws are exceptions to the long-established rule (itself an exception to the general prohibition against propensity evidence) that evidence of a victim's character is admissible to prove self-defense, consent, and the like. In Example 3.14 if Dean were charged with non-sexual assault and battery against Victoria and claimed Victoria had struck him first, he could introduce evidence that, for example, Victoria had attacked other men without provocation on several similar occasions in the past.

Prior acts of defendant: FRE 413-415. As indicated elsewhere (see *Propensity Evidence*), new FRE 413-415 permits the use of propensity evidence to prove the defendant in a sexual assault or child molestation case committed the crime before the court. Although these new rules are motivated by the same general policies as Rule 412, they do not address the same issue. Rule 412 prevents a sexual crime victim from being subjected to exposure of her sexual history, thus curbing abuses in cross-examining such victims and making it more likely they will cooperate in prosecuting sex offenders. Rules 413-415, in contrast, merely make it easier to prosecute and convict those accused of sex offenses. Their lack of a victim-protection justification and direct removal of the traditional protection against unfair prejudice afforded other defendants, especially in combination with the restrictions on cross-examination of the victim imposed by Rule 412, raise questions about their constitutionality which (as of this writing) are yet to be addressed by the courts.

4

Scientific and Probabilistic Evidence

Introduction and Overview of Chapter

Scientific evidence, like character evidence explored in Chapter 3, presents some special kinds of relevance problems. Here, however, it is not a matter of blanket exclusion of evidence we all recognize as marginally relevant but highly prejudicial; rather, the problems concern the ability of the court and the trier of fact to evaluate and make proper use of evidence that goes beyond their common experience and understanding. One party's scientific evidence is another's junk science. The law of evidence struggles to sort one out from the other.

  Although the chapter is divided between the topics of "scientific" and "probabilistic" evidence, the latter is really a specific example of the former;

theories about probabilities and their use in court are, of course, a form of scientific evidence, and as much, if not more, bewildering to the uninitiated as any lie detector test or voiceprint.

A. SCIENTIFIC EVIDENCE: DEFINITION, EXAMPLES, AND USE

Scientific Evidence

Evidence that depends for its relevance on scientific principles, particularly those of the natural sciences. Typically, this type of evidence is presented as expert testimony regarding some scientific process, device, or principle.

Example 4.1: Don is on trial for murder. He allegedly stabbed Vickie with a knife. The prosecution introduces the blood-stained shirt that Don was wearing when arrested and the testimony of Edgar, who states that he has developed a method of determining exactly how long a blood stain has been on an item of clothing. Edgar's testimony would be deemed "scientific evidence" and would have to meet the tests and qualifications set out in this chapter.

Need for expert testimony. In actual usage, the phrase "scientific evidence" has no very precise boundaries. Some would include in the definition, for example, evidence based on the social sciences or technical knowledge in general. One thing that does distinguish "scientific" from most other evidence is that it generally cannot be understood or applied — that is, its probative value cannot be assessed — without the aid of expert testimony. This is because its principles are not within the experience of the average person who lacks training in the particular scientific field. Furthermore, untrained jurors, or even judges, may be overawed by some scientific device or process and be prone to believe it infallible or at least beyond their ability to deny. For these reasons, special rules have been developed for evaluating the relevance and admissibility of so-called scientific evidence.

Example 4.2: Daryl is on trial for murder. The prosecution introduces evidence that Daryl's wife left him to live with Victor, the murder victim, a few days before Victor was killed. It also introduces ballistic evidence that a bullet found in Victor's body was fired by a revolver that Daryl was carrying when he was arrested. The latter evidence, concerning the bullet, is scientific evidence and may be subject to special rules of admissibility.

The relevance of the first item of evidence in Example 4.2 (jealousy as motive) is clear to anyone. The unstated major premise that "men whose wives leave them for another man are likely to harbor ill will toward that person" is a matter of common experience and understanding. (See *Inference (Circumstantial Evidence)*.) The ballistic evidence, however, is different. Without convincing expert testimony, the judge or jury would have no way to evaluate either the validity of the general proposition that guns leave distinctive marks on bullets they fire, or the specific assertion that in this case the marks on the bullet match the gun possessed by Daryl. Thus, in a sense the concept of scientific evidence is merely a special application of the general rules relating to expert testimony (FRE 702-03; see Chapter 9). This is, in fact, the view taken by the Supreme Court in interpreting the Federal Rules. See *Daubert Guidelines*.

Note that although the judge or jury in Example 4.2 might be able to see the actual match between bullet and gun if it were properly demonstrated, as by photographs or diagrams (see *Demonstrative Evidence*), they would still be unable to determine its significance without expert advice. If, for example, all bullet markings are identical, the match in this case is totally irrelevant.

Of course, expert opinion testimony is necessary in many circumstances that do not involve a disputed scientific device or process, but merely the expert's knowledge and experience. Typical is the medical expert testifying to a plaintiff's condition or prognosis. If such testimony does not rely on any new or unusual procedures or disputed principles, the issue of scientific evidence does not arise; the ordinary rules for the admission of expert opinion testimony are applied. For many courts, these same rules are sufficient even for new or controversial devices or techniques, but others have applied special rules to such evidence. For discussion of these specific rules, see *Frye Doctrine; Daubert Guidelines*.

Examples of scientific evidence. Some prominent examples of scientific evidence that have proven particularly controversial over the past several years are listed below.

(1) **Polygraphy** is a method for determining whether a person is lying, using what is commonly called a "lie detector." Although versions of a polygraph machine have been around for decades, for most purposes (and especially in criminal cases) they have yet to be accepted as evidence. (Under the new *Daubert* guidelines, however, some courts are moving from a per se rejection of polygraphy to a case-by-case evaluation.)

(2) **Spectrography** is commonly called a "voiceprint." Like fingerprints, voiceprints (the pattern made by a voice when it is recorded on a spectrograph) are said to be unique to individual voices; thus a person's voice can be identified by the voiceprint it has left. Spectrography is still controversial, but a growing number of courts do permit its use in limited circumstances.

(3) **DNA Typing** (often called DNA fingerprinting or genetic fingerprinting) is the newest identification medium. It attempts to match traces

of bodily fluids (generally blood or semen) with the person who left them behind, by matching aspects of the DNA molecules they contain with those carried by the person in question. Matches are not absolute but are generally expressed in terms of statistical probabilities of the incriminating DNA belonging to the subject. Gradually the principle of DNA typing has gained acceptance (though by no means unanimous approval) in the courts. The main battlefield now is in methodology, rather than theory, as many courts have become wary of the procedures used by both commercial and police-affiliated forensic laboratories to evaluate DNA evidence. In addition, courts are grappling with the proper way to instruct a jury in the application of DNA evidence to the case, specifically the assimilation and use of the sometimes-bewildering, potentially misleading statistical data. See *Probabilistic Evidence*.

(4) **Hypnosis of witnesses**, either before they testify or on the stand, has the theoretical potential to remove many barriers to accurate and total recall of events. In practice, however, courts have become quite skeptical about its efficacy and reliability. A hypnotized witness may accept suggestion too readily, **confabulate** (invent details to fill in gaps in the story, or just to please the hypnotist), or become unable to distinguish actual from hypnosis-induced memory.

Thus far, testimony under hypnosis is not permitted, and while some courts admit testimony previously "enhanced" by hypnosis, many now either have established stringent safeguards or exclude it entirely (perhaps with limited exceptions, as for memories shown to predate the hypnosis). A court, however, cannot constitutionally exclude per se (without specific grounds) the hypnotically-refreshed testimony of a criminal defendant.

(5) **Narcoanalysis** (or narco-interrogation), using what is sometimes popularly called "truth serum," carries many of the same dangers as hypnosis, with the added difficulty of an even greater aura of infallibility in the eyes of a lay jury.

Frye Doctrine

The traditional test for the admissibility of scientific evidence, requiring that the evidence (the disputed scientific principle, technique, procedure, or device) have gained general acceptance in the particular field in which it belongs, that is, in the relevant scientific community. This is also known as the **general acceptance test.**

The general acceptance test, which usually applies only to "novel" scientific techniques, derives from *Frye v. United States*,[1] a 1923 prosecution for murder in which the federal circuit court for the District of Columbia rejected the defendant's attempt to prove his innocence using evidence of an early version of a polygraph test.

1. 293 Fed. 1013 (D. C. Cir. 1923).

Reliance on scientific community.   When a court applies *Frye*, scientific evidence must still meet the usual test for expert testimony (which under the Federal Rules is basically helpfulness to the trier of fact). (See **FRE 702**; Chapter 9.) But its validity must also be determined under the general acceptance test. In other words, to the extent that the validity of a scientific technique bears on its ultimate helpfulness to the trier of fact, the decision whether to admit it is largely taken out of the hands of the trial judge and delegated to the scientific community. This is a point either in favor of or against the doctrine, depending on whom you might ask.

The relevant scientific community.   Critics of the *Frye* doctrine also point out that it is often unclear just how to identify the relevant scientific community that must have accepted the principle or process.

Example 4.3:   In the course of divorce proceedings, Harry and Wanda are disputing the issue of child custody. In attempting to prove Harry a poor risk as a single parent, Wanda introduces the testimony of Emil, who testifies to a new technique developed by Freudian psychologists to aid in the determination of just such questions. In applying the *Frye* test, the judge would have to decide whether to seek general acceptance in the community of scientists, psychologists, or only Freudian psychologists. What if there is only one of the latter in the local community?

Frye superseded.   Whether a good test or not, general acceptance has been challenged and to some extent replaced as the criterion for admitting scientific evidence by the more recent **Daubert guidelines.** In the 1993 case of *Daubert v. Merrell Dow Pharmaceuticals, Inc.,*[2] the Supreme Court held that FRE 702 superseded the *Frye* test in the federal courts. For cases governed by federal evidence law, general acceptance is now only one of several factors by which a court, applying FRE 702, might determine whether an expert would be testifying to, in the Rule's language, scientific knowledge that would assist the trier of fact. Scientific knowledge was defined by the Court as derived by or grounded in "scientific method." Thus, the Court held that evidentiary reliability must be based on scientific validity. And of course the evidence still must be helpful to the trier of fact, as must all expert testimony under FRE 702. The scientific technique, even if valid, must "fit" the purpose for which it is offered.

The Daubert guidelines.   The *Daubert* court offered five "nonexclusive" guidelines for trial judges in acting as "gatekeeper" and assessing the validity of scientific evidence: (1) whether the theory or technique can be or has been tested; (2) whether it has been subjected to peer review and, if possi-

---

2. 509 U.S. 579 (1963).

ble, publication (emphasizing that the latter is not dispositive); (3) its known or potential rate of error; (4) the existence and maintenance of standards; and (5) general acceptance in the relevant scientific community. (The continued presence of the general acceptance criterion, although no longer an absolute requirement, causes some commentators to believe that the ghost of *Frye* will continue to haunt inquiry into scientific evidence.)

The result of *Daubert* should be to make the admission of scientific evidence much more flexible than under *Frye*. The test is less a "bright line" and more dependent on the ability or willingness of a trial judge to make an independent judgment of scientific validity.

Daubert expressly is limited to the "scientific knowledge" prong of FRE 702, and does not apply directly to "technical or other specialized knowledge," although some lower courts have extended it to the latter. Clearly it is not intended to affect, and should not be confused with, the separate test of **FRE 703,** that specific expert testimony must be based on facts or data "of a type reasonably relied upon by experts in the particular field," although that basis need not itself be admissible evidence. See Chapter 9. Balancing under **FRE 403** still operates as well.

Practical effect of Daubert. It should be emphasized that state courts that have followed the *Frye* standard in the past may (and many certainly will) continue to do so, even if the federal courts in that state must now abandon it to follow *Daubert*. This may lead to some forum-shopping for application of whichever rule a party prefers.

Most cases of scientific evidence will likely be unaffected by *Daubert*, reaching the same result under either test (as did the *Daubert* case itself when the evidence was reassessed under the new criteria). For that matter, most routine, well-established scientific evidence from a qualified expert is already admitted with little or no difficulty under the basic principles of Rules 702 and 703. Nevertheless, the *Daubert* guidelines will result in the admission of some scientific evidence that has not gained general acceptance and would have failed the *Frye* test. And there will likewise be occasional cases of generally accepted principles that, applying the other *Daubert* criteria, are ultimately excluded. *Daubert* would appear to be, at least potentially, a two-way street.

Forensic Science

Scientific practice that is directed toward the production or evaluation of evidence, or that pertains to the courts; thus forensic medicine, forensic psychology, and so forth.

Junk Science

The pejorative term applied to scientific evidence that supposedly lacks scientific validity. It is most often encountered as defense counsel's characterization of a purportedly scientific test or technique introduced by a plaintiff, on an issue such as the causal link between the defendant's product and the plaintiff's injury. It exemplifies, however, a more general dissatisfaction on either side with expert testimony that smacks of pop science or sloppy methodology.

B. PROBABILISTIC EVIDENCE: DEFINITION, EXAMPLES, AND USE

Probabilistic Evidence

Evidence that is based on an analysis of probabilities, that is, the mathematical likelihood of the existence or nonexistence of a fact.

Probabilities can be based on statistical or nonstatistical data. It is the use of statistics that tends to be most controversial.

Probabilistic evidence, which typically is based on statistical generalizations, can be contrasted with **particularistic evidence,** which derives from the particular facts of the case before the court, such as eyewitness testimony or the finding of the defendant's necklace at the scene of the crime.

Probabilistic evidence can be as simple as the statistical likelihood of a coin coming up heads or tails on any given toss, or as complex as the likelihood that some discovered trace or observed characteristic belongs to the defendant, out of all the possible persons to whom they could belong.

Example 4.4: Debbie is accused of killing Vance, who was stabbed with a knife. A police officer testifies that a six-inch bloodstained knife was found at the scene of the killing. An expert then testifies that the blood on the knife was type O, and that Debbie also has type O blood. The evidence of the knife and blood types is particularistic evidence, whereas an attempt to prove the incidence in the relevant population of type O blood, and to use this figure to argue the mathematical likelihood that Debbie is the killer, would be an example of probabilistic evidence.

A common use of probability theory is the so-called **paternity index.** This is a calculation, based on serologic (blood analysis) evidence, of the likelihood that a putative father (the defendant) would produce a child with given blood characteristics, as compared to the likelihood that a man selected at random would do so. A paternity index of 150 would mean that the subject is 150 times more likely than a man selected at random to have fathered a child with the given characteristics. (It is not a measure of the probability that the defendant is in fact the father of a particular child. If, for example, the accused is sterile, his actual probability of paternity is zero, no matter what his paternity index might be.)

Risk of misleading jury. Even if, however, Mark Twain's reference to "lies, damned lies, and statistics" is exaggerated, both "probabilists" and "anti-probabilists" would likely agree that improperly used statistics can give a false impression to a person unfamiliar with their use. Because of this, courts tend to be wary of purely mathematical evidence. Although no attempt will be made here to resolve, or even set out, the heated and voluminous debate that persists over the use of probabilistic evidence, a simple example will demonstrate some of the more obvious problems that have been addressed. These concern the difficulty of discerning just what a given statistic proves, and what it does not prove.

Example 4.5:   Dennis is accused of killing Violet. An eyewitness testifies that the killer was wearing a moustache and had a beard. Dennis has these two characteristics. The prosecution offers expert testimony that in the local population, one in five men has a moustache, and one in ten has a beard. Multiplying ten by five, the expert concludes that "the incidence of men with both moustaches and beards is 1 in 50, so the odds are 50-to-1 that Dennis killed Violet."

Among the difficulties with the reasoning in Example 4.5 are the following:

- Are the statistics offered accurate? (Are there really four bare-lipped men for each mustachioed one?)
- If so, what is the "local population," and does it represent all of the persons who could possibly have killed Violet? (For example, what geographic area should be included? Could the killer have driven in from another town or state and then left after the killing?)
- Are the data equally and uniformly applicable to all segments of the local population, regardless of race, age, sex, etc.? (Do Asian men tend to have the same proportion of beards and moustaches as Caucasian men? Which groups are represented in the chosen population, and to which does the defendant belong?)
- Are moustaches and beards independent characteristics (that is, do they have **statistical independence**)? The **product rule** (or **multiplication rule**) states that if the frequency of one factor (like having a moustache) is 1 in 5, and the frequency of another (like having a beard) is 1 in 10, then to get the frequency of having a beard

and a moustache one can multiply 5 by 10 and get 1 in 50. But if having a beard tends to make it more likely that a person will also have a moustache, then the two factors are not mutually independent and the product rule does not apply. At the extreme, if one could not have a beard without also having a moustache, the frequency of having both would be 1 in 10, not 1 in 50.

- Even if all of the statistics are correct, they do not make the odds of guilt 50-to-1. To simplify this point, assume a different but parallel example:

Example 4.6:   I pick a playing card, an ace of clubs, at random out of a hat containing a full deck of 52 cards. I look at it and show it to you, then I put it back into the hat. (This is the equivalent of an eyewitness description of the killer of Violet in Example 4.5 as a man with a beard and moustache. In effect, Violet was "killed by an ace of clubs," and the actual killer has "escaped" back into the deck.) You are now looking for (seeking to "arrest") that same card. You reach into the hat (the "local population") and pull out ("arrest") an ace of clubs. Is it the same one I drew before (the "man who killed Violet")? We know there is only one ace of clubs in every deck of 52 cards; but that does not make the "odds" that the present card is the one in question "1 in 52." On the contrary, if there is only one deck of cards in the hat, then all we can say before you draw one out is that the chance that a card chosen at random from the hat will be an ace of clubs is 1 in 52, which itself is an irrelevant statistic. Once you are holding an ace of clubs pulled from the hat, however, and assuming we are correct that the original card was an ace of clubs, the actual chance that the card just drawn is the one I drew earlier (that "the man arrested is the one who killed Violet") isn't 1 in 52, but 1 in 1. It must be the same card, as there is only one in a deck.

But wait! What if the hat (the "local population") is very large and contains not 1, but 100 decks of cards? The chance that you will choose ("arrest") an ace of clubs at random is still 1 in 52 (actually 100 in 5,200). But having chosen ("arrested") an ace of clubs, the chance that you have chosen the *same* ace of clubs as I did ("arrested the man who killed Violet") is now not 1 in 1, or even 1 in 52, but *1 in 100!*

- Finally, and perhaps most importantly to the anti-probabilists who distrust such evidence, all of this may distract the jury from the crucial initial question: *Did the killer of Violet actually have a moustache and a beard?* ("Was the card initially chosen an ace of clubs?") In other words, the statistical evidence may detract from and lessen the trier of fact's concentration on the particularistic evidence, upon the accuracy of which the validity of this entire exercise depends. See *Bayes' Theorem*.

An important distinction must be made between the admissibility of probabilistic evidence and its sufficiency. It is one thing to use a statistical calculation as one item of evidence, for which a court will consider its validity and usefulness; it is quite another, however, to base a verdict or conviction on a statistical calculation as the *only* item of evidence. One well-known example (suggested by Professor Lawrence Tribe) follows:

Example 4.7: Patty sues Bus Co. for injuries suffered when Patty was struck by a hit-and-run vehicle in a crosswalk. The only evidence Patty presents is that she was knocked down by a blue bus. Bus Co. owns four of the only five blue buses in town. The odds that Bus Co. owns the bus that hit Patty are therefore 4 in 5, or 80 percent in favor of Bus Co.'s liability. This is, of course, well beyond the theoretical "balance of probabilities" upon which a jury is usually required to find liability in a civil case. In theory, therefore, Bus Co. should be held liable on a directed verdict in Patty's favor.

While a famous case directly on point (*Smith v. Rapid Transit*[3]) held that such probability evidence alone is not sufficient to find Bus Co. liable, a heated controversy continues as to the correctness of that holding and the propriety of using bare statistics as the sole basis for decision.

Note that, had the odds in Example 4.7 been merely one of many items of evidence, such as eyewitness testimony that one of Bus Co.'s drivers was driving the bus and records showing that one of Bus Co.'s buses was scheduled to be at the scene of the accident at approximately the time it occurred, there would be little controversy over the admissibility (as opposed to sufficiency) of the 4-in-5 statistical evidence.

Bayes' Theorem

*A formula (named for the Reverend Thomas Bayes) that permits the revision of an estimate of probability (a **prior probability**) in light of some new evidence of probability, that is, some new data.*

Example 4.8: Dan is on trial for killing Veronica. From eyewitness and other direct and circumstantial (particularistic) evidence, the jury is 75 percent convinced — that is, it believes the chances are 3 in 4 — that Dan killed Veronica. The prosecution then produces expert tes-

3. 58 N.E.2d 754 (Mass. 1945).

timony that, because of certain traces of blood found at the scene, Dan is one of only 10 persons who could have killed Veronica. Bayes' Theorem is a means of calculating the new ("posterior") probability of Dan's guilt based on both the prior and the new data.

While the exact calculations involved in Bayes' formula are beyond this work, suffice it to say that its concept is an important qualification to the tendency to give too much weight to supposed chances of guilt or the like. To illustrate using a very simplified example:

Example 4.9: Fred is alleged to be the father of baby Babs. According to blood tests and taking into consideration frequencies of blood types in the population, the odds that Fred is the father are 99 to 1. There is, however, undisputed evidence already in the case that Fred is and always has been sterile. When the new probability of 99 to 1 is combined with the prior probability of 0, the result is still 0.

Whether or not a court admits evidence of Bayes' formula directly, it is likely to recognize the importance of combining new statistical evidence with prior probabilities, including those based on particularistic evidence.

5

Hearsay

Introduction and Overview of Chapter

The subject of hearsay, like that of the Rule Against Perpetuities in estates law, is often both feared and misunderstood by students (and not a few practitioners). But unlike its infamous cousin, it is in fact a relatively simple concept. A diligent effort to understand the hearsay rule's basic premise at the outset of its study will make the rest of the subject (primarily exceptions to the rule) quite accessible. Further, unlike perpetuities, an understanding of the policies and rationale behind the hearsay rule will go a long way toward making the rule itself seem more logical. For this reason, although generally this book eschews lengthy discussions of policy or historical background, this chapter includes a brief foray into those regions.

Over the years, I have encountered and have myself created many devices for making the hearsay rule easier for students to learn and understand. Those that have proven the most successful are set out here. They include both simple diagrams and a basic Rule of Thumb.

All analysis of hearsay problems must begin with the question of whether the proffered evidence (as it is intended to be used) is or is not hearsay; if it is, the next issue becomes the availability of a hearsay exception. The chapter reflects this approach: it is divided into entries (1) for the basic hearsay rule and the difference between hearsay and non-hearsay uses of statements; (2) for exceptions to the hearsay rule for uses of statements that are definitely hearsay but may nevertheless be admissible; and (3) the constitutional limitations on the use of hearsay under the Sixth Amendment's Confrontation Clause.

A word about diagrams: For most people it is easier to understand an abstract concept when they can visualize it in some concrete way. The diagrams used in this chapter attempt to give some visual substance to the fact patterns set out in the various examples. They represent statements to witnesses or to the court by an arrow (———→). It is suggested that you try them if you are having trouble separating out the various statements and declarants, especially in a problem of multiple hearsay.

A. HEARSAY AND NON-HEARSAY

Hearsay Evidence (In General)

Evidence of a statement which was made other than by a witness while testifying at the hearing and that is offered to prove the truth of the matter stated.

There are, in fact, many different formulations of the definition of hearsay and of the hearsay rule (or, more accurately, the rule *against* hearsay, for it is an exclusionary rule that defines hearsay and then excludes it in all cases that do not fit within some exception). The foregoing definition, from California Evidence Code section 1200 (and former Uniform Rule 63), is typical and, because it contains no terms of art that need special definition, is the easiest to use to explain the basic concept: put simply, "hearsay is an attempt to get the trier of fact to believe an assertion that was not made in their presence." (See also *Hearsay Evidence (Federal Rules).*) Following a detailed explanation and several examples, you will find a Rule of Thumb that will make application of the hearsay rule much easier.

Example 5.1: Paul sues Xavier in a jury trial, for injuries when Xavier's automobile struck Paul as Paul was crossing a street. Paul alleges that

Xavier was at fault for driving through a red light. Witness Wanda testifies that while she didn't see the accident, her friend Donald saw it and later told Wanda, "The car ran the red light." The quoted statement, having been made other than by a witness testifying at the present hearing and offered to prove its truth, that is, that the car indeed ran the red light, is hearsay. It is an attempt to get the jury to believe an assertion (by Donald) that was not made (by Donald) in their presence.

Hearsay can be diagrammed as a series of statements, in this case from Donald to Wanda and from Wanda to the court:

$$D \longrightarrow W \longrightarrow Court$$

The person whose hearsay statement is being offered (Donald in Example 5.1) is called the **declarant,** that is, the one who has made the out-of-court declaration. The declarant must be distinguished from the witness (Wanda in the example), the person who relates to the court the declarant's statement. (Note that if Wanda were testifying to a statement that *she* made in the past, it would still be hearsay and she would be *both* witness and declarant.)

At the outset, the rule excluding hearsay must be distinguished from the similar but distinct rule requiring that a witness have firsthand knowledge (also called personal knowledge). See Chapter 8. If, in Example 5.1, witness Wanda had testified, "The car ran the red light," the proper objection would have been not hearsay but lack of firsthand knowledge, because Wanda is stating a fact which she did not observe with her own senses. Since, however, Wanda actually testified, "Donald told me, 'The car ran the red light,'" there is a hearsay but not a firsthand knowledge objection, because while Wanda may not have seen the car run the light, she did personally hear Donald say so, and that is all she is asserting.

Although the term "hearsay" strictly refers to a witness who heard someone else say something, a hearsay statement may be oral, written, or implied by conduct ("see-do" rather than "hear-say," usually called **assertive conduct**). Thus in Example 5.1, if Wanda's friend Donald had written to Wanda saying "The car ran the red light," it would be as much hearsay as if spoken to her; similarly if Donald had acted the statement out in pantomime (see Example 5.5). Hearsay statements, like fashion statements, can be made by appearances as well as words. Finally, the common law definition of hearsay includes assertions that are implied from nonassertive conduct. These are discussed under *Hearsay Evidence (Federal Rules)*, because they represent an important difference between common law and the Federal Rules.

The key to understanding hearsay is recognizing that the definition of hearsay contains two major parts, both of which must be satisfied for a statement to be hearsay: The statement must have been made outside of the present trial or hearing; and it must be offered into evidence with the purpose of proving the truth of the matter asserted. These two parts require some further explanation.

1. Presence at the Hearing

Hearsay is one of those concepts that is easiest to understand when one understands the rationale behind it. When one considers the fundamental reason for the hearsay rule, the distinction between witness and declarant becomes clear.

There are primarily three potential weaknesses of testimonial evidence (hearsay or otherwise) concerning some event or condition: (1) The speaker (or writer) may have misperceived the event in question; (2) the speaker may have forgotten what really happened by the time of the statement; and (3) the speaker may have lied or been ambiguous or otherwise unclear in relating the event. These three deficiencies are sometimes called, respectively, errors of perception, errors of memory, and errors of narration (both intentional and unintentional). They can be illustrated as follows:

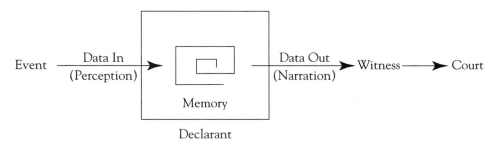

Declarant Donald (1) perceives an event (by sight, hearing, touch, and so forth), the data entering his mind. It (2) resides in his memory until (3) he relates (narrates) it to Wanda, who then, as a witness, repeats it to the court. At each stage of the process, there is a possibility of error.

To overcome these three potential sources of error, the common law developed three methods of detecting or avoiding them: (1) Requiring the speaker to be under oath; (2) observing the speaker's demeanor (appearance and tone of voice) at the time the statement is made; and (3) cross-examination of the speaker to clarify any ambiguities and discover any intentional or inadvertent errors.

All three of these safeguards require at least that the statement have been made at a hearing or trial, and all ideally require (although only the second necessitates) the presence of the speaker at the hearing, testifying in the presence of the jury (that is, **viva voce** (living voice) **testimony**).

65

In Example 5.1, then, Wanda is at the hearing. As to her, all the safe-guards are present: She is under oath; her demeanor can be observed; and she can be cross-examined, all before the same jury that must decide whether to believe her when she states "Donald said that Xavier ran the red light." Therefore the link from Wanda to the court in the diagram is not hearsay. Donald, however, was not at the hearing when he allegedly made the statement to Wanda. As there are no safeguards available, even if the jury decides Wanda is telling it the truth (that is, that Donald indeed made the statement to Wanda), it has no way of deciding whether Donald was telling the truth to Wanda. The **D——→W** link in the diagram is thus hearsay.

Note: It is common to substitute for the awkward "statement made other than by the declarant while testifying at the [present] hearing," the simple phrase "out-of-court statement." As shorthand, the phrase is useful (and this work uses it in that manner). But one must beware of taking "out-of-court" literally: As indicated, hearsay is *not* confined to statements made outside of a court, but includes statements made in some other court or proceeding than the one at which the statement is being offered into evidence. (Such statements may be the subject of the *Former Testimony* exception, discussed in detail elsewhere.) Thus it may help to think of the phrase as more properly "out-of-*this*-court statement."

2. Offered to Prove the Truth

The same fundamental basis for the hearsay rule explains why a statement is hearsay only if it is offered to prove the truth of the matter stated. In essence, there is no need to guard against error in the correctness of the declarant's statement if correctness is irrelevant to its intended use.

In Example 5.1, the only reason to require that Donald's statement be made in court, before this jury, is so that the jury can make use of the three safeguards against intentional or inadvertent error. If Donald is either lying or mistaken, then Xavier did not run the red light. Since the only purpose of Paul's offering Donald's statement (through Wanda's testimony) is to prove that Xavier ran the red light, even if the jury believes Wanda's testimony that Donald made the statement to Wanda, it is crucial that the jury also be able to decide whether or not Donald was telling the truth to Wanda. For this they need the three safeguards of oath, demeanor, and cross-examination. Because Donald's statement to Wanda was made out of the jury's presence, not under oath and not subject to cross-examination, the jury is denied all three ways to assess Donald's statement.

Suppose, however, that the case were slightly different:

Example 5.2:   Same facts as Example 5.1, except it turns out that the whole lawsuit was a fraud by Paul, and that Xavier never did hit Paul with his car. Wanda, the witness, is now on trial for perjury. Wanda maintains that she told the truth when she testified, "Donald told me the car ran the red light." Wanda calls Harold, her husband, who testifies that he was present at the time Donald made his statement to Wanda, and that Donald indeed said, "The car ran the red light."

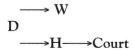

Harold's testimony is not hearsay, because although Harold is testifying to the same exact statement by Donald as did Wanda, in the same words as used by Wanda, Wanda is not offering Harold's testimony to prove the truth of the statement by Donald, but only that Donald in fact said it: If Donald said the words, even if they were false, then Wanda was telling the truth when she so testified. Here the statement is still relevant, but for another purpose than proving its truth.

Note carefully that in Example 5.2, unlike Example 5.1, the jury is not being asked to determine whether the out-of-court statement by Donald is true. Therefore the jury does not need the three safeguards of oath, demeanor, and cross-examination of Donald. So long as it believes Harold (who is in court under oath and subject to cross-examination), it does not have to believe Donald. Similarly:

Example 5.3:   Same facts as Example 5.1, except that Paul alleges that Xavier was negligent in driving with faulty brakes. Xavier counters that his brakes were fine, and even if they were faulty he had no reason to know of it. Paul calls witness Wanda to testify that she was waiting at a local brake repair shop when she overheard Donald, a mechanic, tell Xavier, "Your brakes are faulty."

$$D \begin{array}{c} \longrightarrow X \\ \\ \longrightarrow W \longrightarrow \text{Court} \end{array}$$

If this statement is introduced to prove Xavier's brakes were faulty, it is hearsay; but if it is introduced only to prove that Xavier was on notice that his brakes might be faulty, it is not hearsay.

Video tape problem: Is it hearsay? No!

> Rule of Thumb: In most instances, whether an out-of-court statement is hearsay can be determined simply by answering one question: *Does the jury have to believe the declarant?* That is, from the point of view of the party offering it, is the statement just as helpful if the jury disbelieves it? If the jury has to believe the declarant for the evidence to be of help, the statement is hearsay; if not, it is not hearsay.

A videotape doesn't testify. "while testifying" implies that someone is testifying as to what was said (re the contents of the videotapes)

A videotape is circumstantial evidence it is not testimonial + therefore is not subject to hearsay

If is physical evidence. Since physical evid. subject to hearsay rule?

Let us apply this Rule of Thumb to each of the above examples: In Example 5.1, the jury does have to believe declarant Donald when he said, "The car ran the red light;" if Donald was lying or mistaken, the car did not run the red light and the evidence is of no help to Paul. In Example 5.2, however, as far as Wanda is concerned the jury does not have to believe Donald, because even if (as alleged) Donald was lying, Wanda is safe from prosecution if Donald in fact made the statement to Wanda. Finally, in Example 5.3, if Paul offers the statement to support his contention that the brakes were defective, the jury has to believe the mechanic for the statement to be of any use to Paul; but if Paul offers it only to prove notice (relying on other evidence to prove defectiveness), then so long as it was said it provided notice regardless of whether it was true. (For discussion of the problem of restricting admission of evidence to certain issues, see *Limited Admissibility*.)

Hearsay Evidence (Federal Rules)

Under **FRE 801(c),** hearsay is *"a statement, other than one made by the declarant while testifying at the trial or hearing, offered in evidence to prove the truth of the matter asserted."* The primary way in which this definition, shared by the Uniform Rules, differs from the common law (see *Hearsay (In General)*) is in its definition of the term "statement."

According to **FRE 801(a),** a **statement** is "(1) an oral or written assertion or (2) nonverbal conduct of a person, *if it is intended by the person as an assertion.*

Under the FRE, then, conduct can be hearsay, but only if the actor intended by the conduct to make some assertion. So-called **nonassertive conduct** that is offered as an **implied assertion** is not hearsay. This is consistent with many modern state rules (see, e.g., CEC 225), but it is contrary to the common law, under which (as illustrated in the famous case of *Wright v. Tatham*[1]) conduct that made an assertion was hearsay, even if such an assertion was not intended by the actor. Perhaps the most famous hypothetical example of this distinction is the following:

1. Wright v. Doe dem. Tatham, 7 AD. & E. 313, 112 Eng. Rep. 48 (1837).

68

Example 5.4: In a lawsuit Quincy wishes to prove that it was raining on a certain day in October. Witness William testifies that although he did not notice whether it was raining that day, he happened to look out of his window and see his friend Fiona emerge from the building and open her umbrella. Quincy contends that, since Fiona opened her umbrella, she must have thought that it was raining. Although she was not aware of it at the time, Fiona was, in effect, impliedly asserting to William that it was raining.

$$F \longrightarrow W \longrightarrow Court$$

Fiona's conduct is thus an out-of-court statement that is being offered to prove the truth of the matter asserted (it was raining), seeming to fit the definition of hearsay. However, since she did not intend to make any statement or assertion to William or anyone else, her conduct would not be deemed a statement within FRE 801(a)(2), and thus it would not be hearsay under FRE 801(c). It would, however, be hearsay under the common law definition.

Note that even if Fiona's nonassertive conduct had been verbal and assertive (she had said to William, "I hope I closed my convertible top this morning"), it would not be hearsay under the FRE if offered to prove it was raining, which Fiona did not intend to assert.

Example 5.5: Same facts as Example 5.4, except William testifies that he was sitting at his desk when Fiona came into the office. He asked Fiona whether it was raining, and instead of replying she raised her umbrella (she apparently was not superstitious) and pretended to huddle under it. Again Fiona's conduct of opening an umbrella is being used to prove the truth of the assertion it contains, that it was raining. Now, however, since Fiona *intended* her conduct to be an assertion (to be an answer to William's question), it is hearsay under both the common law and the FRE. See *Assertive Conduct.*

There are other types of statement which the FRE defines as nonhearsay despite the fact that they seem to fit the basic definition of hearsay. These are found in **FRE 801(d)**, and they are discussed separately under the entries for *Prior Statements of Witnesses* and *Admissions of a Party Opponent.*

Hearsay Within Hearsay

A hearsay statement in which not only is an assertion hearsay, but that assertion contains within it another assertion which also is hearsay. (The second assertion may itself contain another hearsay statement within it, and so forth *ad infinitum*.) This is sometimes called **multiple hearsay.**

In order for hearsay within hearsay to be admissible, every level of hearsay must come within an exception to the hearsay rule. See **FRE 805.**

Example 5.6: Daryl is on trial for assaulting Carol. Witness Wendell testifies in court that he was told by his friend Freda that she in turn was told by her friend Betty that Daryl assaulted Carol. Wendell's testimony contains [Betty's] hearsay within [Freda's] hearsay.

Fully written out, Wendell's testimony would read: "Freda said to me, 'Betty told me, "Daryl assaulted Carol." ' " It would be diagrammed:

$$\textbf{B} \longrightarrow \textbf{F} \longrightarrow \textbf{W} \longrightarrow \textbf{Court}$$

Wendell's statement to the court is not hearsay, because although the jury has to believe the statement for it to be helpful, it is made while testifying at this trial. (See *Hearsay (In General)*.) Freda's out-of-court statement to Wendell ("Betty told me, 'Daryl assaulted Carol' ") is hearsay, as it is offered to prove the truth of the matter stated by Freda, that Betty made such a statement to Freda. Freda's statement, however, contains a further assertion by Betty, that Daryl assaulted Carol. That assertion — the **B**$\longrightarrow$**F** link in the hearsay chain — also needs to be believed to be helpful, and so is also hearsay.

Thus for Wendell's testimony to be admissible, there must be an exception to the hearsay rule not only for **F**$\longrightarrow$**W,** but for **B**$\longrightarrow$**F** as well.

Breaking the hearsay chain. When there is a hearsay chain like that above, containing multiple hearsay statements, it is "broken," and there is no need to find another hearsay exception, at any point at which we no longer care whether a statement is true. That is, if any one of the statements in the chain is offered only to prove it was made and not for its truth, none of the statements behind it (that is, further back from the witness) needs to be true either, so none is hearsay.

Example 5.7: Pierre sues Alicia for defamation, for calling Pierre a "thief." Winnie testifies that she was told by her friend Charlie that he (Charlie) was told by Barbara that she (Barbara) was told by Alicia, "According to Judy, Pierre is a thief." (Under the law of defamation, Alicia would be liable even if she was only passing along Judy's remark.)

$$\textbf{J} \longrightarrow \textbf{A} \longrightarrow \textbf{B} \longrightarrow \textbf{C} \longrightarrow \textbf{W} \longrightarrow \textbf{Court}$$

Both **C——►W** and **B——►C** are hearsay, as they must be believed to be helpful. If either Charlie or Barbara is lying or mistaken, Alicia did not make the alleged defamatory statement. Accordingly, Winnie's testimony contains [Barbara's] hearsay within [Charlie's] hearsay. Barbara's statement, however, does not contain anyone else's hearsay within it, because Alicia's assertion is not hearsay. Alicia is liable if she merely made the statement, so Pierre is not trying to prove its truth (and in fact asserts its falsity). Therefore, hearsay exceptions only need be found for the statements by Barbara and Charlie. The chain is "broken" at **A——►B.**

As the chain is now broken, Judy's alleged statement to Alicia (the **J——►A** link) cannot be hearsay. Once the **A——►B** link need not be true (is not hearsay), *no link behind it need be true (that is, can be hearsay) either,* because if it doesn't matter that Alicia was lying (about being told by Judy), then it doesn't matter whether Judy made any statement at all, or whether there is even such a person as Judy, much less whether any such statement by Judy is true.

Finally, note that if Pierre chose to sue Judy instead of Alicia, the break in the chain would move a link back. Pierre would have to prove not only that Alicia said Judy called him a thief, but also that Judy did indeed call him one. Thus the **A——►B** link would be hearsay and require an exception. Judy's statement to Alicia, on the other hand, would remain non-hearsay, offered only to prove it was made.

Verbal Acts

Words, whether assertive or nonassertive, that have operative or legal effect merely by virtue of having been expressed.

Example 5.8:   Bill states to John, "I offer you my autographed Mickey Mantle baseball card for $100." John replies, "I am pleased to accept." According to contract law, these statements constitute an offer and an acceptance, merely because they were uttered. Should John fail to tender $100 or Bill refuse to deliver the card, evidence of these statements would be admissible to prove the contract, because they *are* the contract. They are verbal acts, the acts of offering and accepting a contract.

The reason the offer and acceptance in Example 5.8 are not hearsay is that the truth of their content is irrelevant. Even if Bill could prove that he was only kidding, or John that he really was not pleased at all to accept, the words themselves are enough to bind them.

Other examples of verbal acts are the words that constitute defamation

("Mary is a thief") or the crime of fraud ("This ring is a genuine diamond"). While ultimately it may be necessary to prove whether or not the statement is true, clearly neither would be introduced with the purpose of inducing the jury to believe the truth of the matter asserted by the declarant.

Sometimes the term "verbal act" is used in a broader sense to include any statement that has logical significance wholly apart from the truth of its content, such as "I am alive" to prove that the speaker is still alive or "Jill is a nice person" to prove the speaker likes Jill. Verbal parts of acts, discussed below, might also be included. These statements have no intrinsic significance, however, and therefore do not themselves constitute acts, and including them may unduly generalize the term.

Verbal Parts of Acts

Words that accompany and give a particular significance to otherwise ambiguous acts. Such words are not hearsay.

Example 5.9:   Bill hands his autographed Mickey Mantle baseball card to John. As he does so, he says, "I want this back tomorrow." Bill's words are a verbal part of the act of lending the card to John. They give significance (as a loan) to an otherwise ambiguous act (handing over the card). As such, they are not offered to prove their truth (that is, we don't care if secretly Bill did not want it back) and are not hearsay.

In Example 5.9, other words (such as "Take this, it's a present" or "Would you please see if you have another of these") would change the character of the act from a loan to a gift or an exchange. They too would not be hearsay.

Example 5.10:   Same facts as Example 5.9, except as Bill hands his baseball card to John, he says, "You know, I saw a card just like this last year selling for $100." These words, although they accompany the act of handing over the card, do not give any particular significance to that act. They therefore would be outside of the concept of verbal parts of acts.

Wigmore identified four conditions that a verbal part of an act must satisfy: (1) the conduct must be independently material (for example, the significance of the change of possession in Example 5.9 is at issue in the case); (2) the conduct must be equivocal (without the words, it could be a loan, a gift, or neither); (3) the words must give the conduct significance (under the law, the words can determine the effect of handing over the card); and (4) the words must accompany the conduct.

See also *Res Gestae.*

5. Hearsay

State of Mind (Non-hearsay)

Evidence of assertions, intended to show what the speaker is thinking or how the speaker feels about a matter.

State of mind evidence can be either hearsay or non-hearsay, and if hearsay it may come within an exception to the hearsay rule (see *Hearsay Exceptions: State of Mind*). There are, however, several ways in which an assertion may be non-hearsay if used to prove the state of mind of either the declarant or some third person.

Example 5.11: Dan is on trial for stabbing Vicki in a fight. Dan contends that he admired Vicki and would never have harmed her. Wayne testifies for the defense that, a day before the alleged stabbing, Dan said to Wayne, "That Vicki is the finest person I know." Dan is not attempting to prove that Vicki was, in fact, a fine person, but only that Dan admired Vicki. A person who disliked Vicki would not have said such nice things about her. It therefore is unnecessary for the jury to believe Dan's statement to use it as evidence of Dan's state of mind (admiration for Vicki), and this use is not hearsay. (Of course, the jury need not draw this inference; for example, it may decide that Dan was deliberately misrepresenting his true feelings in order to "manufacture" favorable evidence for just this use.)

Example 5.12: Dick is on trial for kidnapping Kirk. Wilma testifies for the prosecution that she was told by Kirk (who is unavailable to testify) that he was taken by Dick to Dick's apartment and kept there in a room with unusual green and purple striped wallpaper and a picture of Mount Rainier. Dick's landlord testifies that a room in Dick's apartment does indeed have green and purple striped wallpaper and a picture of Mount Rainier. Kirk's statement to Wilma is admissible not to prove what Dick's apartment looked like, but to prove that Kirk was in fact there; how else would he have known what was in it? In other words, Kirk's statement is non-hearsay if used only to prove that Kirk had acquired knowledge of the appearance of Dick's apartment.

Example 5.12 is sometimes called a case of proving a **trace on the mind** of the declarant: showing an awareness or consciousness of facts that could be explained only by the declarant's perceiving them. Note carefully, however, that for the assertion in such a case to be non-hearsay, it must not be necessary to rely upon it (that is, there must be independent evidence available) to prove the fact stated, and there must have been little or no opportunity for the declarant's mind to have acquired the trace or awareness — that is, for the declarant to have learned or guessed the information contained in the assertion — other than the way suggested.

Example 5.13: Descartes said, "Cogito, ergo sum" ("I think, therefore I am"). If offered to prove not that Descartes was in fact thinking, but only that he knew how to speak Latin, it would not be hearsay. For this purpose we need know only that he made the statement (he spoke in Latin); it is irrelevant whether he was telling the truth about thinking (or, for that matter, about being). Moreover, the mere fact that he spoke, in Latin or otherwise, is evidence of his "being," regardless of the content or truth of his statement. It is mere coincidence that he has stated the very fact that we wish to prove. Similarly, if he had stated in Latin "I can speak Latin," it would prove his knowledge of the language because he said it, not because we believe him.

Note that in a case like Example 5.13, the declarant need not even be making an assertion.

Example 5.14: Perry alleges that Dean was negligent in driving with faulty brakes. Dean admits that his brakes were faulty, but he contends that he had no reason to know of it. (See Example 5.3.) Perry calls a witness to testify that she was waiting at a local brake repair shop when she overheard Mike, a mechanic, tell Dean, "Your brakes are faulty." If used only to prove the state of mind of the listener Dean (notice that his brakes were faulty), Mike's statement is not hearsay.

As Example 5.14 illustrates, assertions can be used as non-hearsay to prove the state of mind of either the declarant or some person to whom the assertion is made. Neither use requires that the jury rely on the veracity of the declarant.

Prior Statements of Witnesses (In General)

Statements of witnesses that were made by them prior to (and not while) testifying at the present trial or hearing.

Example 5.15: Dennis is on trial for the murder of George. Witness Wendy testifies for the prosecution that she saw Dennis commit the crime. In rebuttal, Dennis's attorney introduces the testimony of police officer Pat that Wendy told her two days after George's death that Janet, not Dennis, killed George. This is a prior inconsistent statement.

$$W \longrightarrow P \longrightarrow \text{Court}$$
$$W \longrightarrow \text{Court}$$

Example 5.16:   Same facts as Example 5.15. Following Pat's testimony, the prosecution introduces the testimony of witness Constance, who states that one day after George's death (that is, before the alleged inconsistent statement to Pat) Wendy told Constance that she saw Dennis commit the crime. This is a prior consistent statement.

$$W \longrightarrow C \longrightarrow Court$$
$$W \longrightarrow P \longrightarrow Court$$
$$W \longrightarrow Court$$

Prior statements of witnesses occupy a region somewhere between the typical hearsay and non-hearsay statement. To the extent offered to prove their truth, they are hearsay, because they were not made by the witness while testifying at the present trial or hearing. Unlike other hearsay statements, however, the declarant is in court, under oath, and subject to cross-examination. Nevertheless, although the declarant is in court, the statement was not. It was not (necessarily) made under oath, the jury cannot view the declarant's demeanor as it is made, and any cross-examination would be "now for then": months or even years after the statement was made. For this reason, the law has been ambivalent about prior statements, and it remains so.

Traditionally, prior statements of witnesses were admissible only for non-hearsay purposes: inconsistent statements to impeach and consistent statements to support or rehabilitate the witness's present testimony. (In Example 5.15, Wendy's prior inconsistent statement, whether or not true, casts doubt on her veracity; in Example 5.16, Wendy's earlier consistent statement makes it less likely that her present testimony was a recent invention just for trial. See Chapter 8.) It was said that they could not be used for substantive purposes (that is, to prove the truth of their content).

Gradually, most jurisdictions have created exceptions to the hearsay rule for all or some prior statements. (These are discussed separately under *Hearsay Exceptions.*)

Under **FRE 801(d)(1),** however, some prior statements of witnesses (prior consistent or inconsistent statements and statements of identification) are simply classified as non-hearsay, although they are in truth hearsay exceptions. That is, despite the fact that if offered to prove the matter asserted they fit the general definition of hearsay, they are deemed "not hearsay" (and therefore admissible without an exception) so long as they meet certain criteria. See *Prior Inconsistent Statements; Prior Consistent Statements; Prior Statements of Identification.*

B.   EXCEPTIONS TO THE HEARSAY RULE

Hearsay Exceptions (In General)

Rules that permit the use of certain out-of-court statements despite the fact that their purpose is to prove the truth of the matter stated and they are therefore classified as hearsay.

Example 5.17:   Ada sues Boris for battery. Willie testifies for Boris that, at the hospital, Ada told him, "I guess I started the fight with Boris." Ada's out-of-court statement is hearsay because offered to prove the truth of what Ada said; but it is nonetheless admissible for that purpose because it comes within a recognized hearsay exception, that for Admissions of a Party Opponent.

Before there can be a hearsay exception, there must be hearsay. If a statement is not (for any reason) classified as hearsay (see *Hearsay* and *Non-hearsay*), it requires no hearsay exception to be admissible.

By the same token, hearsay exceptions must be carefully distinguished from non-hearsay uses of out-of-court statements that, in some other context, would be hearsay and require an exception. (See *Hearsay Evidence (In General)*.) A hearsay exception is an exception not to the definition of hearsay, but to the rule excluding hearsay uses of statements.

The Federal Rules Distinction.   The Federal Rules (and the current Uniform Rules) have confused the hearsay/non-hearsay distinction by declaring that certain statements that do satisfy the basic definition of hearsay (prior statements of witnesses and admissions by opposing parties), and to which an exception might logically apply, are deemed "not hearsay." FRE 801(d). See *Prior Statements of Witnesses (In General)*; *Admissions of a Party Opponent.* Calling a rose a daisy, however, does not change its fragrance. Unlike a true instance of "not hearsay," 801(d) statements do satisfy the basic definition of hearsay. While they could, therefore, be classified as exceptions to the *exclusion* of hearsay, under the FRE they are exceptions to the *definition* of hearsay. This is particularly confusing in the case of admissions, since (unlike prior statements) they have traditionally been considered a hearsay exception and continue as such in many jurisdictions. In this chapter both types of statement will be considered as hearsay exceptions, where they best fit analytically. The "not hearsay" designation will, of course, be duly noted.

Rationale for Hearsay Exceptions.   Although the list of hearsay exceptions evolved slowly and sometimes without great deliberation, Wigmore offered two unifying rationales that it is now generally agreed justify the existence of most exceptions: A hearsay exception is justified by it special *trustworthiness* and its special *necessity*.

Although these twin rationales serve as justifications for the existence and persistence of most hearsay exceptions, it generally is not necessary for a specific application of a particular exception to satisfy either rationale. Aside from a few exceptions that explicitly require a consideration of trustworthiness, and the so-called residual or "catchall" exceptions that are applied on a case-by-case basis, once a category of exception is established in the law, it applies regardless of whether it appears in the particular case to be either especially trustworthy or especially necessary. (Of course, if it is sufficiently untrustworthy and unnecessary, it may be excluded as overly prejudicial, confusing, or time-wasting under the equivalent of FRE 403.)

The discussion of specific exceptions below will highlight the rationale for each.

The "list" of exceptions. There are approximately 30 traditional exceptions to the hearsay rule, about a third of which are encountered with any frequency. The number cannot be precisely defined, for several reasons. Sometimes several related exceptions are treated together as one (for example, "existing mental or physical condition"; "*res gestae*"). At other times, what the common law calls an exception a codification may designate as non-hearsay (for example, admissions under the FRE). And the addition of "catchall" exceptions such as FRE 803(24), which can encompass virtually any statement that satisfies its general criteria, makes the actual number somewhat fluid. Of course, the number is less important than the substance; but in seeking a given exception, one must be aware that it may not appear in the same guise in every jurisdiction.

Nor does every exception appear in every jurisdiction. There are differences both in the acceptance of certain exceptions and in the scope of particular ones. Significant differences will be noted in the entries below.

Any given statement may qualify for more than one hearsay exception, and some are more easily proven than others. Even if you believe that all of the requirements for a particular exception have been met, check to see if another exception might not be available as well. Have as many "arrows in your quiver" as possible.

The requirement of unavailability. Both at common law and under modern codes, some hearsay exceptions require that the declarant — that is, the declarant's testimony — be unavailable to testify at the present trial, and some (the great majority) do not.

It is said that those exceptions requiring unavailability are less trustworthy and therefore require greater necessity to justify their existence; unavailability supplies that necessity. On the other hand, it is asserted that the hearsay statements that do not require unavailability are, for one reason or another, more trustworthy than would be live testimony, whereas those that require unavailability tend to be less trustworthy than live testimony by the declarant if it could be obtained. Thus, for one class of exceptions the greatest justification is necessity; for the other, it is trustworthiness.

Exceptions for which declarant must be available. Although for some exceptions the declarant must be unavailable, for two exceptions the declarant must be *available*. These are *Prior Statements of Witnesses* and *Past Recollection Recorded*. Both assume that the declarant is a witness in the present proceedings, and the exception relates to something the witness has said or written prior to and outside of those proceedings.

Specific exceptions follow, with examples and rationales.

Hearsay Exceptions (Specific Exceptions)

For convenience, the order of the major exceptions set out below largely follows that of the Federal Rules, merely because it has been so widely adopted. Nevertheless, those exceptions the FRE and many states have designated as "not hearsay" (see section A) are listed and discussed as exceptions, with the FRE's approach duly noted.

1. Exceptions Not Requiring Unavailability

As indicated above, some hearsay exceptions traditionally have not required that the declarant be unavailable, deeming the hearsay evidence sufficiently trustworthy to warrant admission even if live testimony could be obtained.

Prior Statements of Witnesses

Statements previously made by a witness who is now testifying at the present trial or hearing.

Example 5.18: Chris sues Laurel for trespass. Winton testifies for Chris that he saw Laurel on Chris's land. Laurel introduces the testimony of Ann, who states that, two days before the trial, Winton told Ann that to his knowledge Laurel was never on Chris's land. Ann has testified to a prior statement by Winton that is hearsay. Depending on the jurisdiction, Winton's prior statement may be admissible for the truth of the matter stated (that Laurel did not trespass) as a hearsay exception, or only to impeach Winton's testimony.

Rationale: Closer in time to the event than testimony in court; witness available to cross-examine.

There are hearsay exceptions, with very different requirements, for certain prior statements that are inconsistent (like Winton's in Example 5.18) or consistent with the present testimony of the witness (see Examples 5.22 and 5.23). They may also be prior statements of identification (Example 5.24). See section 3 for a general explanation of why prior statements of witnesses fit the usual definition of hearsay.

Prior Inconsistent Statements

Statements previously made by a witness that are inconsistent with the witness's present testimony.

Example 5.19: Julie sues George for battery, alleging that George struck Julie without provocation, and George counterclaims against Julie, contending that Julie provoked him and struck the first blow. Julie calls witness Wally, who testifies to Julie's version of the events. Before trial, however, Wally told Jim, a friend of George, that Julie had "struck George for no reason," a statement inconsistent with Wally's present testimony. On cross-examination by George, Wally denies making such a statement to Jim. George can call Jim to testify to what Wally told him. Wally's prior inconsistent statement is hearsay. It may be used in all jurisdictions to impeach Wally's testimony, weakening Julie's case. In some jurisdictions, however, it is also admissible under this hearsay exception to support George's case and prove that, contrary to Wally's present story, Julie was the aggressor.

Orthodox rule. Traditionally, under the so-called **orthodox rule,** prior statements inconsistent with the witness/declarant's present testimony can be used only to impeach present testimony, but not as substantive evidence. That is, there is no traditional hearsay exception for prior inconsistent statements such as Wally's in Example 5.19. Modern codes, however, generally do permit substantive use of at least some of these statements.

Two modern rules. There are, in fact, two modern approaches to prior inconsistent statements. The first takes the opposite position to the orthodox rule, providing a hearsay exception for every prior statement inconsistent with a witness's present testimony. Under such a rule, Wally's prior statement in Example 5.19 would be admissible for the truth of the matter stated by Wally (that Julie started the fight), provided only that the statement met other technical requirements for admission. See, e.g., CEC 1235.

The other major approach is a compromise between the above two extremes, providing a hearsay exception for certain prior inconsistent statements but not others, based on considerations of trustworthiness and necessity. The provisions of **FRE 801(d)(1)(A)** are an example of such a compromise, the only difference being the statement's classification as "not hearsay" rather than hearsay subject to an exception.

Under the FRE, the only prior inconsistent statements that are admissible for the truth of the matter asserted are those made by a witness (1) presently testifying and (2) subject to cross-examination, if the prior statement was made (3) under oath (subject to a penalty for perjury), and (4) at a prior "trial, hearing, or other proceeding, or in a deposition." The proceeding at which the prior statement was made need not have been related to the present one; nor need the statement have been subject to cross-examination at the time it was made, so long as the witness may be cross-examined now. Wally's prior statement in Example 5.19 would not be admissible for its truth under the Federal Rules; but compare:

Example 5.20: Doris is on trial for selling unlawful drugs to Matt. Matt is called as a witness by the prosecution, but Matt testifies that he purchased the drugs from someone other than Doris. Surprised by Matt's testimony, the prosecution submits evidence that Matt made two prior statements naming Doris as the seller of the drugs: one to a police officer upon Doris's arrest, and one under oath at a grand jury hearing related to an entirely different case. Both prior statements would be admissible to impeach Matt's present testimony by showing Matt to be an unreliable witness. Under the FRE, however, only the second statement would be admissible to prove the truth of the matter asserted, that Doris in fact sold the drugs to Matt.

Definition of inconsistency; lack of memory. A prior inconsistent statement need not be entirely inconsistent with the witness's testimony, if the implication of one version is inconsistent with the other. Further, some statements are considered inconsistent though they are literally and logically quite consistent.

Example 5.21: Witness Wanda is asked whether or not the light was red when plaintiff Pasqual crossed the street, and she states, "I don't recall." In an earlier, unrelated case, Wanda had testified that the light was red. Unless the court is convinced that Wanda's claimed lack of memory is genuine, Wanda's prior statement may be deemed inconsistent with her present testimony and thus admissible to prove that the light was indeed red.

In a strict sense, there is nothing inconsistent between knowing something at one time and forgetting it at some later time; it happens to us all. Yet a witness may easily feign lack of memory. As a result, most courts will consider a later claim of lack of memory as inconsistent and admit the prior statement. If, however, the court is convinced that the claim is genuine, it may well (and should) exclude the prior statement.

Effect on cross-examination. How does lack of memory affect the Federal Rule's requirement that the witness be subject to cross-examination? Lack of memory, of course, can impede or defeat attempts to cross-examine a witness. A claimed lack of memory of the underlying event, however, usually will not preclude questioning about the making of the statement itself (which is all the rule expressly requires). Therefore, probably only a totally unresponsive witness, or one claiming total lack of memory of even the making of the prior statement, would fail the test of being "subject to cross-examination."

Prior Consistent Statements

Statements previously made by a witness that are consistent with the witness's present testimony.

Example 5.22: Pasqual sues Denton for running him down as Pasqual crossed the street. Wanda testifies for the defense that the light was red when Pasqual crossed. Several months earlier, Wanda had told a friend, Fannie, the same thing, that the light was red. Pasqual's attorney, in cross-examining Wanda, implies that just before trial Denton paid Wanda to testify as she did. Denton introduces Wanda's prior consistent statement to Fannie to rebut this implication that Wanda is lying, by showing that Wanda was telling the same story well before the alleged bribe.

As illustrated by the above example, the purpose of introducing a prior consistent statement is not to impeach current testimony (as it is for prior inconsistent statements), but to support it, generally to rehabilitate a witness following an express or implied allegation of recent fabrication. See generally *Rehabilitation* in Chapter 8.

A prior consistent statement may, in fact, be introduced to try to overcome the effect of an opponent's introduction of a prior inconsistent statement:

Example 5.23: Same facts as Example 5.22. On cross-examination by the plaintiff Pasqual, it is brought out that a week before trial Wanda made an inconsistent statement to another friend, Farley, implying that the light was green. Denton now introduces Wanda's prior *consistent* statement to Fannie to demonstrate that Wanda has not, in fact, changed her story since the statement to Farley, but has been telling the "light was red" version all along.

Traditionally prior consistent statements, like their inconsistent cousins, were not admissible for the truth of the matter stated. Most courts now permit their substantive (hearsay) use, although the precise rules may differ.

The broadest rules, like CEC 1236, in effect provide a blanket hearsay exception for any consistent statement that is admissible for rehabilitative purposes, making the hearsay and non-hearsay uses coextensive.

Under **FRE 801(d)(1)(B),** non-hearsay (rather than hearsay exception) designation of a prior consistent statement requires that the declarant (1) testify at the current proceeding and (2) be subject to cross-examination concerning the statement, (3) that the statement be consistent with that testimony, and (4) that it be offered to rebut an express or implied charge of "recent fabrication or improper influence or motive." (Other uses of prior consistent statements, even if admissible for rehabilitative purposes, would not be admissible substantively under the FRE.) URE 801(d)(1)(ii) is to the same effect.

Timing of prior statement.   Since the usual purpose of introducing a prior consistent statement is to overcome a charge or implication of recent fabrication, bias, or the like, most rules for their use require that the prior statement have been made *before the motive or decision to lie arose.* Thus, in Examples 5.22 and 5.23 if Wanda had made the prior consistent statement (that the light was red) only an hour before trial, and the alleged bribe or prior inconsistent statement occurred two days before trial, the taint remains no matter how many times subsequently the "red light" story is repeated. Only a consistent statement made prior to the taint rehabilitates the witness.

Although FRE 801(d)(1)(B) does not mention it, the Supreme Court has held (*Tome v. United States* [2]) that the "postmotive" time requirement was impliedly adopted with the Rule. Whether states that have adopted the Federal (or identical Uniform) Rule will follow suit remains to be seen.

Prior Statements of Identification

Statements previously made by a witness that identified a person as a participant in a crime or other occurrence.

Example 5.24:   Wilomena testifies that she saw someone hold up the First National Bank, but she cannot positively identify defendant Dudley as the perpetrator, as her memory of the crime has faded. The prosecution introduces evidence that just after the crime occurred, Wilomena accompanied an officer on a drive around the neighborhood, and when the car passed Dudley she pointed to him and said, "That's the man who held up the bank." She later made a like statement when she picked Dudley out of a police lineup of seven similar-

2. 115 S. Ct. 696 (1996).

looking men. Both statements are examples of prior identification and generally are admissible.

Rationale: Closer in time to event than in-court identification; in court, defendant is obviously the person the witness is supposed to identify, and the only one from whom to choose.

Specific rules may require that the identification have been made while the incident prompting it was fresh in the declarant's mind, that the declarant believed the identification to be accurate at the time (even if unable to remember now), and so forth.

Under **FRE 801(d)(1)(C)**, a prior identification is deemed not hearsay rather than a hearsay exception. The rule applies only if (1) the declarant testifies at the present proceeding, (2) the declarant is subject to cross-examination concerning the prior statement, and (3) the identification was "of a person made after perceiving the person." The prior statement of identification need not be either consistent or inconsistent with the witness/declarant's present testimony.

At common law identification evidence was more broadly admissible, but some states' rules are more stringent than the Federal Rules (see, e.g., CEC 1238).

Admissions of a Party-Opponent

Statements made out of court by a party that are offered in evidence by an opposing party.

Example 5.25: Jan sues Diana for negligence, following a collision between their cars. Jan offers evidence that a day before the accident, Diana said to witness William, "I need new driving glasses. I haven't been seeing well through these glasses of mine for at least a month." Although the statement fits the basic definition of hearsay, it is offered by the declarant's opponent and therefore is admissible as an admission.

Traditionally admissions are an exception to the hearsay rule; under **FRE 801(d)(2),** they are deemed "not hearsay." They can range from an all-encompassing confession of guilt to a simple statement that later turns out to be beneficial to an issue in an opponent's case.

Rationale: Admissions do not fit the usual rationale for hearsay exceptions, particularly that of special trustworthiness. (This is partly why they are not considered hearsay by the FRE.) The true rationale is probably a combination of the "sporting theory" (one cannot complain of one's own lack of credibility) and the moral imperative that one must take responsibility for one's own acts and statements. There is some necessity in that an opposing party is unlikely to make damaging admissions in court. In any event, a party wishing to explain away an admission is free to do so. Thus even if an admission does not have any particular guarantees of trustworthiness, we are willing to admit it for its truth against the party who made it.

Comparison to Declaration Against Interest. Note carefully that an admission, unlike a declaration against interest, need not have been against the declarant's interest at the time it was made (although almost always that is the case). Thus, do not use the incorrect term "admission against interest."

Example 5.26: Same facts as Example 5.25, except that Diana's statement was made to her mother to justify her request for $200 for new glasses. Although the statement was in Diana's interest when she made it, it is admissible now as evidence against her.

Also unlike a declaration against interest, an admission need not be based on personal knowledge, and the declarant need not be unavailable. See *Declarations Against Interest.*

An admission may be in the form of an opinion, and even a "conclusion of (fact and) law" such as "I was negligent."

Must be "party opponent." The declarant of an admission must be an opposing party; moreover, the declarant is the only opposing party against whom the admission is admissible.

Example 5.27: Same facts as Example 5.25, except Jan has sued both Diana and Diana's eye doctor Ian, the latter on the theory that Ian had negligently given Diana the wrong prescription. As against Ian, Diana's statement that she was having trouble with her glasses would be inadmissible. To prevent the jury misusing it, the judge might have to give a limiting instruction or take other measures to protect Ian.

Confessions. **Confessions** are simply admissions made by a defendant in a criminal case, the "party opponent" of the prosecution. In most respects they are treated the same as other admissions. But because of constitutional considerations, confessions may be scrutinized more closely and subject to various ancillary rules regarding how and by whom they were obtained and how they are employed. For example, statements by an accused person in custody are subject to the *Miranda* doctrine;[3] and a confession that also

3. Miranda v. Arizona, 384 U.S. 436 (1966).

implicates the declarant's co-defendant cannot be admitted against the latter if the declarant is not subject to cross-examination.[4]

Admission by Conduct

In jurisdictions in which a party's nonassertive conduct is defined as hearsay, any statement implied by a party's conduct.

Example 5.28:   Dana is on trial for murder. Officer Ollie testifies that, when during the investigation he approached Dana, Dana turned and ran away. To the extent Dana's flight permits an inference of a guilty mind (and the strength of this inference is always questionable), it is an implied statement "I am guilty," and as such is admissible as an admission.

Under the Federal Rules, if the flight is defined as nonassertive conduct, it would not fall under the basic definition of hearsay. In either event, assertive or nonassertive, it would be admissible.

Admissions by conduct excluded for policy reasons.   Certain forms of conduct are generally not admissible as the basis for an implied admission, whether or not the hearsay rule applies. In each case it is felt that allowing the conduct to be used against the party would be detrimental to the more important policy of encouraging (or at least not discouraging) that conduct. They also tend to be of only marginal relevance (probative value), and they are in fact found in the Federal Rules among the rules on relevance rather than hearsay. The most common examples are the following:

(1) **Subsequent Remedial Measures:** Evidence that subsequent to an event one took measures to prevent its recurrence is inadmissible as an implied admission that failure to take such measures earlier was negligence. Admission would discourage the taking of such precautions or the correction of unsafe conditions while litigation was pending. See **FRE 407.** (Note that, because under the FRE such actions, as unintended implied assertions, are not hearsay, the rule excluding them is in the chapter on Relevance, not that on Hearsay.)

Example 5.29:   Penny sues Daphne for negligently maintaining the stairway in Daphne's store, causing Penny to fall. Evidence that just after the accident Daphne repaired the stairs would be inadmissible to prove that their prior condition was such as to render Daphne negligent.

---

4. Bruton v. United States, 391 U.S. 123 (1968).

There is usually an exception that permits use of the evidence to prove something other than negligence. Thus in Example 5.29, if Daphne conceded the alleged condition of her stairs but claimed that they could not be made any safer, the fact that she did make them safer would be admissible on the issue of feasibility.

Courts disagree whether the exception is limited to cases of negligence, or should also exclude such evidence in strict liability (especially products liability) cases.

(2) **Payment of Medical Expenses:** A defendant's offer to pay or payment of hospital or other medical expenses generally is not admissible to prove (as an admission by conduct) liability for an injury. Public policy favors the encouragement of such acts, whatever logically they may imply. See **FRE 409.**

(3) **Offers of Compromise:** Either party's offer to compromise a pending civil claim is inadmissible to prove the validity or invalidity of that claim. Settlement negotiations would be inhibited if such overtures of offer or acceptance could be used as implied admissions as to the soundness of the pending claim. The evidence is usually admissible, however, for other purposes, such as countering an allegation of undue delay in prosecuting an action. See **FRE 408.**

Likewise, in a criminal proceeding most plea negotiations are inadmissible in later civil or criminal cases, as are withdrawn guilty pleas and pleas of nolo contendere. See **FRE 410.**

Spoliation Admission

A type of admission by conduct in which an inference of guilt or liability is drawn from a party's attempt to suborn perjury, intimidate a witness, destroy evidence, or otherwise interfere with evidence or with the course of justice.

Courts differ on the effect such conduct will have, from generally prejudicing the party's case to specific sanctions such as shifting the burden of proof on an issue.

Adoptive Admission

A statement that a party-opponent has adopted or in the truth of which the party has manifested a belief, by the party's silence or other reaction. See **FRE 801(d)(2)(B).**

Example 5.30: Percival sues Dolly for negligence following an automobile accident. An issue is whether Dolly or Dolly's companion, Cora, was driving at the time of the accident. Warren testifies that when Cora and Dolly emerged from the car, Cora said to Warren within

Dolly's hearing, "Dolly was driving." Dolly, who was standing nearby, said nothing. If a reasonable person in Dolly's position would have denied the assertion had it been untrue, Dolly has impliedly *adopted* Cora's statement, resulting in an adoptive admission against Dolly.

Admission by silence is called a **tacit admission.** Of course, the same result would follow if Dolly had responded, "That's right."

Note that Dolly is the declarant, not Cora, although Cora's statement provides the substance of the implied admission. Example 5.30 would thus be diagrammed:

$$C \begin{array}{l} \longrightarrow W \\ \longrightarrow D \longrightarrow W \longrightarrow \text{Court} \end{array}$$

Like other forms of admission, adoptive admissions are deemed "not hearsay" rather than a hearsay exception under the FRE.

Rationale: A reasonable person in declarant's circumstances, confronted with the statement, would not so act or fail to act if the statement were untrue.

If under the circumstances (for example, a suspect in custody and constitutionally entitled to remain silent) one could not reasonably be expected to respond or deny the statement whether true or not, it will not be considered adopted. Nor is an equivocal response sufficient. Thus had Dolly simply hit Cora on the chin, her action could as easily be interpreted as either "You liar" or "That's right, but here's what you get for telling."

The statement adopted may be written (a letter received, an account offered) as well as oral. Again, the issue is whether, in the context, a reasonable person in the party's position would have replied if the assertion were false.

Finally, before silence alone can manifest adoption, it is usually said that (unlike most admissions) the declarant must have *personal knowledge* of the underlying facts. Personal knowledge should be required at least to the extent that without it, one cannot say that a reasonable person would have spoken up. If Cora had said, "Percival was driving slowly," but Dolly clearly had not been in a position to see Percival's car before the accident, Dolly's failure to disagree with Cora would not mean she agreed with the statement, but merely that she lacked knowledge either way.

Representative Admission

A statement by a person either authorized by a party to make it, or who stands in such a relationship to a party that the party is charged with responsibility for it. It is also known as a **vicarious** or **authorized admission.**

Example 5.31: Perry sues Deanne for negligence after slipping on a banana peel in Deanne's store. Perry testifies that after he fell, Ed, an employee of Deanne, came up to him and said, "My boss sent me to apologize for having left the banana peel there." Ed's statement, if expressly authorized by Deanne, is attributable to Deanne as a representative admission.

Under the Federal Rules, representative admissions, like other admissions, are deemed "not hearsay" rather than exceptions to the hearsay rule.

Scope of employment. Most jurisdictions include not only expressly authorized admissions, but also those made by a party's agent or servant acting within the scope of the agent's employment. Here, however, there is a division of authority: Some rules (like **FRE 801(d)(2)(D)**) include any statement made by an agent or employee while the relationship existed and concerning a matter within the scope of the agency or employment. The traditional rule, however, limits such admissions to circumstances in which making the statement was itself within the scope of the agency or employment, that is, to so-called **speaking agents.** See, e.g., CEC 1222.

Example 5.32: Eric, driving a truck for Dave, is in an accident with Patricia. Just after the accident, Eric tells Patricia, "I'm sorry, it was my fault." Under the FRE, this statement would be a representative admission, admissible against Dave as if Dave had made it. Under the narrower traditional rule, however, unless Eric was employed not only to drive but to make statements about his driving, Eric's statement would not be admissible against Dave. This considerably restricts the number of statements that will qualify as vicarious admissions, especially as employers would be reluctant to give "speaking authority" to most employees.

As with most forms of admission, generally the principal (Dave) need not have personal knowledge of the underlying facts.

Admissions of a **predecessor in interest or title** or persons in **privity** with a party were admissible against the party at common law. The Federal Rules did not retain this aspect of representative admissions. Some states, however, do continue a form of this exception, so that, for example, a grantor's statements relating to land he owns would later be admissible against his grantee in a dispute with a third person over title to that land. Some courts even extend privity to joint (as well as successive) owners.

Judicial (Formal) Admission

A statement in pleadings, stipulations, or requests for admissions that conclusively binds the party making it, in the proceeding in which it was made.

Example 5.33:   Alyn sues Bernard for negligence following an automobile accident. Alyn's complaint alleges, inter alia, that Bernard was driving the car that struck him. Bernard's answer admits driving the car but denies any negligence. Unless the answer is effectively withdrawn or superseded by a later pleading, during the trial the question of whether Bernard was driving is not in issue, and Bernard will not be permitted to prove otherwise. The same result would follow if Bernard's concession were in response to a request for admissions during discovery.

Judicial v. Evidentiary Admissions.   Since judicial admissions are not subject to refutation, technically they are not evidence at all, but under the rules of pleading they define what issues remain open and what are precluded. Judicial admissions are in contrast to garden variety **evidentiary admissions,** discussed above, which are true hearsay exceptions.

Note that to the extent that the party's attorney makes them with the party's express or implied consent, judicial admissions are a form of authorized admission.

Answers to interrogatories generally are evidentiary but not judicial admissions and may be contested. The same generally is true of the pleadings in prior proceedings and those withdrawn or superseded in the same proceeding. A guilty plea in a criminal case is usually admissible as an evidentiary admission in a subsequent civil case, with the possible exception of pleas to minor traffic offenses. A withdrawn guilty plea, however, in most jurisdictions cannot be used civilly or criminally against the defendant; nor is a *nolo contendere* plea usually admissible as evidence in a subsequent case. See also the exceptions for convictions and certain civil judgments, **FRE 803(22),(23).**

If a party has pleaded hypothetically, inconsistently, or in the alternative, to that extent the pleadings generally will not be considered judicial or evidentiary admissions.

A related matter is the evidentiary effect of a party's own testimony at trial. Some jurisdictions consider such testimony merely evidence like any other; some consider it a conclusive admission if it concerns a matter within the peculiar knowledge of the party; and others consider all such testimony conclusive unless, for example, it appears to be inadvertent, mistaken, equivocal, or similarly unreliable.

It is worth noting the relationship between the doctrine of judicial admissions and the concepts of *res judicata* and *collateral estoppel,* usually covered in the civil procedure course. Suffice it to say here that all are capable of carrying the effects of one proceeding over to another, and of precluding a party to a subsequent proceeding from contesting certain facts or issues pleaded or decided in a former one.

Co-Conspirator Admission

A statement by a person who, having participated with a party in a conspiracy, is deemed an agent of the party for purposes of making admissions. In effect a conspiracy is treated like what it is: a "joint business enterprise" for unlawful purposes, to which the agency theory of partnerships applies. See **FRE 801(d)(2)(E).**

Example 5.34:   Don is on trial for the murder of Vera. Witness Wendy testifies for the prosecution that she overheard a conversation between Yusef and Zack in which Yusef stated, "Don has agreed to help us to kill Vera, and in fact has volunteered to pull the trigger." Yusef's statement is hearsay, but it probably is admissible against Don as an admission by a co-conspirator.

Rationale: May be the only evidence available of inherently secretive process; other participants usually protected against testifying by privilege against self-incrimination; declarant in position to know the facts, usually has no motivation to lie.

Course and furtherance.   Generally statements are admissible only if they were made in the course of and in furtherance of the conspiracy. (The business equivalent would be "within the scope of employment.") Courts differ as to when a conspiracy is considered to begin and end; some, for example, extend it into the so-called **concealment phase,** well beyond the actual carrying out of the planned criminal act.

Note that only the declarant (Yusef in Example 5.34) need be a co-conspirator of Don; the person to whom the statement is made (Zack) need not. The declarant need not be indicted, or even charged with a crime.

Proving the conspiracy.   How do we know that Don was a co-conspirator of Yusef at the time Yusef made the statement? If we assume it from the very statement in question, we are guilty of **bootstrapping,** that is, relying upon the truth of the statement as a basis for believing the statement is true. Most courts therefore require extrinsic evidence of the conspiracy. The Supreme Court, however, has permitted use of the statement to prove the conspiracy, at least if it is not the only evidence of it (*Bourjaily v. United States*[5]).

The same rule applies in civil cases, where co-conspirators would in effect be joint tortfeasors.

5. 483 U.S. 171 (1987).

Spontaneous Statements (In General)

Statements made either contemporaneously or in close connection with the event or condition to which the statement relates.

Rationale: Closer in time to event than testimony; little opportunity for mistake, memory loss, or insincerity.

Relationship to res gestae. Spontaneous statements are part of a more general, "catch all" class of statements, also including verbal acts, once referred to as being "part of the **res gestae**" ("the thing(s) done," variously pronounced with the first word rhyming with "face" or "please," and the last syllable of the second with "tee" or "tie"). The phrase has fallen out of favor, and when in general use it was often more confusing than helpful. Although it is still occasionally encountered, especially in older cases, it is best to avoid it entirely and use whatever specific rule applies.

Common attributes. Several exceptions can be grouped generally under the term "spontaneous statements," and in modern rules some have expanded such that actual spontaneity is attenuated or may not even be required. What they share in common is a close connection between some thought, emotion, or sense impression, some impulse of the mind or body of the declarant, and a statement concerning or induced by that condition. Those set out below are the most common examples: present sense impressions, excited utterances, state of mind or physical condition, and statements for medical diagnosis or treatment.

Present Sense Impression

A statement that describes or explains something the declarant is presently perceiving, or has just perceived (in the language of **FRE 803(1),** *"while perceiving" an event or condition or "immediately thereafter").*

Example 5.35: Paula sues Digby for negligence following an automobile accident, alleging that Digby was driving without headlights after dusk. Witness Willa testifies for Paula that she was standing next to Barry just before the collision and heard Barry say, "That red car [Digby's car] ought to turn on its lights." Barry's statement is hearsay, but it is admissible as a present sense impression, a description of an event then being perceived by the declarant Barry.

Rationale: Closer in time to event than testimony; little opportunity for mistake, memory loss, or insincerity; circumstances usually corroborated by in-court witness.

Present sense impressions should be distinguished from excited utterances (discussed next). The latter requires the stimulus of some exciting event, whereas a present sense impression can describe even a mundane circumstance, such as that in Example 5.35.

Time interval. The time interval between event and statement must be negligible, that is, insufficient to permit reflection or forgetfulness. Usually a few minutes is too long, although courts occasionally are more liberal. In addition, the declarant must have perceived the event or condition by sight or some other sense, and the statement must describe or explain it. Thus, in Example 5.35, had Barry said, "Look at that car — I saw it parked near the bank yesterday," the statement would not have been within the exception.

A similar exception found in some jurisdictions (not within the FRE as such) is for a statement explaining or describing conduct in which the declarant is then engaged. See, e.g., CEC 1241.

It has been proposed that there be an exception for a statement explaining or describing an event "recently [as opposed to immediately] perceived" by the declarant, provided certain additional safeguards are present (such as good faith and absence of contemplated litigation). See, e.g., optional URE 804(b)(5). See also CEC 1261 (recent perception, clear recollection, in action against declarant's estate).

Excited Utterance

A statement relating to and made under the stress of some startling or exciting event that the declarant has just perceived. See **FRE 803(2).** Sometimes this is just called a "spontaneous" statement or utterance.

Example 5.36:　Same facts as Example 5.35 (Paula sues Digby for negligence), except that Paula alleges Digby drove through a red light and struck her car. Witness Willa testifies for Paula that she heard bystander Barry shout, "My God, that [Digby's] car just ran the red light and is going to . . ." (remainder drowned out by sound of crash). Barry's statement is hearsay, but it is admissible as an excited utterance.

Rationale: Stress caused by startling event stills reflective capacity, thus makes lying unlikely. (In practice, however, excitement may actually interfere with accurate perception.) Closer in time to event than testimony; little opportunity for memory loss. Circumstances usually corroborated by in-court witness.

Time interval. There need not be strict contemporaneity, as for a present sense impression. The important interval is that period of time during

92

which the excitement would still "reflective thought." This will vary according to such factors as the sensory impact of the event and the age or mental condition of the declarant. For example, courts often assume children's minds are affected by startling events longer than adults'; they have been especially liberal with respect to reports by child victims or witnesses in cases of sexual abuse.

Relation to event. An excited utterance must "relate to" the event that produces it, but in most jurisdictions (and unlike a present sense impression) it need not actually describe it.

Most courts (including federal courts, applying FRE 104(a)) permit the exciting nature of the event to be proved by the statement itself. A few require extrinsic evidence of this foundational fact.

State of Mind

*Statements that describe the declarant's mental or emotional condition at the time of the statement (the declarant's **then-existing state of mind**).* See **FRE 803(3).**

Example 5.37: Tess's will has left her entire estate to her nephew Ned. Tess's sister Sally contests the will, alleging that Ned coerced Tess to make the gift. Ward testifies for Ned that just days before executing her will, Tess told Ward, "I really like Ned. I'm going to leave him all my money." Tess's statement is hearsay, but it is admissible as a statement of Tess's then-existing state of mind. Specifically, the first sentence relates Tess's present feelings about Ned, whereas the second states her present intention regarding her will.

[handwritten margin notes: intent, plan, motve, design, pain, bodily health. make sure declarant isn't talking about his memory. "I am sick" = presently existing physical "I intend to go to NY"]

Rationale: Spontaneity and contemporaneity avoid memory problems, allow little opportunity for calculation; not easily mistaken about own state of mind; present cross-examination regarding witness's previous state of mind would be difficult or futile.

Note that in Example 5.37 if Tess had merely said, "Ned is the finest boy in the world," to justify an inference that Tess was fond of Ned, the statement would not necessarily have been hearsay. It might have been offered merely to prove that it was made, not for its truth (that Ned was in fact "the finest boy"). Nevertheless, courts tend not to differentiate too closely between such direct and indirect assertions of state of mind, since they are admissible either as non-hearsay or under the present exception.

Statements of memory or belief disallowed. Generally the statement of mental condition cannot be one of memory or belief, to prove the fact remembered or believed. In the words of Justice Cardozo in *Shepard v. United States*[6], the statement must not "face backwards."

Example 5.38: Deke is on trial for the killing of Veronica. Wesley testifies for the prosecution that, the day before Veronica was killed, she told Wesley, "Deke has threatened to kill me." The prosecution asserts that it is not trying to prove by Veronica's statement that Deke actually threatened her, but merely Veronica's "state of mind," from which the jury might or might not *infer* that he did so. The statement is not admissible, however, because it relates Veronica's memory of Deke's threat or belief that he made one.

The main reason for the limitation in Example 5.38 is that to admit such statements would virtually destroy the hearsay rule. Almost any statement of fact can be described as a statement of the declarant's memory of or belief in that fact; an exception admitting such statements to prove the truth of the fact "remembered" would render almost all hearsay statements admissible. Compare, however:

Example 5.39: The issue in the case is whether Irving believed his brother Ronnie to be dead at the time Irving married Ronnie's wife. His statement, "I believe Ronnie is dead" would be hearsay (offered to prove the truth of the statement, the existence of the belief) but admissible as Irving's state of mind; it would not be excluded as a statement of belief, because it is not offered to prove the truth of that belief, only its existence.

The one usual exception (included in FRE 803(3)) to the prohibition against statements of memory or belief is a statement relating to the declarant's will:

Example 5.40: As in Example 5.37, Tess has left her entire estate to Ned. Sally alleges that the will is a forgery, and that Tess's true will left her estate to Sally. Ward testifies, however, that two years after the contested will was executed, Tess said to Ward, "I left Ned my entire estate in my will." Under the special exception for statements relating to wills, Tess's statement would be admissible to prove that she did indeed execute such as will.

A narrow additional exception under a very few rules (such as CEC 1251-52) permits statements of *past* states of mind or body if the declarant

6. 290 U.S. 96 (1930).

is unavailable, the condition described is itself in issue, and there is no indication of untrustworthiness.

Statements of Intention. A common use of this exception, as in Example 5.37, is for **statements of intention,** immortalized in the famous case of *Mutual Life Insurance Co. v. Hillmon.*[7] Although a statement may not face backwards to the past, it may face forward to the future. A declarant's intention might itself be an issue in the case (as when the intent to kill is relevant to homicide), or it may serve as the basis for an inference that the declarant in fact carried out the stated intention. The latter use can, however, create difficulties:

Example 5.41: Daisy is accused of the murder of Vance, whose body was found behind Joe's Tavern. Vance was heard to say, just before he was killed, "After work, I'm meeting Daisy at Joe's Tavern." Vance's statement is clearly admissible to prove the truth of his intent to go to Joe's Tavern, from which it can be inferred that he in fact went there. His going, however, is relevant only to the extent he might have met Daisy there. Many courts will admit Vance's statement not only as evidence that Vance went to Joe's Tavern, but that he met Daisy there.

Declarant's state of mind only. Note carefully that although Vance's statement in Example 5.41 actually states both his intention and that of Daisy (to meet at Joe's), only *his own* state of mind can be the subject of this hearsay exception. We must, therefore, prove Daisy's actions not directly from her intent, but indirectly from Vance's. As such, the problem here is really one of relevance, not hearsay: Even if we know nothing of Daisy's intent, Vance's intent makes it at least a little more probable that he met Daisy at Joe's Tavern than if Vance had no such intent. Because of the weakness of this inference, however, and the possible prejudice to Daisy, the court might still exclude the statement or admit it subject to restrictive requirements such as corroborating evidence of Daisy's actions. While some courts freely admit the evidence in cases such as this, applying the Hillmon doctrine expansively, the Federal Rules are silent on this question and the matter has not yet been finally resolved by the federal courts.

Physical Condition

*A statement that describes the declarant's physical state at the time of the statement (the declarant's **then-existing physical condition**).* See **FRE 803(3).**

7. 145 U.S. 285 (1892).

This exception is similar in scope and rationale to that just discussed, and under the FRE it is contained in the same Rule 803(3).

Example 5.42:   Portia sues for injuries to her leg received when she was struck by Daphne's car. Daphne alleges Portia was not injured. Winston testifies for Portia that, the day after the accident, Portia said to Winston, "My leg is killing me!" Portia's statement is admissible under the exception for existing physical condition. (Notice that the statement is not admissible as an admission, as it is not introduced by a party opponent.)

Cause or past conditions excluded.   Statements admissible under this exception cannot describe past physical conditions, nor should they state the cause of the present condition.

Example 5.43:   Same as Example 5.42, except Winston testifies that Portia said to Winston, "My leg is killing me! It's hurt since yesterday, when Daphne's car hit me, after it ran the red light." Only the first exclamation would be admissible under this exception.

Unlike the exception next described, most rules do not require that statements of physical condition be made to a physician.

Statements For Medical Diagnosis or Treatment

A statement made to a physician (or the equivalent), the purpose of which was to aid the physician in the diagnosis or treatment of the declarant's injury or illness. See **FRE 803(4).**

Unlike the exception for statements of physical condition just described, this exception traditionally permits statements of past symptoms and, under rules such as the FRE, even causation, if relevant (or, in the language of the FRE, "reasonably pertinent") to diagnosis or treatment.

Example 5.44:   Same facts as Example 5.43, except the statement is made by Portia to her physician in seeking treatment for her leg. Most courts would admit the first and second phrases (present and past symptoms), and many (including the Federal Rules) the third (causation) as well, as sufficiently pertinent to treatment. None would admit the fourth, placing blame or stating facts irrelevant to treatment.

The only common exception to this last prohibition is many modern courts' willingness to admit statements of child victims of sexual abuse that name the perpetrator of the abuse. A physician or psychologist treating such

(handwritten margin note: Can't be used to show fault.)

8-4942

a child often cannot properly diagnose or treat the child's trauma without knowing its true source; the effect on a child of sexual (or other physical) abuse by a parent or friend is different from the effect of such abuse by a stranger.

Rationale: Strong motivation to be truthful, careful, and accurate to assure proper and effective medical treatment; declarant should know own condition, little chance of mistake.

Treatment v. diagnosis. At common law, only statements made for medical treatment were admissible under this exception. Statements to physicians consulted for diagnosis, especially for the purpose of their testifying for the patient at trial, lack the motivation to be truthful and accurate. Nevertheless, the FRE and some other modern rules now include them in the hearsay exception, primarily because such statements are already admissible as the basis for a testifying physician's opinion under FRE 702-703 (though technically not for the truth of the matter stated). See Chapter 8.

Although most statements under this exception are made by patients to physicians, in some circumstances the statement may be made by a third party (such as a parent of a small child) or to a nonphysician (such as a caseworker).

Past Recollection Recorded

A statement previously recorded or adopted by a witness regarding matters the witness cannot recall at trial. See **FRE 803(5).**

Example 5.45: Wilma is testifying about a hit-and-run accident that she witnessed. She is unable to recall some of the details, including the color of the car. She states, however, that she made some notes just after the incident, according to which the car was blue. She knows the notes were accurate and reflected her knowledge of the facts at the time, even if she cannot now remember them all. Wilma's notes are admissible as evidence of the color of the car.

Rationale: Recorded when memory fresh, witness in court vouches for accuracy and can be examined as to circumstances (if not details). No present memory, so record only evidence available.

Distinguish Present Recollection Refreshed. Past recollection recorded is to be distinguished from *present recollection refreshed,* which refers to notes or other materials used by a witness to refresh in-court recollection. (See Chapter 8.) The latter is not a hearsay exception, for it is the refreshed testimony, not the recorded material, that constitutes the witness's evidence. For this reason, recorded recollection is subject to the Best Evidence

("Original Document") Rule, discussed in Chapter 7, but writings used only to refresh present recollection are not.

> <u>Rule of Thumb</u>: If the declarant is presently a witness in the present proceedings, consider this exception or that for prior statements of witnesses. If the declarant is not, this exception is unavailable.

Not an exhibit. Generally the recorded recollection may be read into evidence, but it cannot be made an exhibit that goes to the jury unless offered by the adverse party. The jury might give more weight to the written words than to the oral testimony.

Degree of recollection permitted. Traditionally, the witness/declarant had to have no present recollection at all. Under modern formulations such as the FRE, however, only "insufficient recollection" to "testify fully and accurately" is required.

Accuracy and Recordation. The witness must testify that the statement is accurate. In Example 5.45, Wilma may state that she remembers accurately writing down the color, or perhaps (if it was signed) that she would not have signed it if she did not believe it accurate. Even one's habit or routine to make accurate notes should suffice.

It is not even necessary that the color have been recorded by Wilma herself. It would be sufficient, for example, if a nearby friend had written down the color and Wilma had read and agreed with it ("adopted" it), or if Wilma had told her friend over the telephone what she had seen, and her friend had written it down. In the latter case, however, both participants in the recordation would have to testify, Wilma that she accurately reported the facts, and the friend that she accurately recorded them.

Time interval. Traditionally the statement had to have been recorded at or very near the time of the matter described, but under modern rules the record need only have been made while the subject matter was "fresh in the witness's memory."

Business Records

Statements recorded as a matter of routine in the records of a regularly-conducted business (or business-like) activity. See **FRE 803(6)**.

Example 5.46: Pamela seeks to prove that she paid Harry's Garage $1,200 for repairs to her car necessitated by Dottie's negligence. Having lost her receipt, she introduces into evidence an entry in the Garage's daily ledger that states, "Paid by Pamela, $1,200.00 for repair of au-

tomobile." There is no indication who made the entry. Harry's book-
keeper then testifies that such entries are routinely made by, or on
information from, the mechanic who performed the work, shortly
after the transaction is completed. The entry likely is admissible as
a business record, to prove Pamela's payment.

Rationale: Trustworthiness assured by regularity and familiarity of practice; likelihood of internal checks; business duty and personal motivation of
recorder to be correct; reliance on accuracy for conduct of business. Necessity due to difficulty or impossibility of identifying maker; unlikelihood
maker will recall particular entry; and (at common law) death or other
unavailability of maker.

Example 5.46 illustrates most of the elements required under the usual
modern business records exception. It must be shown by the testimony of
the record's custodian or other qualified person that: (1) the record is that
of some regularly conducted business activity; (2) it was made in the regular
course of business at or near the time of the matter recorded, (3) by or from
information supplied by one with a duty and personal knowledge; and (4)
it was a regular practice of the business to make such records.

To the above usually is added a qualification, that the record should be
excluded if the circumstances indicate a lack of trustworthiness, for example
if the entry was self-serving and made in anticipation of litigation. (Compare *Palmer v. Hoffman*,[8] which excluded such records as not being made
"in the regular course of business.")

Definition of "business." Modern rules and cases generally interpret
the term "business" expansively, to include virtually any record that is not
purely personal. Similarly, "business" can include nonprofit, charitable, or
even unlawful activities.

Multiple hearsay problem. Often a business entry will contain a statement that itself is hearsay; if so, a further hearsay exception may be required,
unless the recorded declarant was also under a business duty to speak. Thus:

> Rule of Thumb: If a business record reports the statement of any-
> one who is not speaking in the course of business, the statement cannot
> be admitted to prove its truth without satisfying some other hearsay ex-
> ception.

Example 5.47: Porter sues Deidre for injuries suffered when Deidre's car
struck Porter. At the scene of the accident Officer Ozzie interviewed

8. 318 U.S. 109 (1943).

Porter, Deidre, and several witnesses. Ozzie's report states: "(1) Deidre was visibly intoxicated. (2) As measured by my partner Art, Deidre's car left a 20 foot skid mark. (3) Deidre admits that Porter was in the crosswalk. (4) Witness Watson confirms this." All of Ozzie's report would qualify as a Business Record, to prove the truth of Ozzie's statements (what he saw, Porter reported, Deidre and Watson said). Sentences (2), (3), and (4) contain the hearsay statements of others: (2) is admissible for its truth under the present exception, as Art had personal knowledge and a business duty to report to Ozzie; (3) and (4) require other exceptions. Deidre's statement is an admission; but Watson's seems to fall under no exception and likely would be excluded. (See the leading case of *Johnson v. Lutz.*[9])

Computer records are generally treated the same as other media, with respect to such requirements as regular recordkeeping, original entry by one with personal knowledge, and so forth. Of course, certain criteria may require some modification to take into account differences between media. Thus, for example, it is the input of information that must occur "at or near" the time of the recorded event, not the production of the printout based on that input.

Absence of entry. Lack of an entry usually can be offered as proof that no transaction took place. **FRE 803(7)** specifically permits such use.

Public Records

Statements found in the reports or records of public offices or agencies, generally made by public officials with a duty to make them. See **FRE 803(8).**

Example 5.48: Pearl wishes to prove the amount of rainfall in Seattle on May 25th. She introduces a certified copy of the records of the United States Meteorological Service, stating that two inches of rain fell on that day. The records are admissible to prove the amount of rainfall. (Note that this record might also be the subject of judicial notice, as a matter of indisputable accuracy and verifiable certainty. See Chapter 12.)

Rationale: Trustworthy because of maker's official duty to record accurately and likelihood that duty carried out. Necessary because of inconvenience and expense of bringing public officials to court and unlikelihood they would recall specific matters even if called.

9. 170 N.E. 517 (N.Y. 1930).

Comparison to business records exception. While in a sense this exception is a version of the general business records exception (FRE 803(6)) for the "business" of government, it operates differently and generally is easier to use. The records needn't be routinely maintained, and no custodian or similar witness need testify to their authenticity because certified copies are self-authenticating (see FRE 902(4)) and are excepted from the Best Evidence Rule (see FRE 1005). Under the FRE they need not be made contemporaneously with the transactions they record, although other jurisdictions (such as California, CEC 1280) do require contemporaneity.

Categories; Restrictions in criminal cases. Under the FRE, public records are divided into three categories, with different restrictions on each. While other jurisdictions may not have the same express restrictions, usually a requirement of "trustworthiness" serves the same general purpose.

Category (A) under the FRE, "activities of the office or agency," has no special restrictions. Example 5.48 illustrates such a record.

Category (B), "matters observed" pursuant to a duty both to observe and to record, does not include observations of police officers used in criminal cases. (Although it doesn't say so, such observations are probably admissible against the government.)

Example 5.49: Percy sues manufacturer Manfred for injuries suffered when Manfred's widget machine malfunctioned and exploded. Irving investigated the incident and wrote a report for the Product Safety Commission, stating: "Machine's rotary widgetometer observed to be loose." This statement would be admissible under Category (B).

Note that if this were a criminal case against Manfred and Irving had investigated for the police or another law enforcement agency, Irving's report would be inadmissible. An exception is usually made, however, for objective or "nonadversarial" observations, such as a computer record of cars reported stolen.

Category (C), "factual findings" of official investigations, similarly does not apply against a criminal defendant (although here admission against the government is expressly permitted). This is the broadest category and the least likely to be found in other jurisdictions.

Example 5.50: Same facts as Example 5.49. After investigating the incident, Irving writes a report stating his observations and concluding that "the rotary widgetometer was defective, leading to a loss of pressure and the resulting explosion." As interpreted by the Supreme

Court (*Beech Aircraft v. Rainey*[10]), Category (C) includes "opinions and conclusions" such as Irving's, so long as they are "factually based."

There is an express exclusion under Category (C) for lack of trustworthiness. (Although in terms it applies only to Category (C), it is unlikely a clearly untrustworthy report under any category would be admitted.) The Advisory Committee lists four nonexclusive factors to consider: (1) timeliness of the investigation, (2) special skill or experience of the investigating official, (3) whether and what kind of a hearing was held, and (4) any "motivation problems" (bias) of the investigator.

Use of other exceptions to avoid restrictions. In most instances, public records would also qualify as (since they are, in effect) business records under FRE 803(6). It is tempting to use the business records exception, which contains no restrictions on use in criminal trials, to evade the restrictions in FRE 803(8). Courts generally hold, however, that if a record is within the latter restrictions, it is inadmissible under other hearsay exceptions as well (particularly FRE 803(6)), subject to this exception: If the public official (such as a police officer) is present and testifies subject to cross-examination, the record should be admissible under FRE 803(5) as recorded recollection, since the reason for the restriction in FRE 803(8), to compel live testimony by the officer, would not exist. Similarly, such narrow hearsay exceptions as FRE 803(9) (vital statistics) or 803(10) (absence of an entry) should still be available.

Exceptions for specific records. In addition to the general exception for public records, there are several very specific types of public or quasi-public records that are the subject of separate hearsay exceptions. Most of these exceptions date back to the earliest common law and are found in virtually every jurisdiction. Among them under the FRE are (with examples noted) exceptions for records of vital statistics (**FRE 803(9)**) (birth, death, and marriage records); records of religious organizations (**FRE 803(11)**) (church registries); certificates of official ceremonies (**FRE 803(12)**) (certificates of marriage or baptism by clergyman or other who performed it); publicly recorded documents affecting property (**FRE 803(14)**) (contents, execution, and delivery of a deed; note that under the FRE, a local statute must authorize the recordation).

As in the case of business records, there is a specific exception in **FRE 803(10)** for absence of a record or entry, provided a diligent search was made to find one.

10. 488 U.S. 153 (1988).

Judgments

Statements made, in effect, by courts when they render judgment in a lawsuit or criminal prosecution. See **FRE 803(22)**.

Example 5.51:   Dorian is convicted of arson, having intentionally burned down his warehouse on July 1. In a later civil suit between Archie and Bobbie, an issue is whether Dorian's business burned down on July 1. The first jury's "statement" that it did (and that Dorian was responsible) is admissible for its truth.

Limitations.   Judgments of conviction and the facts essential to them are admissible, but usually with some restrictions: they may be limited to felonies or other serious offenses, for use only in civil cases or only by the accused in criminal cases. Thus the Federal Rule is limited to felony-grade crimes, and in criminal cases judgments against persons other than the accused can be used by the prosecution only for impeachment purposes. Acquittals and convictions based on pleas of nolo contendere are not included. CEC 1300, in contrast, permits use of judgments based on nolo pleas, and CEC 1302 contains a separate exception for civil judgments against third persons (non-parties to the present action).

One common use of judgments is to prove conviction of prior criminal acts to impeach a witness. See **FRE 609.**

FRE 803(23) covers the narrow area of judgments (civil or criminal) proving matters of personal, family, or general history, or the boundaries of property, to the extent provable by reputation under FRE 803(19) or 803(20). Some jurisdictions admit a variety of other specific types of judgment.

Family Records

Statements regarding matters of personal or family history, pedigree, or status, recorded in any form such as might be kept by a family. See **FRE 803(13)**.

Example 5.52:   Joleen alleges that she is the great-granddaughter of Gertrude. She offers in evidence a hand-drawn genealogy chart inscribed on the inside cover of her late mother's Bible and purporting to show Joleen's lineage back to Gertrude. The chart would be admissible to prove Joleen's lineage.

Rationale: Likely to be true, especially if taken as such and acted upon by family over time; no better way to elicit information.

The exception for family records covers almost any surface upon which statements concerning a family might be found, such as inscriptions on the back of a family portrait, or on a tombstone in the family burial plot.

The exception for reputation within a family or (under modern formulations) reputation in the community regarding personal or family history, discussed below, is similar. See **FRE 803(19).**

Example 5.53: Same facts as Example 5.52. To prove her lineage to Gertrude, Joleen elicits the testimony of Alicia, her aunt, who states that she has often heard it said among family members that Joleen is the great-granddaughter of Gertrude. This testimony is admissible to prove Joleen's lineage.

Other related exceptions are those for judgments affecting personal or family history (see **FRE 803(23)**) and for statements about family matters by the person affected or by others within or intimately connected to the family (see **FRE 804(b)(4)**).

Ancient Documents

Statements in documents shown to be at least 20 (traditionally 30) years old, and generally exhibiting no suspicious characteristics. See **FRE 803(16).**

Rationale: Unlikelihood of finding witness, or witness recalling facts, after long passage of time; likely written before present controversy arose; has stood "test of time" without correction; writing avoids mistransmission.

At common law this "ancient documents" exception applied only to authentication of the document, and not to proof of its contents, although there was a narrow hearsay exception for recitals in ancient deeds. Gradually a more general hearsay exception developed as well.

Age and unsuspicious appearance. The traditional rule requires that the document be at least 30 years old, be obtained from a place one would expect to find such a document, and not be suspicious in appearance. Some modern rules replace the latter safeguards with a more general one, such as the statement having been acted upon by persons with an interest in the matter (see CEC 1331). FRE 803(16) goes further and not only reduces the age requirement to 20 years, but also it eliminates any explicit safeguard except that the document's authenticity be established. Nevertheless, it would have to meet the general requirement that the declarant have had personal knowledge of the matter recited.

Example 5.54: Rebecca wishes to prove that she is the owner of Sunnybrook Farm, having received an unrecorded deed from Grant. The last record owner was Ole. In a letter sent by Grant's attorney Andrea to Grant and dated 25 years earlier, Andrea states that Grant is the sole heir of Ole. If properly authenticated, under the FRE the letter would qualify as an "ancient document" and be admissible to prove Andrea's statement. Under more traditional rules, however, the letter would have to be at least 30 years old, unsuspicious, and found in a place such as would be expected; if old enough and found in the attorney's files, the letter should qualify. Under a rule such as California's, it would not qualify if not "generally acted upon as true" by persons with an interest, possibly a more difficult requirement to satisfy.

Documents Affecting an Interest in Property

Statements or recitals, found in documents of title (mainly deeds to real property), that are relevant to the document's purpose. See **FRE 803(15).**

While there is no age restriction as for ancient documents, subsequent dealings with the property must not have been inconsistent with the truth of the statement.

Example 5.55: Same facts as Example 5.54, except the statement that Grant is the sole heir of Ole is contained in a deed to Sunnybrook, of which Rebecca is the grantee. As this recital is germane to the purpose of the deed, it probably comes within the "documents affecting property" exception. The age of the deed is irrelevant.

Reputation

That which is said about someone or something by the general community, or by some specific segment of it, such as one family.

There are hearsay exceptions for several kinds of reputation: Reputation of a person's character in the community (see **FRE 803(21)**); reputation as to personal or family history among family members, associates, or the community (see **FRE 803(19)**); reputation concerning the boundaries of real property and the general history of a community (see **FRE 803(20)**); and in some jurisdictions reputation relating to such diverse matters as ownership of property or character of a business. FRE 803(20) covers community reputation as to "boundaries of or customs affecting" land, and events of general interest to the nation, state, or community.

Traditionally reputation as to boundaries had to antedate the current controversy (***ante litem motam***) and had to be at least a generation old; possibly other evidence such as markers or monuments must have disappeared. The Federal Rule retains only the *ante litem motam* requirement, for both boundaries and general history.

Limited to hearsay objection. It should be emphasized that the hearsay exception for reputation deals only with the objection that certain uses of reputation — the collective and nonspecific "statements" of many anonymous declarants over time — are hearsay. There are other rules that govern whether and when reputation, and particularly reputation for character, is admissible apart from problems of hearsay. See generally Chapter 3 (Character Evidence) and Chapter 8 (Testimonial Evidence).

Treatises and Other Authoritative Writings

Statements found in learned writings such as treatises and articles in professional journals. See **FRE 803(18).**

At common law treatises could be used to impeach expert testimony, but there was no hearsay exception. FRE 803(18) created a new exception.

Rationale: Special expertise of authors; no incentive to lie and every incentive to be accurate; evaluated, critiqued, and relied upon by other experts in the field; frequent impracticability (and sometime impossibility) of finding or calling expert witnesses.

Need for expert. Matters requiring expertise are usually testified to by an expert witness (see FRE 701-06), who may but need not rely on a learned treatise as a basis for an opinion. FRE 803(18) provides a party a substitute for calling an expert, but it does not entirely eliminate the need for one at the trial. Under the Federal Rule, the work containing the statement in question must either be relied on by an expert on direct examination or called to the expert's attention on cross-examination; it must be established as reliable by admission, expert testimony, or judicial notice. It may be read into evidence but not received as an exhibit.

Example 5.56: Plaintiff Porfirio wishes to establish the causal link between his injury and his symptoms. Porfirio cannot afford to hire (or cannot locate) an expert witness, but he finds a supportive statement in a medical treatise, Smith on Symptoms. At trial Witness Winona, a medical doctor, testifies for the defendant that there is no causal link. On cross-examination, Winona concedes that Smith on Symptoms is a recognized authority in the field, although she disagrees with the author on the point in question. Under FRE 803(18), Porfirio may then offer the supportive statement in the Smith treatise for the truth of the matter stated, and not just to impeach the testimony of Winona.

Under traditional rules, Porfirio would be limited to impeachment use of the treatise; therefore, if Porfirio was required to offer affirmative, expert proof of the causal link to his injury, his lawsuit would fail.

Some modern rules are more liberal than even the Federal Rules (for example, CEC 1341 (admitting learned works by impartial authors to prove "facts of general notoriety and interest")).

A related exception is for **commercial lists and directories** and the like. Under **FRE 803(17),** such publications need only be "generally used and relied upon by the public or by persons in particular occupations." Examples would be stock market quotations, telephone directories, and price lists.

2.   Exceptions Requiring Unavailability

There are some hearsay exceptions that can be used only if the declarant is dead or otherwise "unavailable," and others for which unavailability of the declarant is not required. In theory, at least, unavailability provides greater necessity for the few exceptions that require it. Unavailability is a term of art, however, and a declarant (or rather, the declarant's testimony) must be unavailable for an accepted reason for the exceptions to apply.

Note that to say a declarant *can* be available is not the same as saying the declarant *must* be available: only two exceptions (for prior statements of witnesses and past recollection recorded) actually presuppose the presence in court of the declarant.

Under the FRE, exceptions not requiring unavailability are all grouped under FRE 803, as set out in the previous section. Those requiring unavailability are all within Rule 804 and are examined in the entries that follow. Not all jurisdictions establish such distinct categories, and unavailability may just be one of the criteria for certain exceptions otherwise undifferentiated.

Unavailability

Inability to procure the live testimony of the declarant because of the declarant's death, incompetence, refusal to testify, or other reason.

Note that under modern rules it is the *testimony* of the declarant, not necessarily the person, that must be unavailable; a declarant who is alive and in court but unwilling or unable to testify may be unavailable, and one who is absent but whose deposition can be obtained may be available, for purposes of the hearsay rule.

At early common law, unavailability was usually limited to death of the declarant; no other excuse would do. Courts no longer draw the definition so narrowly. Under **FRE 804(a),** there are five general situations that qualify as unavailability: (1) a claim of privilege upheld by the court; (2) a refusal to testify in defiance of a court order to do so; (3) lack of memory; (4) death or mental or physical illness or infirmity; and (5) inability of the statement's proponent to procure the declarant's attendance at the hearing by reasonable means. Of these five, all but (3) are common to most modern rules. (4) may be phrased in terms of incompetence of the declarant to testify.

Proponent's procurement of absence.   Of course, witness Wally is not unavailable if his attendance or testimony has been prevented by Patty, the party offering his hearsay statement. This might be through Patty's wrongdoing (for example, killing or kidnapping Wally) or other "procurement," as when she has a privilege not to testify, then tries to invoke her own unavailability to justify admission of her hearsay statements.

Deposition as availability.   One somewhat cryptic passage warrants explanation: FRE 804(a)(5) renders declarants unavailable whose attendance or testimony (as by deposition) cannot reasonably be procured. This does not apply, however, to the former testimony exception (subdivision (b)(1)), since the record of in-court testimony at a former trial or hearing, if available, is considered superior to a deposition. Thus, the effect of the requirement is that before using any Rule 804 exception other than former testimony, an attorney must make a reasonable attempt to take the declarant's deposition.

Psychological unavailability.   Recent additions in many states expressly render a declarant (especially a child victim of a sexual offense) unavailable if severely traumatized by the crime or the prospect of testifying. Under the FRE, this would have to be fit within subsection (4) ("infirmity"). See also 18 U.S.C. 3509 (remote or videotaped testimony by psychologically traumatized child abuse victims).

Former Testimony

Statements made by an unavailable declarant while testifying at a previous trial or hearing (or in a deposition), which need not be related to the present proceedings. See **FRE 804(b)(1).**

Example 5.57:   Sam sues Indemnity Insurance Company to collect the insurance on a building owned by Sam that burned down. Indemnity offers the testimony of Willie, a now-deceased witness in a criminal trial in which Sam was accused of intentionally setting the fire that destroyed his building. Willie had testified as to the time at which the fire began. Whether Willie was a witness for Sam or for the prosecution, Willie's former testimony is admissible against Sam in the present trial.

Rationale: Oath and cross-examination at previous hearing eliminate most hearsay dangers; of usual safeguards (oath, demeanor, cross-examination), only demeanor not available.

Protecting the party against whom offered.   Since Sam will have no opportunity to cross-examine Willie at the present trial, it is important that he had some such opportunity at the previous one. Depending upon the jurisdiction, therefore, Willie's testimony is admissible only if, at the prior proceeding, (1) the party against whom it is now offered (Sam), (2) someone in **privity** with him (perhaps the grantor of property that is in issue), or (3) anyone with a similar motive and interest had an opportunity to examine or cross-examine the declarant.

Uncertain breadth under the Federal Rules. The FRE substitutes "predecessor in interest" for "privity" in category (2) and does not expressly recognize category (3). (To avoid Confrontation Clause problems, in criminal cases only category (1), the identical party, is considered; even a predecessor in interest will not do.) There is considerable disagreement as to the scope of "predecessor in interest," and its legislative history is unclear. Literally it means a person with a prior interest in the subject matter of the litigation. Some federal courts, however, extend it to any shared interest, to a "community of interest" (see the leading case of *Lloyd v. American Export Lines, Inc.*[11]), or even to any person at all, reliance on whose prior cross-examination would be fair. It may, therefore, be interpreted being as broad as category (3), whether or not so intended by Congress.

No mutuality required. Note that in Example 5.57 it is irrelevant that Indemnity was not a party to the former proceedings (the criminal trial) and had no one there with a similar motive or interest to protect its interests: it is only the party against whom the statement is offered (here Sam) who needs the protection, and who therefore must have had the opportunity personally or through someone else to develop or attack the former testimony.

Example 5.58: Same facts as Example 5.57 (Sam sues Indemnity to recover for the fire damage) except that Sam seeks to use Willie's testimony against Indemnity. If neither Indemnity nor a predecessor in interest (nor, where included, anyone else with a similar motive or interest to cross-examine Willie) was a party to the previous action, Willie's testimony cannot be used against it.

Opportunity to cross-examine. Usually only the *opportunity* to cross-examine is required. Except in extreme cases, it does not matter whether the party (or privy) did in fact cross-examine the former witness, or the reason for failing to do so. In a preliminary hearing, for example, it may be best for defense counsel to concede the existence of probable cause and hold back on thorough cross-examination of prosecution witnesses until trial; but if the witness becomes unavailable, what might earlier have been good tactics may turn out later to be an unfortunate loss of opportunity.

11. 580 F.2d 1179 (3d. Cir. 1978).

Same issues. It is sometimes said that the issues in the two cases must be the same. This is, however, more properly another way to state the need for a similar motive or interest: the issues must be such that they gave the earlier party a similar incentive to cross-examine and test the witness's statements as the present party would have now.

Objections. Finally, some objections that might have been made in the former proceeding but were not cannot be made for the first time at the later trial, and some can. The majority rule is that objections to the form of the question to which the former witness responded (such as "calls for an opinion") cannot be made for the first time at the later trial; but substantive objections (such as to relevancy) can. Thus in Example 5.57, if at the earlier criminal trial Willie had been asked for his opinion as to the cause of the fire and Sam had not objected, no such objection can be made by Sam when Willie's testimony is later introduced at the civil trial; but if the question was irrelevant (but escaped objection) at the criminal trial and remains irrelevant at the later civil trial, that objection is still available to Sam at the civil trial.

Dying Declaration

A statement made by an unavailable declarant who believes that death is imminent, relating to the cause or circumstances of the declarant's death. See **FRE 804(b)(2)**.

Example 5.59: Violetta has been mortally wounded and lies dying in the arms of Antonio. Violetta gasps, "I'm dying, and it was that dirty scoundrel Donato who did it." Violetta then expires. Violetta's dying statement is admissible against Donato at his subsequent trial.

Rationale: There is no reason to lie when one is about to die. (On the other hand, a more cynical view is that at death the declarant has nothing to lose, and a lie may even benefit the declarant's successors. This counter-rationale has not, however, gained much judicial favor.)

In the above example, Violetta conveniently indicated her belief she was dying. In many instances, circumstantial evidence will be the only means available to prove whether the declarant had such a belief at the time the statement was made.

Although originally the trustworthiness of a dying declaration was based on strongly-held religious beliefs in damnation and punishment, the exception continues without this rationale and even an atheist can be the declarant of a dying declaration.

Death. The declarant need not actually die immediately, so long as imminent death was expected at the time. In fact, under modern practice (and contrary to that at common law), the declarant need not die at all, but need merely to become unavailable. (Of course, if use is limited to homicide and victim/declarants, see below, death is presumably a prerequisite.)

Restrictions on usage and content. Traditional rules restrict dying declarations to cases of homicide (and homicide of the declarant, at that), and to statements regarding the immediate circumstances of the killing. Modern rules are less restrictive as to use, either limiting use to any homicide and civil cases (like the FRE), or imposing no limitation at all (see CEC 1242 and URE 804(b)(2)). They also permit references to the "cause or circumstances" of death, which is usually interpreted broadly. Like most hearsay declarants, the dying declarant must speak from personal knowledge.

Example 5.60: Same facts as in Example 5.59, except that Violetta states: (1) "Donato shot me." (2) "He often threatened me." (3) "His girlfriend probably put him up to it." (4) "Did you know that he and I pulled the Acme Bank job last month?" Only statements (1) and (at least under modern rules) (2) are admissible as dying declarations, since (3) lacks personal knowledge and (4) is unrelated to the cause or circumstances of death.

If Donato is charged only with attempted murder, or the action is civil, whether Violetta's statement is admissible will depend on the strictness of the usage rule followed by the court.

Declaration Against Interest

A statement by an unavailable person (whether or not a party to the present proceedings) that, at the time it was made, would have been harmful to some interest of the declarant. See **FRE 804(b)(3).**

Example 5.61: There is a dispute over whether Trixi was mentally competent on July 1, when she executed her will. Harriet, the will's proponent, introduces a written statement, a receipt dated July 1 and signed by Sigmund, Trixi's physician, acknowledging payment of $100 for an office visit. Harriet contends that this helps establish Trixi's ability to handle her routine affairs properly at the time in question. Assuming the writing is authenticated as Sigmund's and Sigmund is unavailable to testify, it is admissible as a declaration against Sigmund's pecuniary interest, to prove that Trixi paid Sigmund. At the time he wrote it, Sigmund had a claim against Harriet for payment for the treatment; upon issuing the receipt, he relinquished that claim.

Rationale: Reasonable persons do not knowingly make false statements that are against their interest. Put another way, "Why lie if it will only hurt you?"

What interests? At common law, only statements against the declarant's proprietary or pecuniary interest (as in Example 5.61) were admissible. FRE 804(b)(3) and many other modern rules now include statements against penal interest as well (often within the broad requirement that the statement subject the declarant to civil or criminal liability). The most obvious example is a confession of crime. When, however, the confession of an unavailable third person is used to exculpate (establish the innocence of) a criminal defendant, the Federal Rule excludes the statement unless corroborating circumstances clearly indicate its trustworthiness.

Example 5.62: Dinah is accused of murdering Vince. Dinah's attorney introduces the statement of Consuela, who is unavailable, confessing to killing Vince. Unless there are corroborating circumstances that clearly indicate the trustworthiness of Consuela's statement (such as an eyewitness or circumstantial evidence linking Consuela with the crime, or indications of a strong motivation to tell the truth in the particular circumstances in which the statement was made) is introduced, Consuela's statement will be excluded under FRE 803(b)(3).

Some rules, like URE 803(b)(3), also exclude confessions offered by the prosecution which implicate both the declarant and the accused, regardless of corroborative evidence. The Federal Rule does not address these statements, although there are serious Confrontation Clause implications of using them against a criminal defendant. Compare *Bruton v. United States*.[12] Such statements are almost always looked upon with suspicion, and some courts simply reject them outright without a specific rule requiring it.

Statements that are against some personal or social interest of the declarant generally are not within this exception. A few statutes, however, such as CEC 1330 and URE 803(b)(3), include statements that would make the declarant an object of hatred, ridicule, or disgrace in the community, which essentially are defamatory statements.

When a statement is against interest. A statement is considered against interest if the declarant had personal knowledge of the subject matter and a reasonable person in the declarant's position would not have made it without believing it true. (Of course, evidence that the declarant in fact believed it false could result in rejection; and some older formulations of

12. 391 U.S. 123 (1968).

the exception require an affirmative showing of "no motive to falsify.") Also, it generally is assumed that a person realizes that a statement is against interest if a reasonable person would realize it, without actual proof that this is so.

Example 5.63:   Orlando admits he is the owner of the car being driven by Drew when it hit Lonnie. Under state law, this makes Orlando liable if Drew was negligent. It also exonerates Sybil, who had been suspected of being the car's owner. In a suit against Sybil, Orlando's statement probably is admissible as a declaration against interest, even without proof that Orlando was specifically aware of the law of agency making him liable.

Note that context and circumstances are critical. If in Example 5.63 Orlando had been told, "This car has been selected winner in the lucky license plate contest and we are looking for the owner," it was probably in Orlando's (or any reasonable person's) interest to claim ownership.

The statement must be against interest at the time it is made, regardless of whether it is at the time of trial. Thus in Example 5.63 if Orlando's statement was against his interest (because of tort liability) when made, it is irrelevant that, for example, a week later Lonnie admits the accident was her fault and the car wins the lucky license plate contest.

Of course, many statements are both for and against one's interest: for example, the statement "I just put a million dollars in the bank" may help one to get a loan, but the effect on one's friends and relatives may be less than desirable. Generally, courts look for the predominant motive or effect in the circumstances.

Contextual statements.   If in the context of a statement against interest the declarant also makes other statements, themselves neutral as to interest, they may also be admissible. These are sometimes referred to as **collateral statements.**

Example 5.64:   Same facts as Example 5.61 (a dispute over Trixi's mental competence), except that the receipt from Sigmund is expressly for "treatment for acute depression." The fact that the doctor treated Trixi for a particular disease is not itself against his interest. Yet it is obviously a part of, and helps to explain the meaning of, the against-interest "paid $100." It would therefore be admissible as well, this time to support the will's contestant in proving Trixi's incapacity.

At least for federal criminal cases (and perhaps for others), the Supreme Court has narrowed the exception by rejecting neutral contextual statements unless they somehow add to the adverse effect on the declarant's interest. (*United States v. Williamson.* [13])

Example 5.65: Same as Example 5.62 (Dinah accused of murdering Vince), except that Consuela's confession includes the statement, "Me and Lefty did the job together; Dinah wasn't around that day." Under a traditional, broad application of the collateral statements rule, the statement about Dinah (as well as that about Lefty) should be admissible (under the FRE, if there is corroboration), as "neutral" as to interest but helping to explain and give context to the confession. Under a strict reading of *Williamson*, however, the FRE would not permit use of the language exculpating Dinah (or inculpating Lefty, were that an issue), since only the part inculpating herself is, strictly speaking, against Consuela's interest.

Even after *Williamson*, it might still be argued (as it was successfully argued in a pre-*Williamson* case) that the statements about Dinah and Lefty are also against Consuela's interest, as they add details about "the job" and therefore add to the impression that Consuela was in fact involved in it.

The closer in context the collateral statement is to the clearly against-interest statement, the more likely it will be within the exception. Clearly neutral statements that are necessary to an understanding of the against-interest statement (such as that in Example 5.64, which explains what the payment is for) are much more likely to be admitted than those that add nothing important (for example, "paid $100 by Trixi, who was wearing a lovely pink satin dress"). And it is least likely, except in the most liberal of applications, that self-serving statements contained within the context of a declaration that is generally against interest would be admitted under this exception.

Comparison to Admissions. Declarations against interest are easily confused with admissions, which they resemble. Certainly if the declarant is now an opposing party in the lawsuit, both exceptions may apply. There are, however, crucial differences between them:

(1) Declarations against interest may have been made by anyone, whether or not presently a party (and even by the party now offering them, if the unavailability requirement can be satisfied); admissions must have been made by the offering party's present opponent.

(2) Declarations against interest had to be against the declarant's interest when made, but need not be when offered; admissions need

13. 114 S. Ct. 2431 (1994).

not have been against the declarant's interest when made, nor need they be (although by their nature they almost certainly are) when offered.

(3) The declarant of a declaration against interest must be unavailable; the declarant of an admission, again by its nature, usually will be available as a party.

(4) Declarations against interest require personal knowledge; admissions do not.

Rule of Thumb: If the declarant is not an opposing party, it cannot be an admission but may be a declaration against interest; if the declarant is an opposing party, it probably is an admission but it may be both.

It should now be apparent why it is both incorrect and confusing to refer to admissions as "admissions against interest," but correct and helpful to refer to them as "admissions of a party opponent."

To whom made. Finally, it may or may not be important to whom the statement was made. Courts seem to admit declarations against interest made to friends on the theory that the declarant would likely tell them the truth, and to enemies on the theory that no one would knowingly make false, detrimental statements to someone who couldn't be trusted with them. Clearly, however, the fact that a statement implicating the accused was made by a prisoner in custody, or to police officers during interrogation, might suggest the declarant was merely currying favor and the statement cannot be trusted.

Statement of Personal or Family History

A statement by an unavailable declarant relating to such family matters as the declarant's own birth, marriage, or divorce, and to similar facts concerning other persons either related to the declarant or with whose family the declarant was intimately associated. See **FRE 804(b)(4).**

Example 5.66: Portnoy claims that his late father Fenton was the son of Giovanni. Wynette testifies that she once was told by Fenton that he was Giovanni's adopted son. Fenton's statement is admissible for the truth of its assertion.

Rationale: One is unlikely to be mistaken either about one's own personal history or about that of persons or families to whom one is close. Common law restrictions (see below) assured no contrary motivation.

Personal knowledge. Since one cannot have personal knowledge of many of the facts of one's own life (especially birth or adoption), personal knowledge is not required as it relates to the declarant's own history. And for statements about others' history, there need only be a close enough relationship that the declarant's information, derived from the person or family in question, is likely to be accurate.

Relationship required. At common law this exception was limited to the declarant's own family; modern rules extend it to intimately associated families. Thus in Example 5.66, Wynette could also have testified to statements about Portnoy's parentage made by (if unavailable) Giovanni's cousin, the cousin's husband, or even a close friend of Giovanni's family.

Other requirements. Traditional rules also required that the statement be made *ante litem motam* (before the present controversy arose) and that there be no other apparent motive to misrepresent. Some modern rules retain this requirement or a form of it (see, e.g., CEC 1310(b) and 1311(b), rejecting statements for lack of trustworthiness); the FRE relies on Rule 403 for this purpose.

See also the related exceptions for family-related documents, records, reputation, and judgments in FRE 803(12), (13), (19), and (23) respectively.

3. Beyond the Traditional Exceptions

Residual (or "Catchall") Exception

A general hearsay exception for statements that do not fit any enumerated exception, but that share those exceptions' characteristics for necessity and trustworthiness. See **FRE 803(24)** and **804(b)(5)**.

At common law, unless a hearsay statement could be fit within an accepted exception, it was seldom admissible, regardless of its trustworthiness or necessity. New or expanded exceptions were rarely adopted. (No exceptions were added or expanded in English law, for example, between 1886 and 1968, and then it took an Act of Parliament to make the change.) Thus, the most common results would be rejection of the evidence or sometimes a Herculean attempt to fit it into the closest existing exception (rightly compared to squeezing the stepsisters' feet into Cinderella's slipper).

Enter the Federal Rules. Under the so-called residual or catchall exceptions, evidence is admitted if it passes muster on a case-by-case basis.

The only difference between the two exceptions is that one requires the declarant to be unavailable and the other does not. How this might affect their application will be discussed below.

There are six requirements for applying the catchall exception (plus unavailability for FRE 804(b)(5)). The statement must:

(1) not be covered by one of the existing, enumerated exceptions;
(2) have equivalent circumstantial guarantees of trustworthiness to the enumerated exceptions;
(3) be offered as evidence of a material fact;
(4) be more probative than other evidence its proponent can with reasonable diligence procure; and
(5) serve the general purposes of the rules and the interests of justice.
(6) Proper advance notice and opportunity to meet it must also be provided.

Of these, the most difficult to satisfy (and most flexible in terms of court discretion) are (2) and (4).

Example 5.67:   Drexel is on trial for the murder of Vonda. At a previous grand jury hearing, Wilberforce testified that he sold the pistol that shot Vonda to Drexel. Wilberforce is now unavailable, and after diligent search the prosecution has been unable to locate him or to find other evidence of the sale. Wilberforce's testimony does not fit the former testimony exception because there was no opportunity to cross-examine him; it does not fit the prior statements exception because the witness is presently unavailable. A court might well find that the formal setting, Wilberforce's apparent lack of a motive to lie, and perhaps other factors make Wilberforce's statement seem at least as trustworthy as other Rule 804 exceptions; sale of the pistol is a material fact; proper notice has been given; and the interests of justice would be served by admitting the evidence. If so, the residual exception will apply. This is, in fact, a common use of the exception.

Trustworthiness can be shown by almost any means, from intrinsic or "inherent" circumstances such as spontaneity or motivation, to external ones such as corroborative testimony by another witness. At least for evidence offered against federal criminal defendants, the Supreme Court requires (for Constitutional purposes) that trustworthiness be demonstrated through intrinsic factors. (See *Idaho v. Wright.*[14])

Equivalent to what?   The other exceptions (to which the proffered statement must have "equivalent" guarantees of trustworthiness) are themselves so varied in trustworthiness that courts have considerable discretion in comparing the statement to the strongest, weakest, or (most commonly) average exception. Arguably, however, a statement by an unavailable declarant under FRE 804(b)(5) would need less trustworthiness than one offered under 803(24), since as a whole the exceptions that have the added

---

14. 497 U.S. 805 (1990).

necessity of unavailability are probably making up for a lesser degree of trustworthiness.

"Horseshoes" or "Golf"? The reason a statement does not fit an existing exception may be because it presents a new and unanticipated situation, or because (as in Example 5.67) it simply fails to satisfy one or more of some existing exception's criteria. Most courts seem to accept the latter approach, whereby (as in the game of horseshoes) a "near miss" counts. Other courts treat the exception more like golf, where there is no credit for merely getting close to the hole. They reject the near miss theory, because it tends to make the specific criteria of the traditional exceptions mere suggestions that can be ignored by use of the residual exception.

State equivalents. While states not following the Federal or Uniform Rules generally do not have an equivalent residual exception, they often have other narrow exceptions that cover some of its most likely uses. For example, many states have an exception for hearsay statements of child victims of sexual abuse (the specific requirements for which vary), which is a common use of the residual exception. And CEC 1350 excepts statements in cases of "serious felonies" in which the defendant had the declarant killed or kidnapped, the statement was recorded or written and notarized, the circumstances indicate trustworthiness and lack of inducement or coercion, and the facts are corroborated. All of the above are frequently cited as factors in finding statements trustworthy under the residual exception.

4. Constitutional Limitations

Confrontation Clause

The clause of the Constitution's Sixth Amendment that affords an accused the right "to be confronted with the witnesses against him." In the context of the hearsay rule, it limits the availability of hearsay exceptions that would admit certain statements against a criminal defendant.

A full examination of the Confrontation Clause is beyond the scope of this work. The following discussion is limited to the criteria presently being applied by the Supreme Court and their application to the hearsay rule.

The Confrontation Clause applies only to evidence offered against criminal defendants. Evidence offered in civil cases or by a criminal defendant is not affected, at least constitutionally.

Under recent Supreme Court interpretations, the primary purpose of the Confrontation Clause seems to be that of assuring trustworthiness. The

118

Court has set out the following guidelines and criteria for satisfying this purpose:

(1) A declarant need not be unavailable before a hearsay exception can be applied (*United States v. Inadi*[15]), unless the exception itself requires unavailability (*Ohio v. Roberts*[16]).

(2) If an exception is a "firmly rooted" one, it has sufficient "indicia of reliability" to satisfy Confrontation; but if it is not firmly rooted, it must be shown to have "particularized guarantees of trustworthiness" (*Roberts*).

Example 5.68:   Delilah is on trial for robbery. The prosecution introduces the statement of Wilton that he saw Delilah commit the crime, citing the exception for excited utterances. As this exception is of long-standing and firmly rooted in the common law, it is presumed to have sufficient indicia of reliability for Confrontation Clause purposes.

Example 5.69:   George is on trial for assaulting his wife, Martha. The prosecution offers the testimony of Conway, a marriage counselor, relating statements made to her by George during counselling sessions, under a new hearsay exception just adopted by the state and unknown to the common law. The prosecution will have to demonstrate that the statement has particularized guarantees of trustworthiness before it can be admitted against George. (Compare *Idaho v. Wright.*)

(3) "Particularized guarantees of trustworthiness" cannot be shown by collateral evidence, extrinsic to the statement itself. Rather, there must be inherent or intrinsic factors. (*Idaho v. Wright.*)

Example 5.70:   Same facts as Example 5.68 (Delilah's trial for robbery), except that Wilton's testimony is offered under FRE 804(b)(5), the residual exception. This is not a "firmly rooted" exception (*Wright*), so trustworthiness must be shown. If Wilton's statement was made under circumstances indicating both spontaneity and a strong interest in telling the truth, although it does not fit a traditional exception, these intrinsic factors should be sufficient for constitutional purposes.

Example 5.71:   Same facts as Example 5.68, except the only particularized guarantee of trustworthiness offered by the prosecution is that

15. 475 U.S. 387 (1986).
16. 448 U.S. 56 (1980).

Wilton's statement is corroborated by the testimony of witnesses Yolanda and Zoe, both of whom also claim to have seen Delilah at the scene of the crime. These extrinsic facts, not inherent in the statement itself (that is, not something about the statement or its setting that makes it particularly believable), cannot be used to overcome the Confrontation Clause barrier.

It is not clear yet whether an exception must be firmly rooted in time (back to the common law) or in space (widely adopted) or both; some courts treat the requirement as just another way of stating the trustworthiness criterion. It is also unclear whether exceptions presently not firmly rooted will develop those roots over time, or be forever relegated to the "Johnny-come-lately" category and require case-by-case legitimation.

> <u>Rule of Thumb</u>: If an exception appears in the Federal Rules and traces back to the common law, it should pass muster under the Confrontation Clause. If it is relatively new and untested, however, it probably will have to be demonstrated to be trustworthy, a requirement that can be quite exacting.

Chambers Doctrine

A constitutional doctrine prohibiting as a violation of the due process clause the exclusion of extremely reliable evidence favoring a criminal defendant, even if admission would be contrary to the hearsay rule or some other rule of exclusion. This doctrine is based on the Supreme Court's ruling in *Chambers v. Mississippi*,[17] hence the name it is often given.

The breadth of this doctrine is still unclear. *Chambers* itself was an unusual case of a third-party confession (actually several confessions) excluded by a combination of the state's rigid application of the hearsay exception for declarations against interest and the "voucher" rule, which prevented the defense's cross-examination of its own witness, the declarant (see Chapter 8). How far beyond this narrow holding the doctrine will extend is still the subject of disagreement. The doctrine illustrates, however, that as the admission of certain untrustworthy evidence against the defendant can violate the confrontation clause, at some point the exclusion of important and reliable evidence favoring the defendant can violate the defendant's constitutional right to present a defense and thus to due process.

17. 410 U.S. 84 (1973).

6

Real and Demonstrative Evidence

Introduction and Overview of Chapter

Evidence comes in many varieties, but there are only three basic ways it can be presented: orally, in writing, or in the form of tangible things. The latter are the subject of this chapter. As we will see, the chief distinction with regard to tangible objects is between real and demonstrative evidence, which may appear to be the same but serve different functions.

Real Evidence

Things or objects that can be seen, touched, or otherwise sensed directly by the trier of fact, and which are alleged to have played a part in the incident being litigated.

Example 6.1:   Dick is on trial for the murder of Vern. The prosecution introduces: (1) the testimony of Walt, an eyewitness, who states that he saw Dick stab Vern with a red-handled knife; (2) a signed statement, in which Dick admits owning a red-handled knife; and (3) the alleged murder weapon, a blood-stained red-handled knife. Item (1) is *testimonial* evidence, conveying to the jury information about the knife through Walt's statements. Item (2) is *documentary* evidence, conveying such information about the knife through Dick's writing. Item (3) is *real* evidence, the knife itself, an object that allegedly played a role in the killing and that conveys its information to the jury directly, by sight and possibly touch.

Real evidence is sometimes called **original evidence, objective evidence, autoptic evidence,** or **autoptic proference.** It may also be called demonstrative evidence, when that term is used as the generic designation for the two distinguishable categories of real and demonstrative evidence. In its narrower sense (and the sense used in this work), however, "demonstrative evidence" is an object that did not play a role in the affair litigated, but which is used only for illustrative purposes (see the separate entry below). Thus, in Example 6.1 if the prosecution had introduced a *model* of the alleged murder weapon to illustrate Walt's description of it, this would have been true demonstrative evidence. But even if the term "demonstrative" is used generically, the two distinct types (that which played a role and that which is used for illustrative purposes only) must still be kept in mind, as their foundational requirements are very different.

Examples of real evidence.   Objects like a murder weapon are easy to classify as real evidence. But the category also includes, for example, writings, when it is the document itself, and not its content, that is in issue.

Example 6.2:   Doris is charged with stealing a valuable document, an old letter. The evidence against her includes the object stolen, the letter, recovered from Doris's apartment. The letter is real evidence.

If the letter in Example 6.2 had not been the object stolen but had been offered in evidence because it contained Doris's confession (see Example 6.1), it would have been testimonial and not real evidence.

A witness's demeanor is actually real evidence (of veracity), although it seldom is thought of as such. What a witness looks like while testifying is itself evidence directed to the jury's senses (of sight and sound). In contrast, what a witness might say about the demeanor of an absent hearsay declarant would not be real but testimonial evidence of the declarant's veracity.

Similarly, a view of the scene of the incident in question is real evidence (to the extent it is evidence at all — see *View*), whereas mere testimony about what the scene looked like is not. The fact that the scene is too big to bring into the courtroom does not change its basic function in the case.

A photograph (or motion picture) of an object or scene actually involved in the disputed incident has been called both demonstrative and real evidence, but in truth it has qualities of both. While it is one step removed from the actual thing represented and primarily used to illustrate testimony, with modern technology it has exactly the same features as the original and is virtually tantamount to "being there."

Foundation. To be admissible, real evidence must be shown to be the object it purports to be (that is, authenticated), and to be substantially unchanged in condition from the time it played its role in the litigated drama, at least if substantial change would render it irrelevant. While a simple identifying tag or label often will suffice for this foundation, more may be required if the object is particularly changeable (such as fresh fruit) or volatile (such as alcohol), or if it is fungible or otherwise particularly difficult to identify (such as a plain white powder). A **chain of custody** can be used for this purpose, documenting who had possession of the object, when, and where, from the time it was procured to the time of trial. With the use of sealed containers and other means of identification, it can be established that there was no opportunity for substitution or alteration up to the moment of submission to the court. See generally **FRE 901.**

Demonstrative Evidence

In its broader meaning, *things or objects that can be seen, touched, or otherwise sensed directly by the trier of fact;* in its narrower, more specific sense, *such things that did not play a part in the incident being litigated, but are offered only for purposes of illustration, clarification, or explanation of other evidence.* In keeping with its usual role, demonstrative evidence is sometimes referred to as **illustrative evidence.**

Example 6.3: Dorothy is on trial for the murder of Vince. The alleged murder weapon was a knife, but it disappeared while in police custody. The prosecution offers the following evidence: (1) the testimony of the officer who found the body and the knife; (2) a model of the knife, based on a witness's description; (3) a drawing of the murder scene showing with an "X" where the knife was found; and (4) a computer simulation of the manner in which Vince was stabbed and fell. All except the first are examples of demonstrative evidence in its narrow or specific sense of merely illustrative evidence. The knife itself, if found and offered in evidence, would be real evidence, being the object in question itself. As such, it would still fit the broader, generic use of the term "demonstrative evidence."

Demonstrative evidence is sometimes contrasted with **substantive evidence,** which can be testimonial, documentary, or real. At one time the term "demonstrative evidence" was used to mean evidence that was based on the immutable features of nature (scientific principles, logic, and so forth), as distinguished from "moral" evidence (all other evidence, such as inferences from human experience). The latter term is now out of use, and there is much disagreement over the precise meaning of the rest of these terms. It is best, therefore, to choose one vocabulary while recognizing the existence of the others. In this work, "demonstrative evidence" is used in its narrower sense of primarily illustrative evidence.

Unlike real evidence, demonstrative evidence generally is not admissible in evidence, and without consent of all parties it may not be permitted in the jury room during the jury's deliberations.

Photographic Evidence

Evidence in the form of still photos or motion pictures, offered for the purpose of illustrating testimonial evidence or portraying that which has not otherwise been witnessed. Video tape recordings are, of course, now included with motion pictures in this general category.

Usually the photograph or moving picture is merely intended to illustrate independent testimony, sometimes referred to as **pictorial testimony:**

Example 6.4:   Daryl is on trial for murder. Witness Wanda, who saw the incident take place, describes the scene of the crime in court. She then uses a photograph of the scene, taken just afterward, to illustrate for the jury the relative positions of the defendant and his victim, matters that she has just described.

In Example 6.4, the evidence is really Wanda's testimony, and the photograph is merely an aid to understanding it. Many courts today recognize a "substantive" aspect to a photograph, considering the testimony and the photograph together to be the evidence.

Sometimes, however, the photograph itself is the only evidence, giving mute testimony to that which it observed and recorded; this is the **silent witness** theory of photographic evidence. The oldest and most obvious example is an X-ray, which records that which no one but the camera has seen; but there are many more modern applications of this doctrine.

Example 6.5:   Same facts as Example 6.4, except that there was no one around to witness the crime. There was, however, a hidden security camera filming the scene as the drama unfolded. The film it took, depicting Daryl committing the murder, is (if properly authenticated) admissible as a silent witness. Here clearly it, and not a live witness's testimony, is the evidence.

Different foundations. Because the theories of admissibility are quite different for the two types of photographic evidence, they require quite different foundations and implicate different auxiliary rules. The major differences are these:

(1) *Authentication.* Photographic evidence used to *illustrate* testimony generally is authenticated by the testimony itself, that is, by any witness who is familiar with that which is portrayed and who states that the photograph or film does in fact portray it accurately. See **FRE 901(b)(1).** A silent witness photo or film, on the other hand, by definition must stand on its own. Someone therefore must vouch not for the accuracy of the scene it depicts, but for the reliability of the mechanism that recorded it. Thus unlike illustrative evidence, the silent witness is generally authenticated by testimony as to the nature and accuracy of the photographic process together with the film's chain of custody. See **FRE 901(b)(9).**

(2) *Best Evidence Rule.* Pictorial testimony does not generally implicate the Best Evidence Rule (see Chapter 7), because (in theory) the content of the picture is not in evidence, but only the content of the witness's testimony that the picture illustrates. In the use of a silent witness photo, however, it is the content of the picture itself that is the evidence; thus, the original must be produced unless excused. See Examples 7.16-7.17.

Sound recordings would be treated generally the same as motion pictures, with allowances of course for the different media. Thus, an audio tape recording used to illustrate a witness's testimony about the difference between the sounds of a diesel and a gasoline engine, or a silent witness recording of an audible event no one was around to see or hear, would be authenticated and admitted on similar considerations to those just discussed.

Digital Retouching

Computerized "editing" of photographs, otherwise known as **computer enhancement.**

Unlike some newer scientific devices and procedures (see Chapter 4), photography enjoys wide acceptance for its relatively accurate portrayal of facts. Although photographs could always be "faked" in various ways, in the past this could usually be detected by experts. Moving pictures are inherently more susceptible to tampering and have taken longer to be accepted in court, but they too (together with videotapes) are now routinely admitted using standard authentication procedures.

Enter digital retouching, which can do to a photograph what a word processor can do to a document: the picture is scanned and turned into a digital display; it is then retouched as one would edit a document (for example, a figure is moved from one side of the street to the other, or it is deleted altogether); and the retouched picture is then printed out as if it had never been otherwise.

The potential implications of these processes for evidentiary use of photographs, only just beginning to be encountered by courts, are obvious.

Day-in-the-Life Film

A film or videotape recording depicting the daily routine of a party, in order to demonstrate how illness or injury affects the party's day-to-day life.

Usually day-in-the-life films are presented by plaintiffs, to illustrate the effects of an injury on routine chores and the tasks of everyday living. They can be quite compelling, in a way a mere description cannot. Of course, there is much room for acting or misleading effects for which the court and counsel must be alert. Also, to the extent the plaintiff is consciously implying something (such as "Look how it hurts when I try to do this"), the picture is technically hearsay; however, if the plaintiff is presently testifying subject to cross-examination, courts usually permit the evidence, subject to a cautionary instruction if requested.

Defense use. Similar films are sometimes made by defense counsel, to demonstrate that the plaintiff has less difficulty than alleged, or is simply malingering. Here, of course, the film is taken surreptitiously, and any implied assertion by the plaintiff would not be intended and (under the FRE, at least) not hearsay. See Chapter 5.

View

Firsthand observation, outside the courtroom, by the court or jury of a relevant thing or place.

Sometimes it is impossible or impracticable to bring a thing into the courtroom, but it would be valuable for the trier of fact to see it firsthand, rather than through a description or a picture. In such cases, the court may order a view, in effect a "field trip" to the place where the object or scene resides.

Common subjects of views are real property (especially in eminent domain cases) and the scene of a crime or tort. It usually is discretionary with the judge, but it may in some situations be a matter of right for either party.

The trial judge may accompany the jury on the view, but in most (especially civil) cases the jurors are accompanied by **showers** (those who show), who are appointed by the court to escort the jurors and help assure that nothing improper (such as prejudicial remarks by a party or attorney) occurs.

Parties and their counsel (although sometimes only the latter) generally are permitted to participate in the view, and criminal defendants may in some instances have a constitutional right to be present.

Evidence or not. Still disputed is whether a view is itself evidence, or only an aid to understanding other evidence, with about half the courts taking each position but the modern trend favoring the view as evidence. This distinction generally has no impact on the trial; but on occasion it can be of importance, especially if the only evidence on an issue would be some fact observed during the view.

Example 6.6: Following an auto accident, Paula alleges Daisy was intoxicated, but no evidence is introduced of that fact. The judge orders a view of Daisy's wrecked car, to clear up some questions as to the type of damage incurred. At the scene, several of the jurors detect the aroma of whiskey in the car. On this basis alone they conclude that Daisy was likely intoxicated at the time of the accident. If a view is "not evidence," there is no proof of Daisy's intoxication for the jury to consider. If it is evidence, the jury could consider it, although the court could still rule it insufficient to decide the issue.

Some courts permit the taking of testimony or performing of experiments during a view, while others do not. Certainly if testimony is taken, at least this part is evidence and the view becomes an extension of the courtroom trial.

Computer Simulation

A computer-generated representation of a thing or occurrence, using data supplied by the offering party and relying on the computer's calculations to recreate the image. It is a form of computer-created visual evidence.

Computer simulation may be contrasted with **computer animation,** in which data are also used to create an image, but merely mechanically, without any calculation or assumption being made by the computer itself.

Example 6.7: In issue is the manner in which a complex machine malfunctioned. In order for the jury to understand what the inside of the machine looks like and how the relevant parts interact, a computer animation is created from the precise dimensions of the machine's parts. It depicts on a screen exactly what the machine looks like inside and how the parts look when the machine operates, a view that no camera could capture.

Example 6.8: Same facts as Example 6.7, except the plaintiff offers a computer simulation of how the malfunction occurred. The computer is given the relevant physical and operational characteristics of the machine when new and after the damage occurred. It then calculates what "must have" occurred, and it recreates that process on the screen.

It has been said that a computer animation is just a means of representing visually what a witness describes orally, much as a photograph would do, whereas a computer simulation puts the computer itself in the position of an expert witness, telling the jury (in its "opinion") how it thinks the incident or object appeared. In this use it is a form of *reconstructive* evidence, which purports to recreate conditions substantially similar to those that actually existed at the time in question. For this reason, a computer animation may be treated as ordinary demonstrative evidence, merely illustrating a witness's testimony, but a computer simulation is more of an experiment. As such, the simulation is subject to more stringent rules regarding the similarity of the "inputted" data to that testified to at trial and the reliability of the computer to make its calculated assumptions.

Reconstructive Evidence

A purported recreation of the manner in which an incident occurred, or the way an object appeared, at a relevant point in time. The most common form is **accident reconstruction.** This was once done by the use of charts, photographs of the scene, diagrams, and other such visual aids, illustrating the testimony of an accident reconstruction expert. Today there is widespread use of computer simulation, in which a computer uses actual or assumed data to reconstruct what a party alleges to be reality. See *Computer Simulation.*

Writings and Related Matters

Introduction and Overview of Chapter

This chapter covers rules that govern the presentation of evidence in written form. There are actually only two major rules discussed: (1) that relating to authentication of a document (as opposed to authentication of real or demonstrative evidence, covered in Chapter 6); and (2) the so-called Best Evidence Rule, now often (and more accurately) called the Original Document Rule. Beyond these, documents are treated more or less the same as the other forms of evidence, testimonial or tangible.

Of course there are many instances in which a document is, in essence, either testimony (for example, a deposition) or real/demonstrative evidence (for example, a stolen check). One of the most important (and difficult) issues when dealing with a writing is the initial determination of whether it is being offered as a document, as testimony, or as an object apart from its written content; for it is on the basis of this determination that one knows whether the rules in this chapter are to be applied.

Writing (In General)

In modern rules, any communication or representation by the use of words, symbols, or the equivalent, including electronic or magnetic impulse. Some codes (like **FRE 901**) separately define recordings and photographs. Others (like CEC 250) include photographic images, and even sound recordings, in the general definition of "writing."

Because some definitions are less inclusive than others, reference to a writing in a rule may or may not include photographs, computer programs, or other media, and reference for purposes of evidence may be different than for other purposes, such as probate law; the appropriate definitions should always be consulted.

In this chapter, unless otherwise indicated, "writing" is used in the narrow sense of any recordation of information in tangible form, using words or other symbols intended to be read.

Authentication (Writings)

The process of establishing that a writing is what it purports to be — that is, proving its authenticity. See generally **FRE 901.** For a more detailed definition of the process of authentication see *Authentication (In General)* in Chapter 1.

Authentication of a writing, like that of any other item of evidence, helps to establish some connection between the writing and the issues in the case in which it is offered. It is an aspect of basic relevance and a part of the foundation that must be laid before evidence is admitted.

Example 7.1: Patty sues Indemnity Insurance Co. to collect on a policy issued on the life of Patty's husband Harold. Indemnity alleges that Harold committed suicide, thus voiding the policy under which Harold was insured. It offers into evidence two writings: (1) a standard form life insurance policy containing a clause excepting suicide from the causes of death for which the company was obligated to pay; and (2) a handwritten note, purportedly written by Harold, saying, "Goodbye cruel world, I'm going to kill myself," and signed "Harold." Both writings must be authenticated before they can be admitted into evidence; both must be genuine before they can be relevant.

Authentication does not require that the writing be proven genuine to the satisfaction of the judge or by a preponderance of the evidence. At this preliminary stage, the evidence need only create a sufficient likelihood of the writing's authenticity that the trier of fact could (but need not) ultimately find it genuine.

If authentication is merely a showing that the item of evidence is genuine, meaning, that it is what it purports to be, then in the case of writings the primary task of the offering party usually is to prove that it was written by the person by whom it purports to have been written. That is, the writing must be tied to — a connection must be established with — some person.

There are, however, other aspects of genuineness than authorship that might be significant in a given case, and these too are part of the process of authentication. Thus in Example 7.1, the insurance policy containing the suicide exception clause must be proven to be the one Harold purchased, regardless of who actually wrote or drafted it (although this ultimately may come down to authenticating Harold's signature on a policy application); whereas the suicide note must be proven to have been written by Harold.

In most instances, a writing is not self-authenticating. This means that it must be shown, at some level of proof, to be what it purports to be by evidence other than the writing itself. Thus, although in everyday life we might be inclined to assume that a note signed "Harold" was in fact written by Harold, the rules of evidence generally are not so trusting. As indicated elsewhere, however, there are an increasing number of writings that are admitted on the basis of what they purport to be. See *Self-Authentication*.

Although authentication is still required of most types of documents, in reality it has become something of a formality and quite easy to satisfy in most instances, because it is rare for a document's authenticity to be actually in dispute.

Methods of authentication. There are several accepted methods for authenticating a writing as having been written by a particular person. Using Harold's suicide note in Example 7.1, we can examine each in turn.

(1) The most obvious and most reliable way to authenticate a writing is the testimony of the writer, in this case Harold; however, since Harold is dead, we must forego that method here. See **FRE 901(b)(1).**

(2) Next best would be the eyewitness testimony of someone who actually saw Harold write the note. Again that is unlikely in our case. See **FRE 901(b)(1).**

(3) Probably the most common (if not the most reliable) method is the opinion of someone familiar with the writer's handwriting. Here Patty is the logical person to call, but since she is the opposing party she may not be a cooperative witness. There may be few other people who have seen enough of Harold's writing to be qualified to distinguish it from similar writing (not to mention a forgery). In practice, however, virtually anyone who has ever seen Harold's writing — or, more precisely, what purported to be Harold's writing — and claims thereby to be somewhat familiar with it will be permitted by most courts to testify that Harold wrote the note. See

FRE 901(b)(2) (familiarity must not be acquired for purposes of litigation). See also CEC 1416 (listing means of acquiring familiarity).

Example 7.2: In Example 7.1, Indemnity calls Felipe, a friend of Harold's who once received a letter purporting to be from Harold and asking Felipe for a reference. On the basis of having seen this letter, Felipe will probably be permitted to state his opinion that the note was (or was not) written by Harold.

The extremely lax application of the authentication requirement, as exemplified by lay opinion based on familiarity, has caused many commentators to call for abolition of the requirement and creation of a rebuttable presumption of authenticity in all cases.

(4) Patty may have stated at some time, either outside of court or in response to a discovery request, that the note was in Harold's handwriting. Such an admission, whether evidentiary or judicial, would be a proper method of authentication. In fact, it is quite common for documents to be authenticated by a discovery request for admission of authenticity, covering at least the undisputed documents in the case. In some jurisdictions it is sufficient for an admission that the party acted upon the writing as if it were authentic, in effect an admission by conduct. See CEC 1414.

(5) Expert comparison to a sample (exemplar) of Harold's writing that itself has been proven or admitted to be genuine is an expensive but effective method of authentication. See Example 7.6. It would be especially appropriate in rare cases of truly disputed genuineness. See **FRE 901(b)(3).**

(6) Jury comparison to an exemplar is also permitted, although it obviously is less reliable than expert comparison. Note that although the jury's opinion is strictly nonexpert, handwriting comparison by a lay (nonexpert) witness would be excluded. See **FRE 901(b)(3).**

(7) Circumstantial evidence of various kinds can be used to authenticate a document. (Methods (1) through (6) would be classified as direct evidence, perhaps with the exception of (6).) See generally **FRE 901(b)(4).** Most common would be:

(a) *Custody:* proof that a public or private document came from a public office where such documents are properly kept (see **FRE 901(b)(7)**), or proof that a private document came from some place that connects it with the party in question.

Example 7.3: If the purported suicide note in Example 7.1 was proved to have been found in Harold's safe deposit box, or even the pocket of his jacket, this would be circumstantial evidence that he wrote it.

(b) *Special knowledge:* proof that facts contained in the writing could have been known only to the person in question.

> *Example 7.4:* If in Example 7.1 the disputed suicide note had said, "Goodbye cruel world, I'm going to kill myself just like I told my brother I would," and if it could be proven independently that Harold did tell his brother he planned to kill himself, then assuming no one else knew about what Harold had said, it is likely that the note was written by Harold (or, of course, by his brother).

Similar would be some special pattern or mannerism of language that is shown to be peculiar to the purported writer.

Remember that the "special knowledge" rule requires two things: first, that the matter is something that would be known only to the alleged writer (or to a limited number of persons, the others of whom can be eliminated as authors of the writing); and second, that the information is correct. If in Example 7.4 either Harold did not tell his brother he planned to commit suicide, or if he did so in a crowded room with 20 people listening, the "special knowledge" connection with Harold is broken. See also *Reply Letter Doctrine*.

(c) *Ancient Documents:* The mere age of a writing, combined with a lack of suspicious circumstances, may render it prima facie genuine. The same or similar factors may also provide the basis for a hearsay exception. See *Ancient Documents Rule (Authentication)*.

(d) *Other circumstantial evidence:* There is an endless variety of circumstances, both external to and contained within a writing, that might attest to its genuineness.

> *Example 7.5:* Terry's will contains pages numbered 1 through 7, except page 5, which was found in another location. Carlotta challenges the authenticity of page 5, although she concedes Terry wrote the rest of the will. If page 4 ends in the middle of a paragraph and page 6 begins in the middle of one, and if the disputed page 5 "fits" into both by its syntax and its substance, this internal consistency is strong circumstantial evidence of its authenticity. (It is also a good reason always to end a page of a will in the middle of a sentence.)

Attesting witnesses. Under the common law, if there are attesting (or subscribing) witnesses to a document, like the witnesses who attest a will by signing their names under the testator's, they must testify to its authenticity (or lack of it); only after they have testified, or have been shown to be unavailable, can other witnesses be called. There are exceptions for judicial admissions and for certain documents (such as those collateral to the issues litigated).

Modern codes tend to eliminate this requirement, except where another statute (such as a probate code) retains it.

Judge and jury. Authentication is a matter of conditional relevance: the evidence is relevant only on the condition that it is what it purports to be. Matters of logical probative value (as opposed to the satisfaction of technical admissibility requirements) are generally left to the jury. Usually, therefore, the judge need only make a prima facie finding of sufficiency to sustain a finding, and the ultimate question of genuineness is left for the jury. See **FRE 104(b)**; see generally *Foundation*. Of course, at trial it is still open to the document's opponent to convince the jury to reject it or give it little weight.

Exemplar

A typical or representative sample (example), against which another sample can be compared for identification.

The term is used most often with respect to the authentication of handwriting, but it applies as well to voiceprints, fingerprints, blood samples, and other substances and manifestations whose characteristics are sufficiently unique to permit authentication by comparison.

Example 7.6:   Penny wishes to prove that defendant Dylan wrote a letter libeling her. She has the letter, but Dylan denies writing it. During discovery, Penny has obtained a copy of another letter (the contents of which are unrelated to Penny's lawsuit) that Dylan concedes he wrote. Penny could ask an expert, or the jurors, to compare the letter with the other handwriting sample — an exemplar — to determine whether they were written by the same person.

Judge and jury. Of course, the value of this form of authentication depends on the assumption that the exemplar itself is genuine, and there is some disagreement as to how that preliminary matter is established. Most courts treat the exemplar like the writing in issue, screening it for sufficiency and leaving the ultimate decision on authenticity for the jury. Some, however, make the exemplar's genuineness a matter for the judge's final decision.

Ancient Documents Rule (Authentication)

A rule of prima facie authentication of documents that are of a certain age.

In addition to the requirement of age, usually 20 or (traditionally) 30 years old, ancient documents must have come from proper custody where one would expect to find them, under unsuspicious circumstances. Authentication is subject to later challenge at trial. See **FRE 901(b)(8)** (20 years).

The rationale is not only that age is some assurance of authenticity (if nothing else, it probably predated the present transaction or controversy), but that passage of time makes unlikely the availability of authenticating witnesses who remember the instrument or handwriting.

Note the similar rule, a modern extension of the doctrine, that creates a hearsay exception for ancient documents. While there is overlap, the requirements for both may not be the same, so each rule must be applied separately. See Chapter 5.

Reply Letter Doctrine

A circumstantial method of authenticating a letter by its appearing to respond to an earlier letter received by the person in question. See **FRE 901(b)(4)** (included in general rule — see Advisory Committee Notes).

Example 7.7:   Percy sues Dracena for breach of contract, alleging that in a letter dated June 1, Dracena wrote to Percy stating, "Please send me 12 of those deluxe widgets; perhaps they will indeed reduce my costs." Dracena denies writing the letter. Percy proves that on May 15 he sent Dracena a letter explaining how his new deluxe widgets would reduce Dracena's costs. The fact that the disputed letter followed Percy's by sufficient time to have permitted receipt and reply by Dracena, and that it appears from its contents to respond to Percy's, tends to prove that it was written by Dracena.

The second letter must, as in Example 7.7, refer to or otherwise show that it is responsive to the first. The first must be shown to have actually been sent (with reliance on the regularity of the mails to make receipt probable) or received (as by hand delivery to Dracena).

This doctrine is a form of authentication by content, specifically proof of special knowledge (see *Authentication (Writings)*). As in other such cases, if too many people who might have authored the document have the same knowledge, the content does not authenticate. Thus in Example 7.7 if the May 15 letter was an advertising circular sent to all 1,000 of Percy's customers, the reply could have come from any one of them.

A parallel doctrine has developed relating to reply telephone calls. See *Authentication (Voice)*.

Authentication (Voice)

The process of establishing that a statement was made by the person by whom it purports to have been made.

Recall that some states define writings to include recordings. Most authentication problems are common to both forms of communication. It is not surprising, therefore, that in most instances, authentication of a voice is accomplished by the same types of evidence, direct and circumstantial, as are used for authentication of a writing.

Example 7.8: As in Example 7.1, Indemnity Insurance Co. is trying to prove that a suicide message was authored by Harold, the insured, except that in this case the message was a statement on the telephone rather than a written note. Virtually identical methods of proof would be available as for the note, such as: testimony of the speaker; an "earwitness" who overheard Harold speaking; the opinion of someone familiar with Harold's voice (again requiring very little basis for the familiarity), see **FRE 901(b)(5)**; an evidentiary or judicial admission; expert comparison to a voiceprint, if available (see Chapter 4); jury comparison to a voice exemplar; and circumstantial evidence related to content.

There are even special rules that parallel the reply letter doctrine and rely on the regularity of the telephone service. Thus if Patty had placed a call to Harold at the number listed in the telephone directory, and if the person answering had identified himself as Harold directly or circumstantially, this would authenticate the voice as Harold's. See **FRE 901(b)(6).** And if Patty had left a message for Harold and then received a call back whose contents tied it to Patty's call (such as "This is Harold. You called?"), there would be a true analogy to a reply letter.

Self-Authentication (Writings)

The process of proving that a writing is what it purports to be by reference only to the writing itself, rather than extrinsic evidence. In other words, a self-authenticating writing is able to "pull itself up by its own bootstraps": it is what it says it is, because it says so.

Example 7.9: Pasquale wishes to prove title to realty through a deed he submits in evidence. The deed is acknowledged by a notary public. Both the deed itself and the notary's signature and seal are self-authenticating. Thus Pasquale will not have to call any witness or otherwise offer prima facie proof that the deed is genuine; it is presumed to be what it purports to be.

As in the case of other forms of authentication, self-authentication is only prima facie (sufficient to admit, but not conclusive), and an opponent can challenge the item's authenticity at trial.

At common law and under some modern codes, only such writings as public documents (under seal or certified under seal by an official), certified copies of official documents, acknowledged instruments (as in Example 7.9), and statutes qualify as self-authenticating. See **FRE 902(1),(2),(4),(5).** Foreign public documents are also generally included. See **FRE 902(3).**

Under FRE 902, however, many other official and unofficial writings have been made self-authenticating. They include such diverse items as official publications issued by public authority **(FRE 902(5))** and newspapers and periodicals **(FRE 902(6))**. What they have in common is the difficulty or inconvenience of requiring authentication (how do you prove a copy of the New York Times is not a forgery?) and the unlikelihood that such proof is necessary (what are the chances it is not the New York Times?).

The Uniform Rules have added still another type of document, a record of a regularly conducted activity as defined for hearsay purposes in URE 803(6), certified by its custodian. URE 902(11). It is based on a similar federal statute, 18 U.S.C. §3505, which, however, is limited to criminal cases and to foreign records.

Best Evidence Rule

A requirement that, when attempting to prove the contents of a writing, the original writing be produced rather than a copy or other secondary evidence, unless the original is unavailable or its production is otherwise excused. See **FRE 1001-08.** There are, of course, many qualifications to this basic statement.

Because it is addressed only to writings and not to evidence generally, and only to original writings, the rule is now frequently called the **Original Document** (or Original Writing) **Rule.** Nevertheless, the term Best Evidence Rule is still the more commonly encountered in cases, statutes, and general usage (see, e.g., CEC 1500).

The Federal Rules have greatly liberalized the Best Evidence Rule, permitting use of reliable copies (duplicates) under most circumstances.

The general workings of the Best Evidence Rule are illustrated by the following typical situation:

Example 7.10: Paula alleges Danielle breached a written contract to supply Paula with a certain number of new widgets. Danielle denies that there is or ever was any such contract. Paula therefore needs to establish the existence and terms of the alleged agreement. Because Paula is attempting to prove the contents of a writing, she must either produce the original or account for its unavailability before she will be permitted to use a copy or an oral description of the contract terms. Under the FRE, a duplicate copy may be admissible even if Paula possesses or cannot account for the original, unless Danielle raises a genuine issue as to the copy's authenticity.

Caveat: If taken literally, the name "Best Evidence Rule" is very misleading. *There is no rule requiring a party to produce the "best evidence" that is available.* Other than the Original Document Rule, the only sanction for failing to produce the best evidence is that one's case will be weaker and may, in consequence, fail.

Example 7.11:   Same facts as Example 7.10. Paula has available two witnesses who overheard Danielle admit to breaching the contract in dispute. Witness Wally is a disreputable rogue whose history of lying and cheating makes him a barely credible witness; witness Wilma is just the opposite: honest, respectable, and thoroughly credible. There is no rule that requires Paula to call Wilma rather than Wally, or to call either one, for that matter. The fact that Wilma's testimony is much "better evidence" than Wally's is a matter of tactics, not rules.

Application of Rule.   The Best Evidence Rule applies only under the following circumstances:

(1) *Writing or equivalent.* The evidence must be a **writing,** as that term is defined by the relevant court or statute.

Example 7.12:   Same facts as Example 7.10. Paula introduces a broken widget, which she contends Danielle supplied to her in breach of the contract to supply new, sound ones. If she wishes, Paula may introduce a photograph or oral description of the widget instead of the widget itself; it is not a writing, and the Best Evidence Rule does not apply to it.

Originally, "writing" meant just that: symbols on paper or the equivalent. Most statutes now expand the definition of writing to include also photography and electronic data compilations. See, e.g., CEC 250. Thus in Example 7.12, if Paula tried to use a photocopy of a photograph, and if the photograph were being relied upon to demonstrate the appearance of the widget in question (there being no one available with an independent recollection of it), the Rule would apply and Paula might have to produce the original photograph.

The Federal Rules have separate definitions for "writings and recordings" (**FRE 1001(1)**) and "photographs" (**FRE 1001(2)**). The Best Evidence Rule still applies to both.

Computer records may be separately addressed, because of their relatively recent advent and peculiar characteristics. See CEC 1500.5 (computer programs not subject to Best Evidence Rule). They are not treated separately by the Federal Rules. Writings and recordings include "magnetic impulse, mechanical or electronic recording, or other form of data compilation."

See also *Inscribed Chattels* (objects that may be treated as writings).

(2) *Contents in issue.* The Best Evidence Rule applies only if the **contents** or terms of a writing are sought to be proven. This limitation is explained by the rationale for the Rule, which is primarily the avoidance of fraud or mistake in relating the contents of a writing to the trier of fact. If the contents are not in question, a mistake in them is not crucial. Compare the following three examples, in which, depending on the issue or the manner of its proof, the contents of the same document is or is not being proven:

Example 7.13:   Wanda wishes to prove that she and Herman were married on June 1. Herman claims the date was July 1. Wanda offers only the testimony of Freda, a friend who attended the ceremony and can describe it. Herman contends that, because there is a marriage certificate (a writing) that officially recites the date of the ceremony, Wanda must produce the certificate, not just Freda's testimony. Because, however, it is the fact of marriage on June 1, and not the fact that the certificate says so, that is in issue, the contents of the certificate are not in issue and the Best Evidence Rule does not apply.

Example 7.14:   Same facts as Example 7.13, except Freda is unavailable and Wanda decides to use the marriage certificate to prove the date after all. Wanda must produce the original, because in this case she is attempting to prove the contents of the certificate (what it says), in order to establish a fact recited in it (the date of marriage).

Example 7.15:   Same facts as Example 7.13, except Herman challenges the marriage as invalid because there was never an official certificate issued. Wanda produces the marriage certificate. Again, Wanda must produce the original, because she is attempting to prove its contents. What it says is important to her case.

The use of photographs is another good illustration of when contents are in issue. It also demonstrates an important difference between the "pictorial testimony" and "silent witness" theories of photographic evidence. Compare the following:

Example 7.16:   *Pictorial Testimony.* Doug is accused of robbing the Security Bank. Witness Wilma testifies that she saw Doug commit the robbery, and she describes where she was standing at the time. She is shown a photocopy of a photograph of the bank interior, which she uses to illustrate her statement. Since the evidence is not the contents of the photo but Wilma's testimony, the Best Evidence Rule does not apply and the photocopy is acceptable.

Example 7.17:   *Silent Witness.* Same facts as Example 7.16, except the photograph was taken by a bank security camera; there were no eye-witnesses. Since the issue now is what the photo reveals ("says") about the bank, its contents are being proven and the Best Evidence Rule applies.

> Rule of Thumb: Remember the Rule's rationale, preventing fraud or mistake as to what a writing actually says. Then ask yourself whether it would be important to the party offering the writing into evidence if the contents of the writing were not as represented. If not, the contents are not in issue, and the Rule does not apply.

Applying the above Rule of Thumb, in Examples 7.13 and 7.16, the facts of marriage and of the robbery can be proven quite nicely without resort to the certificate or the photograph, although each would be useful to have. But in Examples 7.14 and 7.15 Wanda is in a position of having to prove what the certificate says; and in Example 7.17 the prosecution has no case unless the robber in the picture is accurately shown to be Doug.

Hearsay distinguished.   The Best Evidence Rule concerns the accuracy with which the contents of a writing are transmitted to the trier of fact; the Hearsay Rule concerns the truth of falsity of those contents. Thus although the hearsay rule may be involved, as when a writing is offered to prove the truth of its contents (see Example 7.14), it does not apply where although the contents are in issue, only the existence of those contents, not their truth, is to be proven (see Example 7.15).

Authentication distinguished.   Authentication establishes that a writing, whether an original or a copy, is what it purports to be. If it purports to be a handdrawn copy of a photocopy of an original certificate of marriage, it must be shown to be just that. (That is, it must be shown that the certificate was an original, that the first copy was in fact a photocopy of that original, and finally that the second, proffered copy is a handdrawn copy of the photocopy.) The Best Evidence Rule then determines whether such a remote copy is admissible in lieu of the original. Put another way, authentication determines whether it is an original or an actual copy; the Best Evidence Rule determines whether it has to be one or can be the other.

Absence of contents.   Generally the Best Evidence Rule does not apply to testimony that the contents of a writing do not contain a certain entry or statement. Thus, in the marriage illustration in Example 7.13, Herman could testify that the marriage records for June 1 do not contain an entry for Herman and Wanda without producing the original records.

(3) *Originals and copies.* If the Rule applies in its common law form, only an **original** is acceptable. "An," because there can be more than one. Of course, if there was one document executed and it is the one in issue, it is the only original. A **counterpart,** on the other hand, is a copy that is intended by the parties creating it to be treated as equal in effect to an original. Often two (or several) are created and signed at the same time and distributed to the parties. Counterparts are treated as originals at common law and under the Federal Rules (**FRE 1001(3)**).

Duplicate originals. In addition, the common law recognized so-called **duplicate originals,** copies made with the "same stroke of the pen" as the original. (An early example was the pantograph, a contraption with pivoting arms that caused a pen moved at one end to reproduce the movement at another.) Carbon copies are the typical modern example, and some courts admit all carbons (not just those intended to be counterparts) as readily as originals. Copies created by xerographic or other photographic processes, however, whether or not admissible in some other capacity, are not technically duplicate originals and at common law are not treated as the equivalent of originals.

What is a copy and what is an original is a matter of function, not form:

Example 7.18: Jim types a letter libelous of Susan and sends it to Bill, keeping a carbon copy in his file. Bill reads the letter and Susan sues Jim for libel. At trial, the letter sent is deemed the "original." But if Jim had mistakenly sent Bill the carbon copy and filed the original, it would be the carbon — that which was read by Bill — that would be the original for purposes of this lawsuit.

What is an original and what a copy is, then, a matter of relevance and of substantive law:

> Rule of Thumb: Ask yourself what, under the substantive law, the proponent is trying to prove with the writing. The answer should tell you which "copy" is the original.

Duplicates under the Federal Rules. Perhaps the most significant departure from the common law by the Federal Rules (and some other modern statutes) is the acceptance of what are termed "**duplicates**" as the equivalent of originals. Duplicates are admissible to prove the writing's contents regardless of whether the original is available, unless there is a genuine question as to the authenticity of the original or it would be unfair under the circumstances to admit the duplicate. **FRE 1003.** The common law had no such category as "duplicates" (only "duplicate originals," see above).

A duplicate, for this purpose, is a copy created by virtually any modern, reliable form of reproduction, chemical, photographic, or mechanical, and as a practical matter excluding only handdrawn copies or the like, where human error is still a significant possibility. See **FRE 1001(4).** In other words, the common photocopy is now admissible the same as an original under modern statutes, so long as there is no good reason shown that it should not be.

For photographs, the negative or a print from it is an original (**FRE 1001(3)**), but a print from a print, a photocopy of a print, or an enlargement would be a duplicate (**FRE 1001(4)**).

A written transcript of an audio recording is neither an original nor a duplicate, but merely secondary evidence of the (original) recording itself. An electronically produced copy of the recording, however, is a duplicate.

Computer printouts or "other output readable by sight," if "shown to reflect the data [stored in the computer] accurately," are considered to be originals. FRE 1001(3).

(4) *Excuses for nonproduction.* The original need not be produced and secondary evidence of it will suffice if its absence is excused. This may be because it is (1) lost or destroyed, (2) unobtainable by process or other legal means, or (3) withheld by the opposing party after notice and a request to produce it. Its absence is not excused, however, if its proponent lost or destroyed it in bad faith. See **FRE 1005(1)-(4).**

If the issue to which the writing is relevant is deemed a **collateral matter,** one "not closely related to a controlling issue" (**FRE 1004(4)**), the original need not be produced. Collateral status is discretionary with the court, and such factors as the complexity of the writing, the practicability of its production, and whether there is a serious dispute over its terms may control.

Example 7.19:   In a dispute over the effects of Manuel's mining operations on the surrounding land, ownership of Lee's land by Lee, not seriously disputed by Manuel, is collateral and need not be shown by production of deeds.

Example 7.20:   In the course of her testimony concerning the condition of a parcel of realty, a witness states that she read and followed a map to reach the place in question. The map is collateral and need not be produced.

Often the basis for permitting testimony about an inscribed chattel (see below) is that the writing on it is collateral and production would be impracticable (for example, the word "Taxi" on an automobile's door).

Public records. In order to avoid the need to remove public records from their place of official custody, generally they may be proved by either certified copies or copies authenticated by one who has compared them to the original. See **FRE 1005.** The Federal Rule permits any secondary evidence to be used if (but only if) the preferred copies are unavailable.

Admissions. Although traditionally any admission by an opposing party as to a writing's contents would excuse production of the original, modern statutes may exclude from this category oral, nontestimonial admissions ("I heard the defendant say that the document said . . . "), as being too unreliable. See **FRE 1007.**

Summaries. If a series of writings is too voluminous to be conveniently examined in court (whether or not they have been admitted into evidence), a summary usually may be presented, so long as the underlying materials are made available for examination or copying by other parties. See **FRE 1006.** Of course, the underlying data must be admissible in order for the summary to be admitted.

Note that summaries used only demonstratively, such as a chart used to illustrate a witness's testimony or to summarize the evidence, are not within the Rule at all.

(5) *Degrees of secondary evidence.* If the Best Evidence Rule applies but production of the original is excused, as for inadvertent loss of the original, then **secondary evidence** of the contents may be admitted. Secondary evidence is simply non-original evidence. As a practical matter, the reliability of types of secondary evidence varies infinitely, from the most reliable (a copy produced by a virtually infallible process, such as a carbon or photomechanical copy) to the least (the faded memory of a witness who once read the original).

Under the so-called **English rule,** degrees of secondary evidence are not recognized; once production of the original is excused, courts revert to the usual rule that one need not produce the best evidence available. An exception is public records, for which a certified or compared copy will usually be required, at least if available. Until recently, this was the minority rule in America.

According to what is still called the **American rule,** there are degrees of secondary evidence. If the "best" evidence (the original) is excused, then at least the "better" secondary evidence must be used or excused before anything else is allowed. Although the exact hierarchy varies, generally a copy is preferred to testimonial evidence, and certain types of copies may be preferred to others. See CEC 1505 (copies preferred to other secondary evidence). Different priorities may apply to public records.

Caveat. Terminology here is confusing. The English rule has become now also the majority rule in America, as the Federal and Uniform Rules do not generally recognize degrees of secondary evidence. See **FRE 1004** (*"other evidence* of the contents . . . is admissible"). Nevertheless, even under the Federal Rules some distinctions are made. Duplicates, which are treated as original and not secondary evidence, are limited to photomechanically produced copies and the like; and for public records, certified or compared copies are preferred to other secondary evidence.

Inscribed Chattel

An object (chattel) that has something written (inscribed) upon it, so that for purposes of the Best Evidence Rule it has the qualities of both a writing and an object.

Example 7.21:   Danny is on trial for robbery. A witness states that the robber wore a blue and white jacket with the word "Jets" on its pocket. Officer Oliver testifies that Danny was wearing such a jacket when arrested. The jacket is an inscribed chattel, having the qualities of a writing (letters on cloth) and a chattel (a jacket).

Note that, were it not for the identifying testimony about the "Jets" logo, the fact that the jacket probably has a manufacturer's label would not make it an "inscribed chattel" unless there was some attempt to use the label as evidence.

Traditionally courts have had wide discretion whether to treat inscribed chattels as objects or writings. The most common factors considered would be the complexity of the writing (how likely is a mistake?); the practicability of producing the object (a jacket is usually easier than a bus); and the importance of the evidence in the case (is this the jacket's only link to Danny? Is there other evidence of the robber's identity?).

FRE 1001 appears not to distinguish inscribed chattels from other writings, but courts probably will continue to apply the traditional test despite the lack of specific language. This is especially so because even if technically considered a writing, often an inscribed chattel's written aspect is collateral to the issues in the case and thus would be excused from application of the Best Evidence Rule on that basis.

Example 7.22:   A witness testifies that Daisy arrived at the scene in "a Greyhound bus." No such bus is produced. Unless there is a genuine dispute over what bus line Daisy used, and unless that issue is central to the case (perhaps theft of a Greyhound bus), the bus is collateral and need not be produced. And even if central, the impracticability of bringing the bus to court (as well as the simplicity of the writing) would probably excuse its production.

Rule of Completeness

A requirement that when a writing is introduced by one party, opposing parties may introduce, or require the offering party to introduce, other parts of the writing (or even other writings) that clarify or put into context the part already introduced. The rule most often is applied to writings and other tangibly recorded statements, but it can be applied in some cases also to out-of-court oral statements. See **FRE 106;** FRCP 32(a)(4)(depositions).

A well-known example of the problem this rule addresses was suggested by Dean Wigmore: It is misleading to quote only the last phrase of someone's statement, "The fool hath said in his heart, there is no God." Sometimes the effect of a quotation out of context is more subtle:

Example 7.23: Perry alleges his airplane, manufactured by Marvin, crashed because of a mechanical failure. Marvin calls Perry as an adverse witness and elicits an admission that just after the crash Perry wrote a letter in which he conceded that the airplane's pilot made a foolish maneuver just prior to the accident. If left at this point, the jury might conclude that Perry's original, prelitigation theory of the crash was pilot error, not the mechanical failure now alleged. The rest of the letter, however, clearly indicates that even at that time Perry believed that, despite the pilot's action, mechanical failure was the true cause of the crash. Perry will be permitted to introduce the other parts of the letter that clarify the first part's misimpression.

Courts disagree whether in a situation like Example 7.23 Perry could require Marvin to introduce the rest of the letter immediately, as part of Marvin's case, or must wait until his own case or cross-examination. The Federal Rule, recognizing that later correction might not be sufficient to dispel the original misimpression, permits the adverse party to require immediate introduction of any part or other writing "which ought in fairness to be considered contemporaneously with" the first part.

Since the only reason for introduction of the additional material is to clarify the original submission, when clearly necessary to avoid unfairness most courts will allow introduction even if it would otherwise violate some other rule of exclusion. Thus although Perry might not ordinarily be permitted to introduce his own out-of-court statement, especially one that expresses his biased opinion of the cause of the crash, the rule of completeness may permit him to do so for its limited purpose, another example of one party opening the door for admission of evidence by the other. (FRE 106 is silent on this point.)

Of course, if the additional material sought to be introduced is not connected to or necessary to avoid unfairness from the original part, this rule does not apply. A party is perfectly justified in introducing only a part of a writing or other statement, so long as it is not misleading or otherwise unfair. To permit or require introduction of the entirety could be both wasteful of time and unfair to the original proponent.

FRE 106 does not afffect another, common-law "rule of completeness": a party's right to cross-examine on the rest of a document or matter testified to on direct. See *Scope of Cross-Examination*.

8 | Testimonial Evidence

A. Presenting the Testimony
    Witness
        Percipient Witness
    Testimony
        Narrative Testimony
        Interrogated Testimony
    Competency (Witness)
        Voir Dire
        Impeachment (Jury Verdict)
        Quotient Verdict
    Dead Man's Statute
    Oath or Affirmation
    Sequestration of Witnesses
        Exclusion of Witnesses
    Order of Examination
        Direct Examination
        Examination in Chief
        Case in Chief
        Accrediting
        Redirect Examination
        Recross-Examination
    Leading Question
        Misleading Question
        Argumentative Question
    Refreshing Recollection
        Present Recollection Refreshed
        Jencks Act
B. Challenging the Testimony
    Impeachment
        Intrinsic
        Extrinsic
    Cross-Examination
    Scope of Cross-Examination
        Beyond the Scope
        American Rule
        English Rule
        Wide-Open Rule

147

Introduction and Overview of Chapter

Most evidence is presented through the testimony of witnesses, either live or using depositions. This is in contrast to writings, covered by Chapter 7, and real or demonstrative evidence, Chapter 6. Even nontestimonial evidence generally must be supported by the testimony of witnesses for authentication, explanation, or other purposes. Thus, testimonial evidence plays a central role in the entire trial process and in evidence law generally.

This chapter sets out the concepts underlying the two principal phases of testimonial evidence: the initial presentation of the witness's testimony (direct examination), and the attempt, if any, to discredit that testimony (cross-examination). There are also subsequent phases for such purposes as rebuttal or rehabilitation, but these basically replicate the primary two. It is important to keep these phases distinct, because although they may sometimes overlap, the rules of engagement are in many ways very different depending on whether one is presenting testimony or challenging it.

The subject of opinion evidence is often thought of as an aspect of testimony, especially expert testimony. Opinion, however, is a *type* of evidence, like character or scientific evidence, and it need not be (although it usually is) presented testimonially. Opinion evidence is covered separately in Chapter 9.

A. PRESENTING THE TESTIMONY

In the usual adversary trial setting, testimony is presented by one party, then challenged by the opposing party. Thus we can speak of "the plaintiff's witness" and "the defendant's witness." What is important, however, is not form but function, and the real question is whether the party "putting on" or questioning the witness is presenting or challenging the witness's testimony. Thus the rules and concepts set out in this first section can apply at any stage of the trial, and whether or not the party doing the questioning is also the party who called the witness.

Witness

One who observes; in the usual application to litigation, *one who gives oral testimony before the court.*

Because most witnesses are expected to testify from personal (or first-hand) knowledge, see Chapter 9 and **FRE 602,** these general and more specific definitions are compatible. A witness is one who, having obtained personal knowledge of a fact through the senses (whether sight, sound, touch, taste, or smell), testifies to that fact before a court or other legal tribunal.

Some witnesses testify to something other than their own perceptions, such as expert witnesses giving their opinions. Even witnesses reporting hearsay statements must have perceived the statement, if not the matter reported in it. The term **percipient witness** may be used to denote a witness to a perceived event, in effect an eyewitness.

Although one who makes an out-of-court statement later reported to the court is called a hearsay declarant, technically that person is also a witness (albeit once removed from the proceedings) and some of the rules governing *viva voce* (live) witnesses, including in most instances the requirement of personal knowledge, apply to the declarant. See, e.g., **FRE 806** (hearsay declarant may be impeached or supported as if a testifying witness).

Testimony

The words spoken by a witness in court or some other legal tribunal.

Testimony is one form of presenting evidence to a court; the other ways include introducing writings and presenting real or demonstrative evidence (objects, charts, and so forth). Thus when it is said that a witness is "giving evidence," what is really meant is that the witness is giving evidence in the form of testimony.

Testimony may be given outside of court, such as in a deposition, and then presented in writing (or possibly by audio or video recording) to the court.

Of course, a witness who cannot speak can testify by other means, such as sign language.

Types of testimony. There are two basic types of testimony. **Narrative testimony** permits a witness to tell his or her own story with little or no interruption from counsel. **Interrogated testimony,** which is more common, elicits the witness's story through a series of questions asked by an attorney (or occasionally by the judge).

Example 8.1:   Patty's attorney Alvin calls Wesley to the stand to testify as an eyewitness to the automobile accident being litigated. After some preliminary questions establishing that Wesley was on the scene and able to observe, Alvin can ask a question calling for a narrative response, such as: "Please now tell us in your own words what you saw." In the alternative, Alvin can use an interrogated approach, asking a series of specific questions designed to bring out all (and only) the facts favorable to Patty's case, for example: "Did you see anyone in the intersection? Who? Was he doing anything? What was he doing? What happened then? What was the color of the car? Did it change its speed?" And so forth.

It is said that narrative testimony is more accurate because it is more spontaneous and less colored by suggestion, but some question this assertion. Interrogated testimony is likely more complete, because the questions bring out details the witness may forget or simply decline to include in the narrative story. It also makes easier the insertion of exhibits, charts, and the like into the body of the witness's statement.

Narrative testimony, whatever its merits, presents certain problems to the court and opposition. A rambling, disjointed narrative wastes time and can confuse the issues. Moreover, because of the lack of questions to warn an opponent that inadmissible testimony is about to be given, a narrative makes it difficult or impossible to object in time to prevent that testimony.

Nevertheless, in most jurisdictions both types of testimony are permitted, and usually the judge has discretion whether or not to allow a narrative. Some courts do not permit narrative testimony if objected to, at least if it is not confined within narrow bounds or limited to uncontested preliminary matters.

If narrative testimony is being given, opposing counsel must be more alert for improper statements than when there are questions to warn counsel they are coming. If an objection cannot be made in time to avert the inadmissible statement, an immediate motion to strike is the appropriate remedy.

Competency (Witness)

The qualification of a witness to testify in a court of law or equivalent forum, under whatever rules govern the proceeding.

Competency of a witness to testify in court may be governed by different rules than competency for other purposes, such as witnessing a will. The chief attribute, however, is always the same: the ability to carry out the task of the witness. Thus, the most basic competency requirements for a witness giving evidence relate to the witness's ability to perceive a fact, to recall it at the time of trial, and to present it in an understandable manner to the trier of fact, including the ability to respond to questions on cross-examination. In addition, the witness must understand the duty to tell the truth and undertake to do so. A **voir dire** (preliminary examination) can be used to establish the competency of witnesses if challenged.

Common law incompetency.   At common law, there were many other requirements for witness competency, meaning there were more grounds for disqualification of a witness. Most of these, however, related to specific instances in which it was believed that certain classes of persons would not meet the above basic requirements of ability and truthfulness. For example, it was thought that a person lacking religious belief (particularly non-Christians) would not feel compelled to tell the truth under oath; a person interested in the outcome of the proceedings, or the spouse of such a person, would be motivated to lie; children under a certain age would not have the ability to perceive and relate their perceptions accurately; and so forth. In some jurisdictions these latter disqualifications still exist, but in most only the basic requirements themselves are still specifically enforced, without generalizing about classes of people.

Some jurisdictions still list at least minimal qualifications for witness competency, such as the ability to express oneself so as to be understood (see, e.g., CEC 701). Under the Federal Rules, however, with minor exceptions, everyone with personal knowledge to impart who is willing to take an oath is technically "competent" to testify, even the visibly intoxicated, the morally incapacitated, and the certified insane. **FRE 601.**

Nevertheless, even under the Federal Rules, every witness (except expert witnesses) must have personal knowledge (**FRE 602**) and all must swear or affirm they will tell the truth (**FRE 603**). Questions of competency such as mental or physical capacity are generally considered matters of weight for the jury to determine. In an extreme case, they may lead a court to exclude the testimony for lack of relevancy (**FRE 401, 402**), or at least lack of sufficient relevancy to outweigh the usual dangers of prejudice, misleading the jury, or wasting time (**FRE 403**).

Qualifications specific to an issue.   In addition to qualifications that are general to all testimony, there are those that are specific to the testimony to be given. Thus, an expert witness must have the requisite expertise, and every percipient witness must have personal knowledge. A witness authenticating business records must have a sufficient connection with the business and its processes. These may or may not technically be considered matters of "competency"; however, whatever they are called, their effect is still to render the witness qualified or unqualified to testify in these proceedings, on this subject.

Other uses of the term "competency." Evidence in general, and not just testimonial evidence, may be spoken of as being competent or incompetent. As explained in Chapter 1, for example, the distinction between technical foundational matters and those relating to the logical relevance of the evidence, found in FRE 104(a) and (b), is sometimes referred to as the distinction between competency and conditional relevancy; and indeed such foundational requirements for witnesses as the sufficiency of the oath are matters of competency under **FRE 104(a),** while sufficient personal knowledge is a matter of conditional relevancy under **FRE 104(b).** But often "incompetent" is used simply to mean that the evidence, like an incompetent witness, lacks some qualification or suffers some disqualifying feature and thus is inadmissible. (Recall the trilogy of "incompetent, irrelevant, and immaterial.") In such a case "inadmissible" is a more accurate and descriptive term, and it illustrates why a general objection that evidence is incompetent is both uninformative and futile: It is merely an objection that the evidence should not be admitted because it is inadmissible.

Distinguished from privilege. Incompetency disqualifies witnesses whether they want (or a party wants them) to testify or not. Privilege, on the other hand, allows the witness to decline to testify, or sometimes gives someone else a right to prevent the witness from testifying. (See Chapter 10.) Thus a privileged witness can testify if the privilege holder wishes it; at least in theory, an incompetent witness cannot testify, no matter who wishes it. (As will be seen, some forms of incompetency could be waived.)

The early forms of incompetency often included an aspect of privilege as well, in that a class of witnesses (such as parties to the action) was disqualified both to testify if they wanted to (in their own behalf) and to be called to testify against their will (as by their opponent). This latter "privilege" aspect of incompetency has virtually disappeared.

State cases in federal courts. As indicated, many states still retain aspects of competency requirements that have been abolished, at least nominally, by the Federal Rules. When, however, an issue in a case in federal court is based upon state law (generally in diversity cases), FRE 601 defers to the state's rules of competency.

Judges and jurors. Traditionally, judges were competent to testify in a trial over which they presided. While this remains the law in some jurisdictions, the modern view is that judges cannot properly both testify and preside. **FRE 605** disqualifies the presiding judge absolutely, without even the need for formal objection. Some rules take a middle ground, such as making the judge competent unless objection is made to the testimony. See CEC 703.

Jurors are generally treated the same regarding testimony in a case in which they are sitting. **FRE 606(a)** bars juror testimony; the objection is not automatic, but it can be made out of the jury's presence. Again, some rules specifically permit juror testimony if no objection is made. See CEC 704.

Impeachment of jury verdicts. An attack on a jury's verdict based on some irregularity in the process of deliberation is called **impeachment** of the verdict. With certain exceptions, jurors generally are not permitted to testify to anything that affected the verdict, such as what was said or done during deliberations, what influenced the outcome, or what the juror's thought processes might have been. See **FRE 606(b).** Some rules (not including the FRE) distinguish between testimony that impeaches (attacks) the verdict's validity and that which supports it, the latter being permitted. In any event, exception is typically made for, in the Federal Rule's language, "extraneous prejudicial information" or improper "outside influences."

Example 8.2: Dolly is tried for robbery and is convicted. After the trial, Janet, who was one of the jurors, tells Dolly's attorney that: (1) juror Warren was intoxicated during most of the deliberations; (2) juror Xena flipped a coin to decide; (3) juror Yves went out during dinner and checked out the scene of the crime for himself; and (4) during deliberations the prosecutor came by and spoke to juror Zoe. At least under current federal law, Janet could not testify to (1) or (2), but she could testify to (3) (extraneous prejudicial information) and (4) (outside influence). She could not, however, testify to the effect of even these latter two matters on her mental processes in reaching her verdict.

Note that this rule is one merely of competency of jurors as witnesses (or, under FRE 606(b), as the maker of any statement). It does not affect any other form of relevant evidence regarding the jury's verdict. Thus, if a bailiff or a member of the public had seen juror Warren drinking alcohol during deliberations, they would be competent to testify to that fact. Also, the rule does not affect what would or would not be a proper or valid verdict, but only what evidence of it is admissible. For example, a **quotient verdict,** in which jurors add together their estimates of damages and divide by their number to reach a compromise amount none may believe to be the actual damages, is generally improper, even though a juror could not testify to its having occurred.

Attorneys. Attorneys usually are competent witnesses in proceedings in which they represent a party. The rules of professional conduct, however, generally prohibit such testimony except in very limited circumstances (such as substantial hardship to the client). Courts have discretion to exclude attorney testimony that violates ethical standards, and some courts may require the attorney to withdraw from the case before testifying.

Children. Children generally are competent to testify if they have sufficient intelligence and ability to express themselves and understand the duty to tell the truth. Often so-called "children of tender years" are presumed competent at a certain age (such as 10) or may be presumed incompetent under a certain age (such as 7). It is common for a voir dire to be used to determine actual competency. See, for federal courts, 18 U.S.C.A. §3509(c) (procedures for voir dire of child witness).

In cases of child abuse and sexual molestation, special legislation in many jurisdictions permits various special forms of testimony by children (by remote camera and the like), with provisions for protecting the child from undue emotional trauma. In some, child victims under a certain age (usually 10) are deemed or presumed competent. (For new federal rules concerning similar fact evidence in child molestation cases, see *Propensity Evidence,* Chapter 3.)

Dead Man's Statute

A rule of competency that disqualifies a party from testifying to transactions or conversations with (in effect) an opposing party who is now deceased. (In effect because, of course, the actual opposing party would be the deceased person's estate or other representative.) Spelling here is somewhat arbitrary; you will also see "deadman's," "deadman," and "dead man" statute or act.

These statutes are a survival of the old incompetency of parties. Their theory is that if the lips of one party to a transaction have been sealed by death, it is only fair that the other party's be sealed by law. (That this may be unfair to the surviving party is not taken into consideration.)

A majority of states have abolished dead man's statutes, but several remain. **FRE 601** applies them if the state substantive law is involved (as in a diversity case). Actual provisions vary greatly, but typically they affect only a party whose opponent is the estate of a decedent, and they preclude only testimony as to transactions or conversations with the decedent. If "transaction" is construed broadly, however, it may include even automobile accidents in which the decedent was killed and the survivor sues for damages.

Again, this is merely a rule of competency of the party. A third person with knowledge of the transaction or conversation can testify to it; and

154

usually the protected estate can waive the prohibition, as by calling the opponent to testify.

Some states have abrogated the dead man's statute but admit the hearsay statements of the decedent to counter the opponent's testimony and "even the balance" between the parties.

Oath or Affirmation

An undertaking to tell the truth, either invoking a deity ("swearing to God") or solemnly declaring an intention to be truthful.

At common law an oath, and a belief in (the accepted understanding of) God, was required to make a witness competent to testify. Modern law usually retains the oath but offers the alternative of a non-religious affirmation. See **FRE 603.**

The form of the oath or affirmation varies among courts, and there usually is no mandatory language. The primary requirement is that the witness somehow indicate an understanding of the duty to tell the truth and undertake to carry it out. A statement that omits the latter commitment would seem to be inadequate but sometimes is accepted.

An oath is generally considered one of the three major assurances that the witness will tell the truth, the others being observation of the witness's demeanor and cross-examination. See Chapter 5.

Sequestration of Witnesses

Exclusion of witnesses from the courtroom so they cannot hear the testimony of witnesses who testify before them. It is also commonly called simply **exclusion of witnesses** or the rule on witnesses.

Traditionally sequestration was discretionary with the court, and it still is in many states. **FRE 615,** however, makes exclusion mandatory if requested by a party.

Rationale. The rationale for sequestration is generally and most tellingly demonstrated by the apocryphal Story of Susannah. In brief, Susannah was accused by two "eyewitness" elders of sexual misconduct with a man, which allegedly took place beneath a tree. Daniel exposed the elders' falsity by asking each of them separately, out of the hearing of the other, under what type of tree it was Susannah and her lover had lain. When they gave different answers, Daniel knew they were lying and they were punished instead of Susannah. The beauty of the procedure, as Wigmore pointed out, is in its simplicity.

Who cannot be excluded. Certain classes of witness cannot be excluded. They generally include the parties themselves if natural persons, designated representatives of nonnatural (such as corporate) parties, and others whose presence in the courtroom is deemed essential to a party's case. Statutes may expressly include others, such as the complaining witness in a criminal case.

Order of Examination

The order in which the parties' witnesses are examined in a typical case.

Whatever the stage of the trial, and whichever party is putting on its case (see Chapter 1), the pattern for calling and examining that party's witnesses is the same. The party presenting (calling) the witness — plaintiff, prosecution, or defendant — begins with **direct examination,** endeavoring to bring out whatever story counsel wishes the witness to tell. This process is also known as **examination in chief** (sometimes hyphenated: examination-in-chief), or as the party's **case in chief** (or defense case in chief). It begins with an introduction of the witness and the bringing out of background information, a phase called **accrediting,** and it proceeds to the substance of the testimony. The opposing party (or parties, if there is more than one) then may, but need not, begin cross-examination. Cross-examination is intended to test the truthfulness, accuracy, and completeness of the direct testimony, and under some conditions to bring out new facts that the cross-examiner wishes the jury to hear. See generally *Cross-examination.*

Although this usually ends the questioning, the calling party may engage in **redirect examination,** the opposing party in **recross-examination** (sometimes just called recross), and so forth until all questions have been asked and the witness is, literally and figuratively, exhausted. The subject matter of each phase, especially the later ones, is limited by separate rules and gets narrower with each successive phase. See *Scope of Cross-examination.*

The trial court has broad discretion to control both the order in which the parties' cases are presented and the examination of witnesses within those phases. **FRE 611(a).** The court will adjust the rules as necessary to avoid confusion, delay, or undue harassment or embarrassment of witnesses.

For a more complete description of the trial process see *Adversary System,* Chapter 1.

Leading Questions

Questions of a witness that suggest or supply the answer desired by the questioner. See **FRE 611(c).**

Leading questions are permitted only in certain circumstances, discussed below. Whether a question is leading may depend not just on its form, but on the amount of detail that it contains: if too detailed, it may result in the witness merely assenting to what is really the interrogator's testimony.

Example 8.3:   Pete's attorney asks a witness, (1) "Where were you at noon on June 12?" (2) "Tell us whether or not you saw the plaintiff Pete there." (3) "State whether or not you saw D make a threatening gesture toward Pete, who was walking south and just minding his own business." (4) "Isn't it true that you saw D strike Pete without provocation?" Question (1) is not leading, as it in no way suggests the answer desired. Question (2) is somewhat suggestive that counsel thinks Pete was there, but it probably would be permitted. Question (3) gives the witness a choice of "whether or not," but it supplies so much detail that it both suggests the answer desired and supplies the substance of that answer. Question (4) is a classic leading question.

When leading permitted.   The problem of leading the witness generally exists only on direct examination. On cross-examination, leading usually is permitted because even if an answer is suggested, an adverse witness is hardly likely to accept it if it is untrue.

Even on direct, however, leading questions are permitted in certain instances, primarily for uncontroverted preliminary matters ("You are John Jones, of 486 Crenshaw Drive, Sunnybrook?") and for witnesses who cannot properly express themselves without some prompting (such as a child or a mentally disabled person). This is referred to in FRE 611(c) as the necessity of "developing" the witness's testimony.

Remember that it is the nature of the witness and not when or by whom the witness is called that determines whether leading is permitted. Thus on direct it is permissible to lead a hostile witness or one identified with the opposing party, and on cross one may not be permitted to lead a friendly witness, that is, one who is too friendly to the examining party.

Leading can be subtle as well as overt, and counsel has to be alert to the possibilities of the nuances of both oral and body language. Examples of subtle suggestion are the difference between "How *long* was the wait" and "How *short* was the wait," or between "Did you see *a* car parked there" and "Did you see *the* car parked there."

To be distinguished are so-called **misleading questions,** the cross-examination equivalent of leading, in which the interrogator's question assumes facts that are still in controversy. The classic example, of course, is "Have you stopped beating your wife?" Also to be distinguished are **argumentative questions.** Encountered mainly on cross-examination, these argue to the jury, often drawing the interrogator's own conclusions from the evidence. Typical examples would be, "Isn't it a fact that because of the train schedule and flat tire, the defendant could not have arrived there in time?" or "Do you honestly expect us to believe that the officer was mistaken about the gun?" Like leading questions on direct, misleading and argumentative questions are improper and an appropriate subject of objection.

Finally, some attorneys use what has informally been called reverse leading, in which the interrogator on direct suggests the answer that is not desired, in order to make more credible the witness's strong disagreement: Q: "Then you're suggesting that the police officer fired the shot?" A: "No, that's not what I'm suggesting at all! How could he, given where he was standing?"

Refreshing Recollection

The process of helping a witness to remember facts, in order that the witness may testify from present knowledge and recollection.

Example 8.4: Wanda is testifying for Perry to her recollection of witnessing an automobile accident between Perry's car and a car allegedly driven by the defendant. She is asked on direct examination whether she recalls the license number of the car that struck Perry. She replies that she is not certain, but she might recall the number if she could consult some notes she made later that day. If the requirements discussed below are met, Wanda will be permitted to use her notes to refresh her recollection, so she can then testify to the license plate number from present memory, that is, from first-hand knowledge.

The process described in Example 8.4 is generally known as **present recollection refreshed.** It assumes that Wanda is using her notes not as the basis for her testimony as to the license number, but only as a means of jogging her memory so that it — her present recollection — can serve as the basis for her testimony.

"Past recollection recorded" distinguished. Present recollection refreshed is similar in appearance and name to, but very different in effect from, past recollection recorded (sometimes also called, confusingly, "refreshing recollection"), a hearsay exception discussed in Chapter 5. Past recollection recorded assumes that the witness has little or no present recollection of the matter in question, and that the writing consulted does not bring that recollection back. The writing itself then becomes the evidence.

Example 8.5: Same facts as Example 8.4, except even after consulting her notes Wanda still has no recollection of the license number. She can, however, testify to how and when she made her notes and her belief that they are correct. If she satisfies the requirements for past recollection recorded (particularly as to having made or adopted the writing when the events were fresh in her memory — see **FRE 803(5)** and Chapter 5), her notes will be admissible as evidence of the license number.

In other words, in past recollection recorded, the notes are the evidence; in present recollection refreshed, the testimony is the evidence. See generally *Past Recollection Recorded*.

Application of Best Evidence Rule. Because writings used to refresh recollection are not the evidence itself, they are not subject to the Best Evidence Rule's requirement that the original document be produced if available. See *Best Evidence Rule*. A writing admitted under the doctrine of past recollection recorded, however, for the truth of the matter asserted, *is* the evidence and is subject to the Rule. The distinction is similar to that, explained in Examples 7.16-7.17 in Chapter 7, between the use of a photograph for pictorial or silent witness purposes.

What may be used to refresh. While past recollection recorded allows introduction only of a writing that records a witness's past knowledge or recollection, present recollection refreshed permits use of virtually anything that helps the witness to remember. This is because, as we all have experienced, memory of an incident can be brought back by virtually anything: a word, a sound, a scent, a picture.

Example 8.6: Same facts as Example 8.4, except instead of notes, Wanda wishes to dab some Chanel No. 5 perfume on her wrist, because "every time I smell Chanel No. 5, which I had just purchased and applied the day I saw the accident, it all comes rushing back in my mind." Wanda should be permitted to use the perfume aroma to refresh her recollection.

While ordinarily a witness like Wanda would be shown a writing to refresh her recollection, and perfume scent would be somewhat unusual, it makes the point that what the object or device might be is unimportant, so long as it has the effect of refreshing Wanda's present recollection. For example, counsel might sometimes use a suggestive question to try to jog a witness's memory on direct examination, and courts generally have discretion to permit this departure from the usual prohibition on leading. See **FRE 611(c)** ("necessary to develop the witness's testimony"). The use of hypnotism to refresh recollection, still generally prohibited, is discussed in Chapter 4.

While theoretically, then, anything may be used for refreshing recollection, it obviously would be improper for Wanda to refer to a note from her attorney saying, "Tell them the number was ABC 322." But the court's discretion to reject testimony that is not truly from present memory, and the right of opposing counsel to see the writing (or presumably to smell the perfume), discussed below, generally prevents such a subterfuge.

Production for opponent.   If recollection is refreshed, the rules usually permit opposing parties to request that any writing so used be produced for inspection and use in cross-examining the witness (for example, to highlight discrepancies between the writing and the testimony supposedly refreshed by it), and even to introduce pertinent parts into evidence. (The party whose witness consulted the writing may not, however, introduce it into evidence unless it is otherwise admissible.) This is an important safeguard against abuse of the procedure by a witness or attorney and generally creates no difficulty, at least if the writing is used during trial.

Refreshing before trial.   As a matter of trial tactics, the preferred and sensible time to refresh a witness's recollection, with previous statements or memoranda or otherwise, is before trial, not in front of the jury. Many modern rules, including **FRE 612,** now require production of writings used by a witness to refresh recollection before or after trial. This can cause some problems if the writings used are privileged, no longer available, or the like, or if the opposing party attempts to use this as an excuse for a wide-ranging perusal of opposing counsel's files.

To avoid such problems, rules that require production of materials used before trial give courts discretion to waive the requirement where production is not practicable or fair. See, e.g., **FRE 612** (production required only if "necessary in the interests of justice"); CEC 771 (production required unless not in possession or control or reasonably procurable). These rules also limit production to materials specifically used by the witness for the purpose of testifying.

Although the FRE and many state rules refer only to production of writings used to refresh recollection, non-writings (like the perfume in Example 8.6) probably would be treated similarly. URE 612 and some state rules specifically include both writings and objects.

Requirements for use.   Other than the requirement of production, most courts impose few limitations on the process of refreshing recollection. Some, perhaps confusing the process with past recollection recorded (see above), limit refreshment to a writing made or adopted when the facts referred to were fresh in the witness's memory. Whether or not specified by rule, the witness's memory should appear to be exhausted before refreshment is permitted, and the court should try to assure itself that subsequent testimony is actually from a refreshed memory and not from the materials consulted.

Notes used to refresh memory should be read silently by the witness; as they are not themselves admissible evidence, neither the witness nor the examining attorney may read them aloud to the jury. Some courts will permit the witness to consult the notes while testifying, while others require that once the notes have been consulted, the witness then testify without their aid, lest the notes be read into evidence in the guise of refreshed present memory. Courts have inherent discretion to forbid refreshing or reject the testimony to avoid this or any other abuse of the procedure.

Privileged documents. It is generally agreed that use of a document to refresh recollection on the stand waives any privilege to prevent its disclosure to the party's opponent. The same is true of the attorney's work product protection. See generally Chapter 10. With respect to documents used before trial only, however, at common law they would retain any privileged status, and most likely the same is true under the Federal Rules (although there are some contrary decisions). As a practical matter, it would considerably diminish the effectiveness of work product protection and attorney-client or other privileges if they were waived by a witness's use of a document to prepare for trial.

Sanctions. FRE 612 leaves to the judge's discretion what sanction to impose on a party not complying with an order to produce a writing used to refresh recollection, except that in criminal cases a refusal by the prosecution must result in striking the relevant testimony or declaring a mistrial. Other rules, such as CEC 771, make striking the pertinent testimony mandatory in all cases of unexcused noncompliance.

Criminal cases. There may be different rules applied to criminal cases, such as the mentioned difference in sanctions under FRE 612. A major difference is in a party's ability to demand production of materials used to refresh the recollection of opposing witnesses. In federal trials this was previously governed by the **Jencks Act**[1], to which FRE 612 specifically gives priority. Because the Jencks Act was superseded by the similar but not identical Federal Rules of Criminal Procedure 17(h) and 26.2, without any corresponding change in FRE 612 (which still refers to the Jencks Act), it is unclear just what version of the federal restrictions now applies. The Act/Rule denies access to all but a narrow class of statements of opposing witnesses, and even those available (at least those used before trial) need not be produced until after the witness has testified on direct examination. Many aspects of the intersection of the Act, the Criminal Rules, and the FRE, such as the status of statements that are not within the narrow defini-

---

1. 18 U.S.C. §3500.

tion of the Act, are not yet clear and are beyond the scope of this discussion.[2]

States vary in their treatment of refreshing recollection in criminal cases, but many draw distinctions similar to those in the federal law.

B.   CHALLENGING THE TESTIMONY

Direct testimony generally presents the jury with only one side of the story, unless of course the interrogator "shoots himself in the foot," inadvertently helping the opponent's case. It also presents only one side of the witness's testimony. Once a witness has testified, the opposing party has an opportunity to cross-examine and also to present other evidence, all in an attempt either to discredit the witness, to lessen the negative impact of the witness's story, or to elicit positive testimony in aid of the cross-examiner's own case. A witness thus may be challenged both by a direct attack and by the more indirect means of contradicting or adding to the witness's story with an opposing party's own version.

Impeachment

An attempt to discredit a witness's testimony.

Impeachment need not utterly destroy the testimony, but it may be aimed merely at lessening the weight to be given it by the jury.

This may be done by **intrinsic** means, from the witness's own mouth, or by **extrinsic** means, from external sources such as other witnesses. It may be an attack on the witness personally (showing bias due to such factors as familial relationship or racial prejudice, pecuniary or other interest in the case, hostility toward the opposing party, a mental or physical incapacity, or an unsavory character); or the attack may be merely on the witness's testimony (presenting a prior inconsistent statement by the same witness or a contradictory version of the facts through another witness). It may impugn the witness's credibility regarding this specific testimony (bias, interest) or in general (untruthful character). Most courts do not permit impeachment on the basis of religious beliefs. See **FRE 610.**

Whether impeachment is extrinsic or intrinsic may be of importance. A court will, for example, permit contradiction of collateral facts (those not related to a substantive issue in the case) intrinsically on cross-examination, but not extrinsically by calling other witnesses. And the vouching rule may prohibit attacking one's own witness on cross-examination but permit the witness's story to be contradicted extrinsically by another witness.

---

2. See generally, e.g., Meuller & Kirkpatrick, Evidence §6.26.

Cross-Examination

Interrogation of a witness, intended to challenge the truthfulness, accuracy, or completeness of testimony the witness has already given on direct examination. It is sometimes called "cross-questioning" or merely "cross."

Cross-examination is not limited to breaking down the witness or demonstrating that the direct testimony was false or mistaken. Filling in an incomplete or one-sided (and therefore misleading) story is a lesser but still important use of cross-examination, especially necessary when interrogated direct testimony has brought out only selected, favorable facts. An example, based on a similar scene recounted by Wigmore, illustrates the distinction:

Example 8.7: David is on trial for stealing Vickie's red leather purse. David's attorney has called eyewitness Ward and asked him, inter alia, "Did you see David take Vickie's red purse?", to which Ward answered "No." The prosecutor cross-examines and asks, "You have told us your did not see David take a red purse. Just what *did* you see?", to which Ward responds, "I wasn't there in time to see him take it your honor, but I did get there in time to see him throw it away." Case closed.

Even if intending to conceal nothing, the witness may have further information valuable to the cross-examiner's case. Thus, in Example 8.7, even if he didn't see David dispose of the purse, as an eyewitness Ward can be asked whether he saw David in the vicinity, who else was about, and so forth. A witness who has placed the defendant at the scene can be asked to affirm on cross-examination that the defendant was doing nothing suspicious, carried no bulky objects, and was only one of several persons then in the vicinity.

Wigmore called cross-examination the "greatest legal engine ever invented for the discovery of truth." Certainly it is an essential counterfoil to the necessarily one-sided testimony of the witness on direct. For this reason the right to cross-examine is generally absolute, and in criminal cases it is constitutionally guaranteed to the defendant.

Scope of Cross-Examination

The subject matter respecting which a party may cross-examine a witness. Cross-examination as to any other subject matter is said to be **beyond the scope** of cross.

Example 8.8: Philip sues Douglas and Douglas's employer Ernestine for negligence following an automobile accident. Philip calls Winston, who testifies that he saw Douglas's car run a red light and strike

Philip's. On cross-examination, Douglas asks Winston whether a week later Philip had admitted to Winston that he was intoxicated at the time of the accident. Whether Douglas's question is permitted will depend on the rule as to scope of cross-examination applied in the jurisdiction, as discussed below.

Note that the rules governing the scope of cross do not generally dictate whether a particular question may be asked of a witness, but only when, that is, as part of whose case. Thus unless some rule such as privilege prevents Douglas from calling Winston during his own later case in chief, if Douglas is prevented from asking his question now, he can and probably will call Winston later and ask about Philip's statement.

Two primary rules. There are two competing rules governing the scope of cross-examination: the **American rule** (also called the Federal rule) and the **English rule.** The American, or restrictive rule, limits the scope of cross-examination to matters covered in the witness's direct examination: thus the limitation is to the scope of direct. The English (and traditional American rule prior to the mid-nineteenth century), also called the **wide-open rule,** does not limit the scope of cross-examination at all, except for the usual requirements such as relevancy. Thus in Example 8.8, Douglas's question on cross-examination about Philip's admission of intoxication would clearly be beyond the scope of direct in a restrictive American-rule jurisdiction and clearly be within the scope in a wide-open jurisdiction. Winston testified only to his eyewitness account of the accident, whereas Douglas is asking about a later incident that might help to establish an affirmative defense of contributory negligence.

The American rule, at its most strict, limits cross-examination to the very same facts, or same subject matter, as testified to on direct.

Example 8.9: Same facts as Example 8.8. Douglas may ask Winston about what he saw, heard, or otherwise perceived at the time of the accident. He may not, however, ask him (assuming he has the information) about such matters as Douglas's employment relationship with Ernestine or Philip's later statements to him, although they are relevant to the case and can be asked of Winston on direct if Douglas calls Winston during Douglas's case in chief.

Compromise rules: between the extremes. A majority of American jurisdictions follows some form of the American rule. In addition to the two extremes just mentioned, however, some jurisdictions have adopted slightly to somewhat more liberal versions of the American rule. They may, for example, permit questions that are connected with the subject matter of direct, or those that tend to rebut an inference or presumption created by the witness's testimony. Cross-examination may be permitted if it explains or contradicts what the witness said on direct. Further, if the testimony has established a prima facie case for one party, the other may be permitted to rebut that case on cross-examination, even if the rebuttal facts were not mentioned on direct.

Example 8.10:   Same facts as Example 8.8. Douglas testifies for the defense and mentions that he was on his way home at the time of the accident. This creates an inference that he was not acting within the scope of his employment by Ernestine. In any but the most restrictive jurisdictions, it should be permissible to ask Douglas on cross-examination whether he had earlier dropped off a package for Ernestine, if under the substantive law this would put Douglas back into the scope of his employment at the time of the accident.

By one older rule, questions are permitted on any matter except the affirmative case of the cross-examining party. This would still exclude the question in Example 8.8.

Whatever the rule followed, if a witness testifies to a part of a transaction or event, it is always permissible to elicit (if relevant) the rest of the story on cross-examination.

FRE 611(b) adopts the restrictive American rule, limiting cross to "the subject matter of the direct examination" and witness credibility, although it expressly gives the judge discretion to permit questions on "additional matters as if on direct." While this could be read as giving the judge great latitude to permit wide-open cross-examination, this is not how it was intended or has generally been interpreted. As at common law, the judge has some discretion, in the interests of fairness or efficiency, to permit an interrogator to go beyond the scope. Also as at common law, however, questions that are beyond the scope of direct are treated as direct examination themselves, with the usual restrictions on leading questions and, where still applicable, on impeaching the witness.

Restrictiveness depends on interpretation.   One must keep in mind that all of these rules are only as restrictive as the court's interpretation and application of their standards. The same rule may be applied very differently in two jurisdictions that purport to follow it. For example, if the rule is that only the same facts and circumstances are within the proper scope of cross-examination, the term "circumstances" can be interpreted narrowly as the very same thing testified to (the collision in Example 8.8) or broadly as the general transaction to which the testimony related (the collision plus its immediate origins and aftermath). Similarly, under FRE 611(b) there is a lot of play in the phrase "subject matter of the direct examination."

Impeachment always permitted.   One thing that is always within the scope of cross-examination, whatever rule is followed, is impeachment. Questions that address the witness's credibility (bias, interest, capacity, and so forth) may be asked on cross-examination whether or not they were mentioned on direct. Since impeaching facts would seldom intentionally be brought out by the party calling the witness, without this exception to the rule there could be little or no cross-examination for impeachment. As indicated, FRE 611(b) makes this exception explicit.

Testimony on preliminary matters.   An accused may wish to testify on a preliminary matter such as the admissibility of an item of evidence but retain the right not to testify to substantive issues. Under **FRE 104(d),** an accused who does testify to a preliminary matter may not be cross-examined as to any other issue in the case, unless the direct testimony itself raises such an issue.

Vouching Rule

A prohibition against impeaching one's own witness.

Example 8.11:   Portia sues Darren for battery. Portia calls witness Wiley and asks him who started the fight, expecting Wiley to say "Darren." Wiley, however, says "It was Portia who struck Darren first." Under the vouching rule Portia cannot use the usual methods of impeachment (showing bias, mental defect, a prior inconsistent statement, and so forth, with the exception of contradiction — see below) to attack the credibility of Wiley, her own witness.

Rationale.   In theory, parties should not call witnesses whom they do not expect to tell the truth. It is also theoretically possible to coerce a witness to behave by the threat of impeachment that publicly impugns the witness's character. Thus the rule arose that parties are held to "vouch" for the truthfulness of any witnesses they call, and in any event cannot impeach such witnesses' testimony.

Reality.   Theory, however, is not always consistent with reality. Mainly because its premises are faulty, the vouching rule has disappeared in many jurisdictions and under the Federal Rules (**FRE 607**). Litigants often have little or no control over whom they must call as witnesses and may even have to call the opposing party. The idea of vouching for an opponent's veracity, or even that of neutral witnesses, or of coercing an opposing party/witness into favorable testimony, is somewhat implausible.

Surprise and damage.   Where it still exists, the vouching rule usually is qualified to permit impeachment if the calling party is genuinely surprised

166

by the witness's testimony (had no reason to expect it) and, in some jurisdictions, if the party also is damaged by it. (In some courts this applies only to the use of prior inconsistent statements to impeach, and not to evidence impugning the witness's character or motives.) Thus in Example 8.11, if Portia reasonably expected Wiley's answer to be "Darren" but got "Portia," a clearly damaging answer, Portia would be allowed to impeach Wiley, especially by any prior inconsistent statements he may have made. If, however, Wiley had answered "I don't recall," a court requiring both surprise and damage would disallow the impeachment, since Portia's case was not helped but also was not affirmatively damaged by Wiley's testimony.

Contradiction distinguished. The rule against impeaching one's own witness does not apply to impeachment by contradiction.

Example 8.12: Same facts as Example 8.11 (Wiley's testimony that Portia struck Darren first). Even if Portia is not permitted to impeach Wiley by showing bias, proving a prior inconsistent statement, or the like, she is nevertheless free to call other witnesses to testify that it was Darren who struck the first blow, contrary to Wiley's testimony. See *Contradiction.*

No "mere subterfuge." In many jurisdictions, prior inconsistent statements are admissible to impeach a witness but not to prove the truth of the matter stated (that is, not as a hearsay exception). See Chapter 5. In a jurisdiction that has rejected or modified the vouching rule, it is possible for a party to call a witness only as an excuse to get in an impeaching prior inconsistent statement, hoping that the jury will misuse it and give it substantive effect. Because of this, it is generally held that in a criminal case, the prosecution may not impeach its own witness with a prior inconsistent statement if calling the witness was a mere subterfuge, that is, if such impeachment was the primary purpose for calling the witness.

Contradiction

Evidence that tends to refute other evidence previously given, generally prior witness testimony. It is sometimes called **specific contradiction,** especially when it directly refutes a very specific point in the witness's testimony.

Example 8.13: Woody testifies for the plaintiff that Dahlia's car ran the red light. On cross-examination Dahlia is unable to change Woody's story. Dahlia then calls witness Monica, who states that the light was still green when Dahlia drove through it. Monica's testimony contradicts that of Woody. Dahlia has raised doubts about Woody's testimony not by proving it necessarily mistaken, but by proving that either it or Monica's testimony, or perhaps both, must be mistaken.

167

If contradiction is by introduction of the witness's own prior inconsistent statement, it is called **self-contradiction.** The rarer case of eliciting contradictory testimony from the same witness on cross-examination would be similarly designated.

The Federal Rules do not specifically address the topic of impeachment by contradiction, but it is an established practice under federal common law.

Prior Inconsistent Statements (Impeachment)

Written or oral statements made by a witness prior to testifying at the present proceeding, which are used to impeach (contradict or cast doubt on) the witness's present testimony. See **FRE 613.**

Example 8.14:   Priscilla sues Desdimona for battery, alleging that Desdimona struck Priscilla without provocation. Priscilla calls witness Winifred, who testifies to that effect. On cross-examination by Desdimona, however, Winifred is forced to concede that a week earlier she told a friend that it was Priscilla who first struck Desdimona and that Desdimona acted in self-defense. Thus Winifred has been (self-) contradicted by her prior inconsistent statement. Had Winifred denied the prior inconsistent statement, under proper circumstances it could have been proved by the testimony (extrinsic evidence) of the friend to whom it was made.

The use made of the prior inconsistent statement in Example 8.14 is merely to impeach, or cast doubt on, Winifred's present testimony. Jurisdictions vary as to whether Winifred's statement may also be used substantively (for the truth of the matter stated), which would require an exception to, or exemption from, the hearsay rule.

Possible substantive use of a prior inconsistent statement is discussed in detail in Chapter 5; here only its impeachment use is illustrated. Keep in mind, however, that even if substantive use is technically prohibited, there is almost always a danger that a prior inconsistent statement nominally admitted only for impeachment purposes will be improperly used by the jury for the truth of the matter stated. See discussion of "mere subterfuge" under *Vouching Rule*.

Degree of inconsistency.   Strictly speaking, a prior statement is not inconsistent with a later one unless the two logically cannot both be true. Most modern courts, however, interpret "inconsistent" somewhat flexibly. If making the prior statement reasonably casts doubt on the truthfulness of the present testimony, the two are sufficiently inconsistent.

Example 8.15:   Same facts as Example 8.14, except that Winifred's earlier statement to her friend was that she could not remember the incident. While earlier lack of memory is not entirely inconsistent with present recollection, barring unusual circumstances (such as hypnotic enhancement) it is sufficiently unlikely to allow the prior statement to be shown.

Usually a prior recollection and present lack of memory, although far more likely, is also considered sufficiently inconsistent, but sometimes only if the court disbelieves the claim of forgetfulness. Also generally deemed inconsistent is the earlier omission of some significant detail included in the later (testimonial) version of the story.

Foundation.   Traditionally, before a witness could be cross-examined about a prior inconsistent statement, the interrogator had to lay a foundation by asking whether the witness had made the alleged statement. The witness had to be told the substance of the statement, when and where it was supposedly made, and to whom. Many courts still require such a foundation, and some that do not nevertheless permit the judge to require it in the interests of justice. **FRE 613(a)** requires only that, on request, the contents be "shown or disclosed to opposing counsel." CEC 769, by comparison, goes even further and requires no disclosure at all. (Regardless of the applicable rule, however, a reference to the statement and its contents during cross-examination and before introducing the statement will often be the better trial tactic.)

Usually if the witness admits to making the prior statement, it cannot be shown again by extrinsic evidence. Requirements for introducing extrinsic evidence of a denied prior statement are discussed below.

Under the **Rule in Queen Caroline's Case** (also called simply **The Queen's Case**), named after an English case from 1820, if the prior inconsistent statement was in writing, the interrogator had first to show the actual statement to the witness and allow the witness to read it over before asking about it. This gave the witness time and opportunity to fashion an explanation before having to respond to any embarrassing questions about the prior statement. England abrogated the rule in 1854, but it still persists in some American states. It is expressly abolished by FRE 613(a).

Extrinsic evidence.   Unless it is on a collateral matter (discussed elsewhere), once a foundation is laid and a prior inconsistent statement is denied — or at least "not admitted" — by the witness on cross-examination, it can be shown by extrinsic evidence.

Under traditional doctrine (also deriving from Queen Caroline's Case) the witness must be given an opportunity to explain or deny the prior inconsistent statement, whether written or oral, prior to its being proven by extrinsic evidence. **FRE 613(b)** relaxes this requirement, requiring only that the witness have an opportunity to explain or deny the statement, and opposing counsel have an opportunity to question the witness about it, but not necessarily before proof of the statement is given. Even this can be altered if "the interests of justice otherwise require."

Many courts, however, including federal courts, will require a prior foundation anyway where it seems appropriate. This is especially likely if the only proper use of the prior inconsistent statement is for impeachment and therefore there is the danger of its misuse by the jury if introduced "cold" and without prior explanation.

Inapplicable to admissions. The traditional foundation requirements generally do not apply when the witness whose prior inconsistent statement is in question is a party and thus the statement is also an admission (admissible under the hearsay rule for substantive purposes). FRE 613(b) follows this course as well.

Application to out-of-court witnesses. Witnesses who are not in court, such as hearsay declarants and those who testify by deposition, may be impeached by prior inconsistent statements just as in-court witnesses may. See **FRE 806** (hearsay declarants). In such a case, courts that apply strictly the traditional foundation requirements, including an opportunity to explain or deny the statement, effectively preclude introduction of a prior inconsistent statement unless the foundation was laid on the prior occasion, as when the statement was part of an earlier hearing. Some courts will relax the rules in such cases, and FRE 613(b)'s exception for the "interests of justice" provides a federal court discretion to do so. Moreover, FRE 806 expressly eliminates the "explain or deny" requirement in the case of hearsay declarants.

Finally, it should be noted that although most inconsistent statements used for impeachment were by definition made prior to the witness's testimony, statements made subsequent to the testimony (especially if the testimony itself was given before the trial, as in a deposition) can also be used effectively to impeach. The key is inconsistency, not antecedence (although "subsequent inconsistent statement" has not entered the lexicon).

Collateral Facts Rule

A prohibition on contradicting a witness's testimony by extrinsic evidence if the proof has no other purpose than to show that the testimony was incorrect.

Example 8.16: Pamela sues Darnell for breach of an oral contract. Wally testifies for Pamela that he heard Darnell make the promise in question. Wally states: "I was there, standing right by Pamela and her sister that day, when Darnell said, 'You have a deal.' I remember particularly how Pamela then broke out a bottle of French champagne and we all toasted the agreement's success." On cross-examination, Darnell wishes to demonstrate that Wally was wrong about Pamela's sister being there, as it was actually Pamela's cousin who stood next to Wally. Darnell hopes that the jury will conclude that if Wally could be mistaken about such a detail, he might be mistaken about the more important matter of the promise. The identity of Pamela's companion, however, has no other bearing on the case and no other use than to show that Wally could be mistaken (or lying) about that detail, and therefore it is deemed *collateral*. Darnell will be permitted to ask Wally about it on cross-examination, but if Wally continues to maintain that it was Pamela's sister who was there, Darnell must take Wally's answer as conclusive and cannot introduce extrinsic evidence (such as another eyewitness or a prior inconsistent statement) to prove otherwise.

If, however, the contradictory evidence has some other purpose in the case than merely to show that the witness has made a mistake, such as to impeach him in some other way or to prove a relevant substantive issue, the fact is not collateral and may be proven by extrinsic evidence.

Relevant to substantive issue. The most obvious type of noncollateral fact is one that is relevant to the substantive issues in the case and therefore could have been proven — that is, would have been relevant — even if the present witness had not testified to its contrary.

Example 8.17:   Same facts as Example 8.16, except that Darnell alleges that Wally was mistaken not just about who was there, but what was said. In fact, according to Darnell, he said, "You *haven't* got a deal." As this is a matter crucial to the substantive issue of existence of a contract, if denied by Wally it can be proven by extrinsic evidence, just as it could have been if Wally had not testified at all. It is not collateral.

Bias.   Even if a substantive issue is not involved, impeachment by showing bias is not considered collateral. It impeaches other than merely by demonstrating that the witness can make mistakes.

Example 8.18:   Same facts as Example 8.16, except that the reason Darnell wishes to show that Wally is incorrect about the person who was with Pamela is that the person was Sue, Wally's sister, who was there as a partner with Pamela in the alleged transaction. The con-

171

tradiction thus would show bias toward Pamela, an entirely separate basis for impeachment of Wally than merely the ability to make a mistake. As such, it would be open to Darnell to introduce extrinsic evidence of this fact if it were denied by Wally.

Incapacity.   Like bias, physical or mental incapacity or inability to perceive impeaches other than by the mere fact of contradiction. Thus, if Darnell in Example 8.16 wished to dispute where Wally was standing, this would be noncollateral if in truth Wally was too far away to hear what was said.

"Linchpin."   A matter is also noncollateral if, although it has no other connection to impeachment or an issue in the case, it is a fact about which, if Wally's story were true, he could not reasonably have been mistaken. This is sometimes called the **linchpin exception,** because the fact contradicted is the linchpin of the witness's entire story.

Example 8.19:   Same facts as Example 8.16, except the fact that Darnell wishes to contradict is whether Pamela broke out a bottle of French champagne and they all drank a toast. In fact, both Pamela and Darnell are allergic to alcohol, and the last thing they would have done was drink a champagne toast. While the toast (or lack of it) has no intrinsic effect on the deal, it is the kind of detail about which, if Wally were telling the truth about the meeting, he would not likely have been mistaken. (Wally here has been caught in the kind of gratuitous embellishment of a lie that Poobah, the pompous Lord High Everything in Gilbert & Sullivan's *The Mikado*, defended as "merely corroborative detail, intended to give artistic verisimilitude to an otherwise bald and unconvincing narrative." Liars often talk too much.)

Prior convictions.   Unlike most matters of fact that are unrelated to the substantive issues and are considered collateral, a prior conviction is easily proved by irrefutable evidence and therefore considered noncollateral; if the witness denies it, it may be proven by introduction of the record of conviction. See **FRE 609.** If, however, for impeachment purposes a witness is asked about specific acts *not* amounting to a conviction, they are collateral and the witness's answer is final, as they would take too much time to prove and would be likely to confuse the issues. See **FRE 608(b).** See generally *Character Evidence (Impeachment).*

Inapplicable to cross-examination.   The collateral facts rule is concerned only with the introduction of extrinsic evidence and has no application to cross-examination. Collateral questions may be asked on cross-examination, but the interrogator must take the answer of the witness as final. (Of course, the judge may place reasonable limits on cross-examination, but this rule is not one of them.) Thus, all of the matters stated by Wally in Example 8.16, as well as any regarding prior inconsistent statements or past bad acts and the like, may be inquired into on cross-examination; but only those deemed noncollateral may be contradicted or proven by extrinsic evidence if denied.

Character Evidence (Impeachment)

Evidence of a witness's character used as a means of deciding whether the witness is testifying truthfully. Like other character evidence, it may be in the form of reputation, opinion, or specific acts. See **FRE 608-609.**

Example 8.20: Warner testifies for the plaintiff in a negligence case. On cross-examination, Warner is asked by the defendant: (1) "Do you cheat on your income tax?" (2) "Were you ever arrested for assault?" (3) "Were you once convicted of grand theft?" Warner answers "No" to each question. After Warner's denials, the defendant calls another witness, Vera, to testify to her low opinion of Warner's veracity and to Warner's poor reputation for truthfulness in his community. A record of Warner's conviction for grand theft is then produced. All of these efforts by the defendant are attempts, more or less logical, to discredit Warner's testimony by demonstrating that Warner's character is such that he is the type of person who should not be believed.

Which of the questions in Example 8.20 are proper forms of impeachment depends on the jurisdiction. As explained below, a court might distinguish between reputation and opinion evidence, whereas the admissibility of specific acts may depend on the nature of the act and whether there was a conviction for it.

Distinguish other uses. Impeachment use of character, the present topic, applies of course only to the character of a witness. It is very important to distinguish this use of character evidence to impeach from other, substantive uses of character. These might include, for example, a criminal defendant's good character introduced to dispute the accusation of criminal conduct; the defendant's prior crimes to establish the element of intent for the crime presently charged; or a libel plaintiff's unsavory character as justifying the disparaging statements made by the defendant. All of these are covered in detail in Chapter 3. As there explained, certain uses of character evidence are improper, particularly evidence of a defendant's propensity to commit bad acts as proof the defendant committed the one charged. When a party is also a witness, however, the opposing party's attempted impeachment by proving the party/witness's bad character may be only an excuse for putting before the jury just such propensity evidence; and whether so intended or not, it inevitably does put that damaging information before the jury.

Example 8.21: Dan is on trial for burglary. The prosecution would like to produce evidence that several years earlier Dan was convicted of theft, merely to show that Dan is the type of person who would commit such a crime; however, such use is improper propensity evidence (see Chapter 3), and the prior crime would be excluded. If, however, Dan takes the stand to testify in his own behalf, subject to certain limitations the prosecution will be able to prove Dan's prior conviction, not as evidence that Dan would steal, but as evidence that Dan would lie (that is, for impeachment only). It is doubtful the jury would be able to distinguish the two uses and consider Dan's prior conviction only with respect to his veracity on the stand and not with respect to his tendency to commit crimes.

Types of evidence admissible. As in other instances of the proof of character, traditionally only evidence of the witness's reputation for veracity was admissible to impeach, whereas under many modern rules, including **FRE 608(a),** a character witness's opinion is now admissible as well. See generally Chapter 3.

Generally testimony about a witness's character is limited to reputation or opinion as to truthfulness or untruthfulness. In a few states a character witness may testify to traits other than veracity, or to the witness's general moral character.

With respect to specific acts bearing on character, an important distinction is made between those that have and have not resulted in a criminal conviction, with convictions generally being much easier to admit.

Specific acts, no conviction. A few courts take the extreme position that a witness can be asked in cross-examination about virtually any bad act, whether or not it directly relates to one's propensity to tell the truth (for example, an armed assault). Their theory is that a person who would commit any bad act would be more likely to commit perjury. Other courts prefer the other extreme and allow no impeachment by (non-conviction) bad acts. They consider the possible prejudice to the witness or the party to outweigh any tenuous benefit in the truth-seeking process. Between these extremes are the majority of courts, which allow impeachment only by prior acts that are probative of the witness's credibility, such as those involving dishonesty or deception. **FRE 608(b)** is in this latter category.

Example 8.22: Delilah is on trial for murder. She testifies in her own defense and denies guilt. She is impeached with evidence that she once assaulted her parents, and that she cheated on school examinations. The assault would be admissible only in a jurisdiction allowing any bad act to impeach; the cheating should be admissible also where only credibility-related acts are permitted to impeach. In some jurisdictions neither would be admissible, there having been no conviction of crime.

Criminal convictions. At common law, conviction of what were termed **"infamous crimes"** (felonies, treason, obstruction of justice, and those involving dishonesty or false statement — so-called ***crimen falsi***) rendered a witness incompetent to testify at all, so the question of such a witness's credibility never arose. Later the incompetency was abolished and these crimes became merely grounds for impeachment. What crimes now qualify for impeachment varies among states, from virtually any crime at all to only *crimen falsi,* such as perjury or fraud. Some states limit the crimes to those involving moral turpitude, some to felonies. The definitions tend to be vague and their application can be quite flexible.

The Federal Rules establish two different categories of convictions. **FRE 609(a)(1)** admits any crimes which, under the law where convicted, can be punished by death or by prison for more than one year (the usual equivalent of felonies), but only under certain conditions. If the witness is the accused in a criminal case, the crime's probative value for impeachment must outweigh its prejudicial effect. This is a reversal of the usual FRE 403 balance, under which evidence is admitted unless its prejudicial effect substantially outweighs its probative value. In other words, it is made much more difficult to admit prior crimes against a witness accused than it is to admit almost any other evidence. Factors to be weighed usually include the type of crime and how long ago it occurred, the importance of the accused's testimony and credibility, and the similarity of the prior and the presently-alleged crimes. If the witness is not a criminal accused, only the usual FRE 403 weighing is applied under FRE 609(a)(1).

Under **FRE 609(a)(2),** crimes involving dishonesty or false statement are admissible to impeach *any* witness, regardless of the seriousness of the crime or its punishment. There is no provision for weighing probative value against prejudice, and courts have held that even FRE 403 is inapplicable. Although some courts have held that crimes like theft are "dishonest" and so qualify under Rule 609(a)(2) even if they do not involve a false statement, most have limited this category to *crimen falsi* (see above). This usually eliminates crimes of violence and others (like drunken driving) unrelated to truthfulness. Courts generally will, however, look at the facts of the particular conviction and admit the crime if false statement, deceit, or the like was actually involved in its commission.

Example 8.23:   Diane is accused of murder. She wants to testify on her own behalf, but if she does the prosecution intends to impeach her with two prior convictions in the state of Georgia, for assault and fraud, occurring within two years before the present trial. Diane's own testimony is the only evidence she has in her defense. Most if not all jurisdictions should admit the fraud conviction as very relevant to credibility and unlikely to prejudice Diane unfairly. Under the Federal Rules it would come in under FRE 609(a)(2). The assault might or might not be admitted at common law, depending on the jurisdiction and whether it was a felony, whether considered a crime of "moral turpitude," and so forth. Under FRE 609(a)(1), the assault would be admitted only if under Georgia law assault is punishable by death or more than one year in prison (regardless of the actual sentence Diane received), and if the court found its probative value outweighed its prejudicial effect on Diane. Here the importance of Diane's testimony to her case (thus increasing the possible unfairness of discouraging her from taking the stand), and the fact that assault is not particularly probative of credibility, all weigh against admission, whereas the relative recency of the conviction and the dissimilarity of assault to murder (as opposed, for example, to a prior murder conviction that might unfairly label Diane as having a propensity to kill) favors its admission. Given the need for probativeness to outweigh prejudice, the evidence probably would not be admitted. But in the unlikely event that the assault was carried out in a manner that employed deceit (such as luring her victim with a false promise to protect her), a Federal Rules court might admit it under Rule 609(a)(2) regardless of its punishment limits and without any weighing of probative value against prejudicial effect.

Note that in Example 8.23 the witness is a criminal accused. If instead Diane called a witness to testify for her who had the same background of convictions as indicated for Diane, under the Federal Rules the fraud conviction would be treated exactly the same, but the assault conviction would not. While it would still have to be a death/one-year-imprisonment crime, as generally under FRE 403 it would be presumptively admitted unless its probative value was substantially outweighed by the danger of unfair prejudice or the other balancing factors such as confusion of the issues.

Lapse of time.   **FRE 609(b)** contains a special restriction on crimes if the conviction (or release from jail, if later) was more than 10 years prior to the date of testimony. Here still a third weighing formula is employed, the most restrictive of all: Probative value must not only outweigh prejudicial effect (as under 609(a)(1)), but it must *substantially* outweigh it. Also required are the proponent's written notice of intent to use the conviction and an express finding by the court of specific facts and circumstances supporting admission. Stale convictions are very difficult to admit.

Effect of collateral facts rule. When a witness is asked about specific acts other than convictions on cross-examination, the matter is collateral — the interrogator must take the answer of the witness and cannot introduce extrinsic evidence of those acts. Prior convictions, however, may be proven, usually by introduction of the record of conviction. See generally *Collateral Facts Rule*.

Miscellaneous provisions. Pendency of an appeal usually does not preclude use of the prior conviction (see **FRE 609(e)**). Nor generally does a pardon, although under **FRE 609(c)** use is precluded by a pardon (or the equivalent) based on rehabilitation with no subsequent serious convictions, or a pardon based on a finding of innocence. Juvenile adjudications are inadmissible against an accused under **FRE 609(d),** but admissible in limited circumstances against other witnesses in criminal trials.

Ideally, the question of whether a criminal accused's prior convictions will be usable to impeach is settled by a *motion in limine,* before trial. The Supreme Court has ruled, however, that unless the defendant actually does testify and prior convictions are used to impeach, the trial court's pretrial ruling permitting such use cannot be reviewed on appeal. (*Luce v. United States.*[3])

FRE limitation to character impeachment. It should be noted that the provisions of FRE 608 and 609, although they are phrased in terms of "credibility," apply only to credibility as demonstrated by evidence of good or bad character for veracity. They do not affect impeachment by contradiction, showing bias, or the like, *even if these other forms of impeachment are accomplished using evidence of character.*

Example 8.24: In a criminal trial Wilbur testifies for the prosecution and is impeached with a prior conviction for assault. If that conviction were offered not to show Wilbur's tendency to lie, but to show that he had a grudge against the defendant, who just happened to be the judge who convicted him in the assault case, it would not be subject to the limitations of FRE 609 just because it incidentally involved a conviction and the witness's character.

---

3. 469 U.S. 38 (1984).

Rehabilitation

Supporting or repairing a witness's credibility after it has been attacked. This may simply be called **support** of the witness.

A witness's testimony may be supported only if first attacked, and then only with evidence that fairly and directly meets the thrust of the attack. See **FRE 608(a)** (evidence of good character); **FRE 801(d)(1)(B)** (prior consistent statement). In McCormick's metaphorical terms, a wall attacked at one point may not be fortified at another. To extend the metaphor, defenders must "hold their fire" until the wall is actually attacked.

Example 8.25: Wade testifies for the plaintiff Penny that Penny was "in the crosswalk at the time Donald's car struck her." On cross-examination by defendant Donald, Wade is asked (1) whether he cheats on his wife, (2) whether he was ever convicted of fraud, and (3) whether he is related to Penny's family. He either admits these or they are proven (where allowed) by extrinsic evidence. Following this, Penny may attempt to rehabilitate Wade. Wade may on redirect examination attempt to explain the circumstances of items (1) and (2), or even of (3) ("We never got along and I haven't seen any of them in years!"). And since items (1) and (2) assert, directly or indirectly, Wade's bad character for truth, evidence of his good character for truth is admissible in support. Item (3), on the other hand, does not necessarily allege bad character, just "innocent" bias due to family ties; therefore if it were the only form of impeachment used by Donald, Penny could not counter with evidence of Wade's veracity, just of his lack of bias. Nevertheless, if the tone and thrust of the impeachment suggests bad character, even if the exact words do not, evidence of good character will generally be admitted.

Prior consistent statements. Use of prior inconsistent statements to impeach is common, and prior *consistent* statements may sometimes be used to rehabilitate the witness impeached in this manner. The rules still follow the metaphor of the wall, that the defense must meet the thrust of the attack.

Example 8.26: Same facts as Example 8.25, except Wade is impeached by evidence that he previously stated, on June 1, that "Penny *was not* in the crosswalk." In such circumstances some courts will always permit counterproof of Wade's good (truthful) character; others will not unless the context of the prior statement suggests that his character for truthfulness has been attacked. Traditionally, a prior consistent statement cannot be introduced at this point, because it does not answer or eliminate the inconsistency. Some courts, however, will permit introduction of a prior consistent statement made at about the same time, to the extent it supports Wade's denial that he made the inconsistent statement, or that his memory is poor.

If a prior inconsistent statement or any other form of impeaching evidence asserts or implies some bias, influence, motive to lie, or plan to testify falsely, or what is loosely called **recent fabrication,** a prior consistent statement may be introduced in response.

Example 8.27:   Same facts as Example 8.26 (Wade's prior inconsistent statement), except that Wade is also asked, "Did you have lunch with Penny on June 2, the day after saying 'Penny *was not* in the crosswalk,' after which you changed your story and said she *was?*" Now Donald has implied that Penny bribed, threatened, or otherwise influenced Wade to change his story, as demonstrated by the difference between Wade's prior and later versions. Therefore, Penny may rehabilitate Wade by showing that on May 25, even before the meeting with Penny, Wade had said that Penny was in the crosswalk.

Note that in Example 8.27, even if Donald had not raised the issue of Wade's prior inconsistent statement, an implication that Wade had recently fabricated his story or changed it for some improper reason ("Didn't Penny recently give you a large amount of cash?") would still permit introduction of Wade's prior consistent statement.

"Pre-motive" statements only.   Logically the prior consistent statement is relevant to rebut the charge of recent fabrication only if it was made before the supposed motive to lie arose; if it was made after, it is still tainted. But because of the difficulty of determining just when such a motive actually arose, courts sometimes do not enforce this limitation strictly. The Supreme Court has held that FRE 801(d)(1)(B), the hearsay exception for prior consistent statements, does incorporate the "pre-motive" limitation. See *Prior Consistent Statements,* Chapter 5.)

Character witnesses.   A party may attempt to rebut an assertion or implication of the witness's bad character for truthfulness with a **character witness** who testifies that the principal witness (Wade in Examples 8.25-26) is in fact credible. (The initial attack on the witness's veracity may itself, of course, have been by use of a (bad-)character witness, like Vera in Example 8.20.) Character witnesses may themselves then be impeached by questions that attack not only their own character, but that of the principal witness whom they have supported. See **FRE 608(b).** (Impeaching good-character witnesses is discussed generally in Chapter 3.).

Example 8.28: As in Example 8.25, Wade is impeached with evidence, inter alia, of his conviction for fraud, which impugns his character for truthfulness. Penny now attempts to rehabilitate Wade by calling character witness Melinda. Melinda testifies that she knows Wade to have a good reputation for truthfulness in his community, and that her own opinion of Wade's veracity is similar. On cross-examination, Melinda is asked, (1) "Have you heard about Wade's arrest for tax evasion?"; and (2) "Do you know about the time Wade was caught cheating at cards in Las Vegas?" These questions, provided the interrogator has a good faith belief that the incidents mentioned are true, are considered proper tests of (1) Melinda's knowledge of what is being said by others about Wade (Wade's "reputation") and (2) the basis for Melinda's own opinion about Wade's veracity. (See generally Chapter 3.) Of course, other questions going to Melinda's acquaintance with Wade and Melinda's own veracity would also be appropriate.

Anticipatory Disclosure

A tactical decision to disclose potentially impeaching information about a witness (particularly a criminal defendant's prior convictions) during direct examination, in order to "take the wind out of the sails" of the cross-examiner when that information is used to impeach.

Anticipatory disclosure is as close to a preemptive strike as one can come on direct examination, since one may not bring out a witness's good character in anticipation of a cross-examiner's bringing out the bad. (See *Rehabilitation.*) A court will not, however, necessarily permit all such impeaching information to be "anticipated." For example, it may not be possible to anticipate and deflate the effect of a prior inconsistent statement.

9 Opinion Evidence

Introduction and Overview of Chapter

This chapter examines the rules that govern witnesses' testimony to their opinion regarding a matter in issue. It first explains the different meanings of the term "opinion," and then it discusses the concept of opinion evidence in the context of both lay and expert witnesses, including consideration of the ultimate issue rule. Also explained is the relationship between opinion and the personal knowledge rule.

Opinion Evidence (In General)

Evidence in the form of an inference or a conclusion, rather than a statement of the facts from which the inference or conclusion has been drawn; or evidence of facts based on conjecture or belief, rather than personal knowledge. "Opinion" is a slippery term that can include both inferences and other non-factual evidence. See **FRE 701.**

    Traditional approach: rule of exclusion. At common law, opinion testimony was excluded because it "usurped the province of the jury" to draw its own inferences from the facts. As the doctrine developed (and as it still is applied by some courts today), opinions expressed by lay witnesses were almost always inadmissible, whereas opinion testimony by qualified expert witnesses was permitted upon the laying of a proper foundation.

Example 9.1: Paul has sued Don for negligence following an automobile accident. Witness Wilma testifies that, while she did not actually see the accident, based on the relative positions of the cars when she arrived she believes Paul's car was the first to enter the intersection. While Wilma can properly testify from her observation to the relative positions of the cars, her conclusion from that fact as to which car first entered the intersection is an opinion. As such, it generally would be excluded, unless Wilma is an expert on accident reconstruction and a proper foundation has been laid for her expert opinion.

Modern approach: rule of preference. Although at one time the above distinction between admissible and inadmissible opinion evidence was fairly clear, today most courts are willing to admit even lay opinion when it is necessary or merely helpful to do so. Thus **FRE 701** admits lay opinion if it is both rationally based on personal knowledge and helpful to the trier of fact (see below). This makes the admission of opinion very much a matter for trial court discretion and case-by-case analysis and makes the opinion rule not one of strict exclusion so much as one of preference — for the specific and concrete over the general and conclusory when the latter is not helpful. Some courts, however, still follow the traditional exclusionary concept somewhat strictly.

If the opinion rule is one of preference for specificity, it will be enforced most strictly where the preferred specific form of testimony can most easily be obtained. Thus, a witness on the stand can be asked to restate a response in more specific terms and without expressing any opinion or drawing any conclusion. But a witness not in court, whose statement is offered by deposition or hearsay testimony, cannot generally be asked to rephrase an answer, and in such circumstances an opinion may be permitted to stand, rather than lose the testimony altogether for lack of the proper form.

Personal knowledge and opinion. The **personal knowledge** (also called the **firsthand knowledge) rule** remains the heart of the opinion rule. A witness should state perceived facts (personal knowledge rule), rather than inferences or conclusions from those facts (opinion rule). Note also that while the opinion rule has largely been discarded or become a rule of preference, the personal knowledge rule has been retained and remains a strict rule of exclusion. See **FRE 602.**

Facts and opinions. It is easy to talk about the difference between facts and mere opinions, but the distinction is not as clear as it seems. In reality, the difference between description of a fact and giving an opinion or conclusion is a matter of how general or specific is the description. The more fact-specific the description, the less it seems like just a general conclusion from the facts. It is, like most evidence questions, a relative matter.

Example 9.2:   Witness Wally is testifying for the plaintiff, who was allegedly injured by Daniel's blue automobile. Daniel denies he was there. Wally testifies that: (1) he saw *a blue car* pass him on the street just before the accident; and (2) Daniel was driving the car. Statements (1) and (2) both seem to be facts. Yet a color that one person calls "blue" may be called "blue-green" by another and "greenish-blue" or even "green" by a third. It is, after all, just a matter of opinion. That "Daniel was driving" is also just Wally's inference or conclusion from perceived clues as to the driver's appearance, as compared in Wally's mind to his recollection of what Daniel looks like or his present perception of Daniel in court. Even regarding what Daniel was doing, as the victim of Daniel's incompetence might well respond to statement (2), "You call that '*driving*'?"

More factual with respect to Wally's identification of the driver would be a statement (a verbal sketch, if one were possible) of all of the features of the person he saw driving the car, leaving to the jury whether to conclude that it was indeed Daniel. This would be difficult at best, and such a description of the car's color would be even less likely. (Wally would, however, generally be permitted to testify to these two "opinions," as there is usually no practical alternative. See *Collective Facts Rule*.)

Could it also be only opinion that Daniel was driving a *car*? While no doubt allowed to pass in a case like this, the statement would probably be a prohibited opinion if Daniel were being sued for failing to pay a tax on trucks and the only issue was whether the vehicle Daniel was driving (a passenger car with a pickup truck bed in back) was indeed a car or a truck. The court would want only the most specific descriptive facts, and not Wally's legal conclusion as to what type of vehicle he saw.

Lay and expert opinion.   In this area of the law it is crucial to distinguish between so-called lay and expert opinion. As set out separately below, the rules that apply to opinion testimony by the two types of witness are quite different. Lay (non-expert) witnesses are generally supposed to testify only to what they have perceived; they are, in a sense, "expert" on that narrow subject. Expert witnesses, on the other hand, because of their experience and training, are able to contribute useful opinions based on the observations of others as well as themselves. In both cases, however, the witnesses' opinions are admitted only if and to the extent they are likely to aid the trier of fact in reaching its ultimate conclusions on the evidence.

Sometimes it is difficult to tell whether a witness is offering lay or expert opinion testimony. The witness who opines that the loud noise he heard "was a gunshot" may be classified as a lay or expert witness depending on whether the court believes that such an opinion requires some special training or experience (perhaps as a hunter). Regardless of the label attached, therefore, counsel presenting such a witness must be prepared to establish his qualifications in this narrow field.

Because lay and expert opinion may be admitted or excluded in different circumstances, it is useful to distinguish those situations in which: (1) lay opinion is permitted; (2) lay opinion is not permitted; (3) expert opinion is permitted; (4) expert opinion is not permitted; (5) both lay and expert opinion are permitted; (6) neither lay nor expert opinion is permitted; and (7) expert opinion is required. While these are not rigid (and indeed are overlapping) categories, they can easily be gleaned from the materials that follow.

Lay Opinion

Opinion evidence given by a witness who has not been presented as, or is not qualified to be, an expert on the subject matter of the evidence.

Traditionally, lay (that is, non-expert) witnesses are not supposed to give their opinions or conclusions about the facts, but only to state those facts from their own personal knowledge.

Example 9.3: Lay witness Larry observed plaintiff Patricia just after she was injured by Donna. Larry can testify to facts he observed, such as Patricia having a "flushed complexion" or a "black eye." Larry may not, however, opine that, based on these observations, Patricia was feverish or had been struck in the eye. A qualified expert, on the other hand, here a doctor, might be permitted to draw conclusions as to causation from the observed facts.

Under modern formulations like **FRE 701,** however, the opinion rule as it applies to lay witnesses has become more of a rule of preference — preference for the concrete over the abstract, the specific over the general — than a strict rule of exclusion (see *Opinion Evidence (In General)*). FRE 701 does not proscribe lay opinions, or even attempt to distinguish between "fact" and "opinion," but it limits opinions to those that are rationally based on personal knowledge ("on the perception of the witness") and are helpful to the trier of fact. (As discussed later, expert witnesses need not base their opinions on personal knowledge.) Thus, the opinion rule under the Federal Rules is a rule of preference for specificity, unless under the circumstances the witness's more general "opinion" would be helpful.

Usually it would not be helpful for a lay witness (or, for that matter, even an expert witness) to offer an opinion on that which is within the understanding of, and just as easily inferred by, the jury. Nor would a lay opinion usually be helpful in elucidating that which is beyond the ken of the ordinary juror and therefore within the province of an expert. Sometimes, however, it is helpful for a lay witness who has stated particular facts to state as well the inference the witness draws from them.

Example 9.4:   Lay witness Leonard testifies to the color, texture, and taste of a substance he found and examined. If it is likely that he could identify the substance, he should be permitted to state as well his opinion as to what it was. Almost any witness, therefore, should be able to state that "it looked and tasted like sugar"; but only a witness with a particular background and experience could helpfully opine that "it tasted like cocaine."

Collective facts.   Even the common law recognized that some "facts" cannot so easily be separated from the conclusions we draw from them. The **collective facts rule** (also called the **shorthand rendition rule**) takes this into account.

Example 9.5:   Same facts as Example 9.3, except Larry is asked whether Patricia appeared to be "angry." This requires that Larry draw a conclusion, or give his opinion, regarding Patricia's state of mind. In theory, we could require Larry to state all of the physical indications he observed that lead him to conclude that Patricia was angry, such as Patricia's flushed complexion, narrowed eyes, agitated movements, downturned mouth, and so forth. Most likely, Larry could not do so, since these factors would have registered on Larry's mind subconsciously and collectively, and not as individual observations. Even if Larry could so testify, it would take too much time and the jury might find it very difficult to draw its own conclusions from Larry's description. In effect, "you had to be there." Under the collective facts rule, Larry will be permitted to state his conclusion about Patricia's anger, either with or without some of the more obvious facts he observed.

See also Example 9.2. When a witness testifies to a conclusion rather than specific facts, as in the above example, the opposing party always may examine further the basis for the witness's opinion on cross-examination.

The collective facts rule satisfies, of course, both the "rationally based on perception" and "helpfulness" standards of FRE 701.

Opinion on sanity.   One subject on which lay witnesses have traditionally been permitted to state their opinion is another person's sanity or mental competence. The witness must, however, be sufficiently well acquainted with the subject to have a basis for such an opinion. Because sanity is also a proper subject for expert testimony, this is one of the unusual situations in which both lay and expert witnesses may properly exress their opinions.

Ultimate Issue Rule

A prohibition against a witness expressing an opinion on the final conclusions of fact or law in a case, which the judge or jury is ultimately charged with deciding.

The traditional prohibition against witnesses testifying to their opinions or conclusions (as opposed to "facts" — see *Opinion Evidence (In General)*) was enforced most vigorously with respect to the so-called "ultimate issues" in a case.

Example 9.6:   A building owned by Denise catches fire and damages Perry's adjoining building. (a) Perry sues Denise for causing the fire. Witness Wilma testifies that Denise was operating certain machinery on her premises "negligently." (b) Same, but negligence is conceded and only causation is contested by Denise. Wilma testifies that Denise's operation of the machinery "caused the fire." (c) Denise is also prosecuted for operating the machinery without a license in violation of a criminal statute. Wilma testifies that Denise's operation was "unlawful." Wilma's testimonial statements in (a), (b), and (c) are not just opinions, but they can be characterized as the very conclusions that the jury is charged with drawing. Moreover, that Denise acted "negligently" is a legal conclusion (or one of mixed fact and law), as is the opinion that Denise's actions were "unlawful." Both are considered strictly the province of the jury after appropriate instruction on the law from the judge. It thus has been said that permitting such testimony would allow the witness to "usurp the jury's function" and in effect tell it how to decide the case.

As a separate rule, the ultimate issue rule has largely been discarded by modern codes. See, e.g., **FRE 704(a).** Thus statement (b) in Example 9.6 would generally be permitted. To the extent, however, that the rule prohibited a witness from merely telling the jury what result to reach, that is, expressing an opinion on the very issue that the jury is ultimately charged with deciding, and when the jury is in just as good a position (or better) to draw that conclusion without the witness's assistance ("defendant was negligent" or "defendant acted unlawfully" in Example 9.6), the opinion will still be rejected. The Comments to FRE 704, for example, contain the following illustration, taken from a well-known pre-Federal Rules case:

Example 9.7:   Tess's will is challenged on the ground that Tess lacked sufficient mental capacity. Witness Wanda testifies for the will's proponents. Even where the ultimate issue rule no longer exists as such, Wanda may not give her opinion on the ultimate issue of whether the testator had capacity, because "capacity" is a legal term of art and the witness's and jury's understanding of capacity may be different from that of the law. The opinion would be, in the Advisory Committee's words, "phrased in terms of inadequately explored legal criteria." But Wanda may state her opinion on the criteria upon which the legal concept of capacity is based: "whether the testator had the capacity to know the nature and extent of his property and the natural objects of his bounty and to formulate a rational scheme of distribution." Here the jury would be unlikely to misunderstand the intended meaning of the terms used by the witness, as all are matters of common usage rather than terms of art.

Under the FRE, and despite FRE 704's abolition of the ultimate issue rule, opinions on such ultimate issues as "negligence" or "capacity" would simply be classified as unhelpful to the jury under either Rule 702 (experts) or Rule 701 (lay witnesses). And in FRE 403 terms, they would generally only confuse the issues, waste the jury's time, and be more prejudicial than probative.

Opinion of accused's mental condition. **FRE 704(b)** contains one major exception to the FRE's abolition of the ultimate issue rule: An expert witness may not state an opinion as to a criminal defendant's "mental state or condition" that constitutes an element of the crime or a defense. The Rule was aimed at the defense of insanity, but by its terms it covers the mental element of any crime or defense. In other words, as a practical matter FRE 704(b) seeks to abolish expert testimony as to whether the defendant intended the act, acted under duress, or was legally insane at the time.

Example 9.8: Dick is on trial for murder in federal court. His defense is insanity. Expert witness Elton may not testify that Dick was "unable to appreciate the nature and quality or wrongfulness of his acts," a test of legal insanity. Elton may, however, testify to Dick's symptoms and his diagnosis of Dick's disease based on those symptoms, as well as other details pertinent to Dick's condition or the characteristics of the affliction in question. It is for the jury to decide, in light of such facts, whether Dick had the requisite "inability."

Because the distinction between facts and opinions and the classification of ultimate issues is so vague, it remains unclear how FRE 704(b) affects many borderline areas of testimony. For example, it is questionable whether Elton can testify that "one with Dick's condition might well" lack the ability to appreciate the wrongfulness of his conduct, or that "it is in the nature of the disease" to have such an effect. Both seem indirectly to state the same "ultimate" opinion as "Dick lacked the ability," yet they do leave the final inference about Dick to the jury.

Expert Witness

A witness who, because of specialized knowledge, skill, training, experience, or education, is particularly qualified to give an opinion or draw an inference about a matter within that area of expertise. See **FRE 702.**

As the above definition indicates, expertise need not be acquired by formal education. A man who has worked as a plumber all his life, or a woman whose lifelong hobby has been breeding German Shepherd dogs, may be as qualified to give an opinion in their respective fields as is a doctor who acquired his expertise in medicine through post-graduate education and years of practice.

Although there are a few areas of overlap, in general an expert witness may give an opinion on a subject on which the opinion of a lay witness would not be helpful to the jury, and on which the jury themselves would not be qualified to draw an inference without the expert's assistance. This is traditionally said to be any subject which is "beyond the ken" of lay jurors, or beyond their "common knowledge and experience"; and in the terminology of the Federal Rules, the test is whether the testimony will "assist the trier of fact" to understand the issues or determine the facts. In most instances, these come to the same thing, except in those few circumstances in which an expert's opinion is deemed helpful even though the subject matter is also within the competence of the jury.

Notice that if a subject is within the competence of the jury, generally neither expert nor lay witnesses will be permitted to state their opinions about it, as neither would be helpful to the trier of fact. A jury should be perfectly capable of deciding without assistance whether it is negligent to drive without headlights on a dark and stormy night, or whether it was reasonable for a doctor to leave a surgical sponge inside a patient.

Basis of opinion. Traditionally an expert's opinion could be based on personal knowledge (for example, the doctor who examined the plaintiff) or on facts in the record which the expert learned by listening to the testimony or by being asked a hypothetical question containing those facts. See *Hypothetical Question.* The opinion could not be based on otherwise-inadmissible evidence (although sometimes this was permitted if the opinion was also based on firsthand knowledge). This practice still continues in some jurisdictions.

Under modern rules such as **FRE 703,** however, the facts underlying an expert's opinion need be neither in the record nor even admissible in evidence, so long as they are "of a type reasonably relied upon by experts in the particular field" in forming such opinions. (Whether the expert can be relied on in deciding whether this standard has been satisfied is still unsettled.)

Example 9.9: Dr. Ann testifies as an expert on cardiovascular trauma. She states her diagnosis respecting the plaintiff Phil's illness. She then is asked the basis for her diagnosis (opinion). Among the data on which Ann relied are the statements of the people who were with Phil when he became ill. Even if these statements would be inadmissible hearsay, so long as they are of a type reasonably relied on by doctors such as Ann in making diagnoses, Ann can testify both to them and to her opinion based on them.

Note that this ability to rely on (and testify to) inadmissible data does not make FRE 703 an exception to the hearsay rule, as the underlying statements are admissible only as a basis for the expert's opinion. As a practical matter, however, the effect is sometimes the same.

Disclosure of underlying data. Under **FRE 705,** the expert may state an opinion without first stating any of the facts or data underlying it, unless the court requires otherwise. Thus if the calling party chooses to present the opinion "cold," it is left for cross-examination to bring out and challenge the basis of the opinion. Of course, if the opinion rests on a solid foundation, the calling party will probably want to bring it out and opposing counsel will not.

Some jurisdictions generally following the federal model retain the traditional right of opposing counsel to explore the basis for the expert's opinion on voir dire before the opinion itself is stated.

Limitations on expert opinions. There are a number of specific doctrines that affect or augment the basic requirements for expert testimony (qualification, helpfulness, proper basis). For example, an expert may not be permitted to present certain scientific evidence unless it meets the *Frye* or *Daubert* standards for relevance and scientific validity (see Chapter 4); or the expert may be permitted to state scientific or technical information but required to stop short of an opinion on the ultimate issue in the case (see above and FRE 704); and of course the probative value of the expert's evidence may be outweighed by its tendency to waste time, confuse the jury, or create undue prejudice, under FRE 403 or its equivalent.

It used to be said that an expert's opinion must not be "based on another opinion." Like the old prohibition against basing an inference on an inference, this rule fails to take account of what is common practice, and it probably would not be seriously enforced today even in a traditional jurisdiction. It clearly is not a limitation under the Federal Rules if the reasonable reliance standard is satisfied.

When expert opinion required.   The above rules tell us when expert opinion is permitted. For the same basic reason that it is traditionally permitted, however — the subject is beyond the ken of the average juror — expert opinion may also be a requirement, without which an issue cannot be decided in favor of its proponent.

Example 9.10:   Patrick sues Dr. Dean for malpractice. Patrick alleges that Dean used an unsuitable surgical procedure when operating on Patrick, thereby causing the incision to become infected. A jury generally would not be permitted to conclude either that the procedure used by Dean was unreasonable or that the procedure caused Patrick's infection, in the absence of expert opinion testimony to that effect. Expert testimony is thus a required element of Patrick's case on this issue.

Medical malpractice has traditionally been an area in which juries are not considered competent to draw inferences without expert assistance. Even here, however, if the issue is considered to be within lay jury competence (such as leaving a sponge inside a patient, mentioned above), expert testimony will not be required.

Note that even if expert testimony is required to draw a particular inference, a jury is not usually required to accept that testimony or draw that inference.

Court-appointed experts.   The court has discretion to appoint its own expert, who then can be called to testify by either party. This might be useful where the parties' own experts strongly disagree on important and complex technical issues, or perhaps where no adequate expert witness has been called (or perhaps found) by either party.

Under **FRE 706,** the court may appoint experts on its own motion or that of a party, and it may select its own expert or one nominated or agreed upon by the parties. The expert must consent to the appointment, may be deposed, called, or cross-examined by any party (including the calling party), and must advise the parties of any findings. The parties may still call their own expert witnesses. Importantly, the court may prevent disclosure to the jury of the fact that the expert is court-appointed, to avoid giving the expert the (often unjustified) appearance of greater objectivity than the parties' own experts.

Hypothetical Question

A question containing a series of assumed facts, upon which an expert witness is asked to state an opinion or draw a conclusion.

At common law a hypothetical question was the only proper way in which to elicit the opinion of an expert who was not testifying from first-hand knowledge. Moreover, the facts contained in the question had to be those properly introduced in evidence, although they might be disputed. All of the relevant facts had to be included in the question, or at least those facts relevant to and necessary for an understanding of the opinion sought. The process was (and is) cumbersome and possibly confusing to the jury — one court referred to it as "soporific" — at least where the facts are complex; but it had the advantage of setting out "up front" the data behind the expert witness's opinion. (Stating the "hypothetical" facts also gives the interrogating attorney an early opportunity to sum up those facts for the jury.)

Although hypothetical questions are no longer required under many modern rules such as **FRE 703** and **705,** they are still permitted and sometimes can be quite helpful. Under these rules, however, since there is no requirement that the facts underlying the expert's opinion be otherwise admissible, the hypothetical facts presumably are not restricted to those already admitted (or even those potentially admissible) in evidence, provided they meet the requirements of Rule 703.

Under either approach, if the hypothetical facts are not clear or would be confusing to the jury, the court can require that they be more fully or more clearly stated.

If the expert has viewed the previous testimony on which an opinion is sought, the hypothetical question may only have to refer to that testimony (assuming it is clear to what testimony the question refers) and ask the expert's opinion on the facts contained in that testimony.

10

Privileges

Agency Policy Deliberations Privilege
Law Enforcement Investigatory Files Privilege
Official Information Privilege
Governmental Information Privilege
Privilege for Required Reports
Freedom of Information Act
Graymail
Classified Information Procedures Act
Informer's Privilege
Informer
Police Surveillance Sites Privilege
Grand Jury Privilege
Privilege Against Self-Incrimination
Self-Incrimination
Testimonial Self-Incrimination
Compulsion
Required Records Exception
Immunity from Prosecution
Use Immunity
Derivative use Immunity
Transactional Immunity
Miscellaneous Privileges
Journalist's Privilege
Shield Law
Accountant's Privilege
Victim-Counselor Privileges

Introduction and Overview of Chapter

Privileges are something of an anomaly in the law of evidence, in that they (together with only a few other evidence rules) exclude certain items of evidence regardless of their trustworthiness, relevance, or importance. This chapter examines first the general principles behind the concept of evidentiary privilege, and then the individual privileges that the law has recognized. Some privileges that are usually omitted from or given limited treatment in evidence courses (such as the informer's and grand jury privileges) are similarly limited in their coverage here. Separately discussed (but also only briefly) is the privilege against self-incrimination, which, unlike most privileges, is constitutionally mandated for all state and federal proceedings.

There is some overlap between privilege and incompetence (see Chapter 8), particularly with respect to testimony for or against a spouse. This chapter will refer to the marital testimonial privilege, but its relationship to marital incompetency will be explained at an appropriate point.

Because the Federal Rules of Evidence do not codify specific privileges for federal courts, this chapter makes more frequent reference to the Uniform Rules of Evidence (URE) and California Evidence Code (CEC) for examples than do other chapters. There are also references to the Proposed Federal Rules on privileges, which were not ultimately adopted.

A.   GENERAL CONCEPTS OF PRIVILEGE

Privilege (In General)

A rule that gives a witness the option not to testify, or gives another person the option to prevent the witness from testifying, with respect to some particular subject.

Example 10.1:   Don is on trial for murder. The prosecution has evidence that, the day after the crime, Don voluntarily but confidentially confessed the crime to his wife, his attorney, and his clergyman. If these statements were all made under the circumstances required for them to be considered privileged, none of the three confessions is admissible against Don.

As illustrated by Example 10.1, privileges, unlike most exclusionary rules of evidence, are not based on the relevance, trustworthiness, or relative importance of the evidence excluded. Instead, they are generally intended to further some other social (or perhaps political) policy regardless of the effect of that policy on the truth-seeking process. Moreover, privileges are not, like most common law exclusionary rules, primarily aimed at keeping from the jury information that they might misuse; a privilege is designed to keep any trier of fact, whether judge or jury, from learning potentially useful but privileged information.

Terminology.   The person who has the right to keep privileged information from being revealed is the **holder** of the privilege. The holder may or may not be the witness who is asked to reveal the information. The holder **exercises** the privilege by objecting to disclosure or otherwise seeking its enforcement. A failure to exercise it is among the ways a privilege can be **waived,** or lost. These terms are further discussed below or in separate entries.

Types of privilege.   Most privileges are **communication privileges,** that is, they protect from disclosure confidential communications between certain persons. A few privileges, however, are concerned not with communications but with particular information or types of testimony. Thus the marital testimonial privilege is a privilege not to testify against one's spouse regardless of the subject matter of the testimony. Whether the subject matter of a privilege is confidential communications or some other information may determine various of its attributes, from its rationale to how it can be waived.

Communications and facts.   One common thread in communication privileges is that it is the communication itself, not the facts communicated, that is privileged.

Example 10.2: Clyde tells his attorney Ann that he was driving 100 mph when his car hit Paul's. In a lawsuit between Paul and Clyde, Clyde can refuse to reveal, and prevent Ann from revealing, the contents of the attorney-client communication, *qua communication*. In other words, Clyde need not disclose what he told Ann. If, however, Clyde is a witness, he can be asked at what speed he was driving when his car hit Paul's. He cannot claim a privilege just because he told the same fact to his attorney.

Rationale. The impetus for privileges has been traced to the Roman law and such lofty concepts as moral duty and honor. Today, however, the basic justification for most evidentiary privileges, whether protecting communications or other information, is what is usually called the **utilitarian theory**: A privilege exists to protect some relationship, usually through the protection of communications between persons within that relationship, where it is believed that in the absence of the privilege the relationship would be harmed or defeated. Thus, as will be seen in more detail in reference to the specific privileges, the marital privileges protect marriage by protecting confidentiality within it or by preventing the forced testimony of one spouse against the other; the attorney-client privilege protects the attorney-client relationship by encouraging full and candid disclosure by the client; and so forth.

Example 10.3: Dick is uncertain whether he has acted properly in a business transaction and how he should act in future transactions. He explains what he has done to Alice, his attorney, and asks Alice's advice. Alice advises him that his actions probably were lawful, but a court could find otherwise. To be safe, an immediate rescission might mitigate any potential liability. Dick follows Alice's advice. According to the utilitarian theory, were there no privilege for Dick's statements to his attorney, he would be inhibited from giving Alice a full and frank account of his actions, for fear that Alice would divulge, or be forced to divulge, his confidences should the matter ever come to court. Without that full and frank communication, Alice would not be able to advise Dick accurately as to his potential liability or mitigating actions. At best, Dick would have to choose between receiving competent legal advice and preserving his secrets.

Wigmore's four conditions. Dean Wigmore expressed this utilitarian theory for privileges that protect communications (which means most privileges) in the form of four conditions necessary for the establishment of such a privilege: (1) The communication must be intended to be confidential; (2) confidentiality must be essential to maintenance of the relationship

196

between the communicating parties; (3) that relationship must be one that the community strongly desires to encourage; and (4) injury to the relationship from disclosure of such communications must outweigh the benefits of disclosure to the correct disposal of litigation. If all of these conditions are generally satisfied, a privilege should be established. And once established in a jurisdiction, the privilege should be applied in all cases, regardless of whether or not, in a particular case, they seem to be met.

Caveat: Do not confuse the rationale for a privilege and the determination whether it should be adopted, with the application of that privilege once it is adopted. Most privileges, once adopted, are absolute and are not weighed against the need for the evidence in a given case.

Wigmore's four conditions apply equally well in assessing noncommunication privileges, such as the marital testimonial privilege, if we simply ask whether the privilege furthers the policy behind it, and whether that policy outweighs the loss of the evidence.

Lately another, **nonutilitarian theory,** the *protection of privacy,* has been proposed that is not the original basis for most privileges but provides another reason to retain them. For example, it is said that whether or not one believes that protection of confidentiality is necessary to the existence of a healthy marital relationship, to force or permit one party to a confidential marital communication to breach that confidentiality and testify to its contents is a violation of the other communicant's right of privacy.

Related to the above privacy theory is what has been called the **repugnance theory**: The spectacle of a court wresting from a witness the confidential communications of a spouse, a client, or a patient would be repugnant to the public and destroy confidence in the judicial system.

Because privileges are very much a matter of general social and political policy, their scope varies among jurisdictions more than is true of such strictly evidentiary doctrines as those excluding hearsay or opinion. State legislatures are far more likely to agree on the unreliability of hearsay than on the extent to which, for example, confidentiality is necessary to the physician-patient relationship and the fostering of that relationship in general outweighs the search for truth in individual lawsuits.

Compared to similar rules. There are a few rules other than privileges that exclude evidence for policy reasons extraneous to the search for truth. These are primarily the rules found in **FRE 407-410** and similar state rules, concerning evidence of certain acts or statements (such as subsequent repairs, offers to compromise, and plea negotiations) that would be discouraged if they could later be used as admissions of fault. These are discussed in Chapter 5, as *Admissions by Conduct.*

The primary difference between admissions by conduct and privileges is that most privileges are not limited to parties or to a particular proceeding, but they generally may be asserted by any person who fits the description of a holder of the privilege, at any time. This is because most privileges involve the confidentiality of communications necessary to certain relationships, and the relationships would be damaged by revelation whether or not the holder of the privilege were a party or a particular case were pending. In the case of admissions by conduct, once the threat of losing a case is removed, the party's conduct will not be inhibited.

Comment and inference. Courts disagree whether it is permissible for opposing counsel to comment to the jury on the fact that a party has invoked a privilege not to testify or to reveal a confidence, or to urge the jury to draw an adverse inference from that fact. When an accused has a constitutional privilege, such comment or drawing of inferences is prohibited in order not to make assertion of the privilege (such as that against self-incrimination) too "costly" for the defendant to be effective. Nor need the defendant assert the privilege before the jury. The modern trend is to treat nonconstitutional privileges similarly. See, e.g., URE 512, CEC 913, Proposed FRE 513.

Federal Rules. Although a complete set of federal privileges was proposed for the Federal Rules, they were rejected by Congress. See Proposed FRE 501-513. Many were incorporated into the Uniform Rules and some states have adopted them. Under what became **FRE 501,** privileges in federal courts (when applying federal law) are "governed by the common law" as interpreted "in the light of reason and experience." Federal courts can thus look to either federal or state precedents to discover or formulate the appropriate common law rule. They can recognize new privileges or amend existing ones. Where, however, state substantive law applies (primarily in diversity suits), the Rule directs application of state rules of privilege.

Constitutional considerations. In theory, the withholding of relevant evidence to further some public or social interest might be a violation of the rights of the litigant whose case is in need of that evidence. When that litigant is a criminal defendant, those rights are of constitutional magnitude. Nevertheless, at least to the present time, traditional evidentiary privileges that exclude evidence favoring an accused have not been declared per se unconstitutional by the Supreme Court, and in most cases the privilege will be upheld. When, however, there is a direct clash between a defendant's rights and a privilege, a court may either override the privilege completely or interpret it as qualified, weighing the policies on both sides in the particular case. See, e.g., *Governmental Privilege.*

Incompetency distinguished. Although the incompetence of a witness to testify is related to (and may be the origin of certain) privileges, the concepts are analytically distinct. Perhaps the most important difference is that incompetency relates to classes of persons and is absolute; the incompetent person is considered unworthy or unable to give reliable evidence and simply cannot testify. Privileges are rights that are held by certain persons, relating to types of information. In the absence of exercise by a holder, a privilege is waived and the information may be disclosed.

Approach to analysis. When considering any privilege, it is important to ask certain questions about it and apply the answers to the facts of your case. This can be expressed as a

> Rule of Thumb: Analysis of a claim of privilege should include consideration of the subject matter, the holder, the time limitations of the subject matter and time and forum limitations of exercise, and any applicable exceptions or possibility of waiver.

More specifically, one must ask

1. What is the *subject matter* of the privilege? What types of statements, conduct, or testimony does it cover?
2. Who is the *holder* of the privilege? Who is entitled to invoke the privilege, or have it invoked on their behalf? There may be more than one holder of a particular privilege. Note, however, that just because one person is able or required to claim the privilege on behalf of the holder (as an attorney can and usually must on behalf of a client), the holder is still the person on whose behalf it is claimed, and who alone can decide not to claim it.
3. Are there any *time limitations* relating to the privilege? This encompasses both the subject matter (the time period, if any, during which the statement or conduct privileged must have occurred) and the exercise of the privilege (the time period, if any, during which testimony about the subject matter is privileged). In addition, there may sometimes be general *forum limitations* on the privilege's exercise, such as a limitation to criminal cases. (Inability to invoke a privilege in a more specific type of case, such as civil commitment proceedings, or where certain persons are parties, is considered under "exceptions.")
4. Are there any applicable *exceptions* to the exercise of the privilege, or has the holder in any way *waived* it?

These questions can be illustrated by the following example, relating to marital privilege, which is discussed in detail elsewhere:

Example 10.4: Delia is on trial for murder. She confessed the murder to her husband Harry, and the prosecution wishes to call Harry to testify against her. The *subject matter* of the marital testimonial privilege is anything that would be considered against Delia's interest in this proceeding. The subject matter of the spousal communication privilege, on the other hand, is limited to confidential communications between the spouses. The *holder* of either form of privilege may (depending on the jurisdiction) be either Delia, Harry, or both. With respect to *time limitations*, usually the testimonial privilege applies only if Delia and Harry are presently married and may sometimes be limited to facts arising during marriage; the communication privilege requires that the communication took place during marriage, but it applies even if Delia and Harry are not presently married. The testimonial privilege is often limited also to criminal trials. An *exception* might exist if, for example, Delia were being prosecuted for physically abusing Harry or their children. A voluntary disclosure by Delia to her brother might constitute a *waiver*. (Note that some of these considerations would be different in a jurisdiction with marital incompetency instead of a marital testimonial privilege.) See generally *Marital Privilege*.

As each privilege is discussed below, these considerations (to the extent they are applicable or relevant to that privilege) will be listed in abbreviated, checklist form, under the heading "Essentials."

Waiver of Privileges

Intentional or inadvertent surrender of the right to invoke a privilege.

Privileges can be waived by their holder, either deliberately or by inadvertence. If, for example, the holder of a communication privilege voluntarily reveals or consents to the revelation of a significant part of the communication in an unprivileged setting, the privilege may be considered waived as to the entire communication. (Some courts will apply full waiver only if selective waiver would be unfair.) See, e.g., URE 510, CEC 912, Proposed FRE 511. It does not matter that the holder did not intend to waive the privilege.

If, on the other hand, the revelation itself is involuntary (for example, by theft or compelled by a court after rejection of a claim of privilege), it is not a waiver. But if it was accidental in the sense that there was no intention to make the communication at all (such as inadvertently including the privileged document with unprivileged ones in response to a discovery request), some courts will consider the privilege waived, while others will look to the circumstances and considerations of fairness. (Here waiver would probably be of the material disclosed only, not of related materials.)

Waiver can usually be effected only by the holder or by an agent (including the attorney) of the holder, so long as it was an act within the scope of the agency. Most deliberate waivers by an attorney would be attributed to the client.

Eavesdroppers. At common law, **interception** of a privileged communication, as by an eavesdropper, rendered it no longer confidential and so the interceptor could testify to it. In effect, permitting interception (even inadvertently) was like waiving the privilege. Modern rules and decisions treat intercepted communications in different ways. Some prohibit revelation of any privileged communication by an eavesdropper, provided the holder of the privilege took reasonable steps to avoid interception, while others may protect only certain privileges in this way. Thus rules such as CEC 954, URE 502, and Proposed FRE 503 (all respecting attorney-client privilege) allow the holder to refuse to disclose *and to prevent another person from disclosing* the privileged communication. On the other hand, URE 504 (marital privilege) does not protect against disclosure by third parties, whereas CEC 980 does. These distinctions are discussed in detail in specific privilege entries.

B. SPECIFIC PRIVILEGES

Attorney-Client Privilege

An evidentiary privilege for confidential communications between attorney and client. See URE 502; CEC 959-962. See also the related *Work Product Doctrine.*

Essentials:

Holder: Client.

Subject matter: Confidential communications by client to attorney, attorney's response.

Time limitations (subject matter):   From first consultation, whether or not leading to employment.

Time or forum limitations (exercise):   Survives termination of relationship; usually survives client's death.

Principal exceptions: Furtherance of crime or fraud; claimants through same deceased client; breach of duty by attorney or client; lawsuit among joint clients.

Example 10.5:   Cathy is uncertain about the legality of a recent business transaction. She goes to see Alan, an attorney recommended by a friend. During an initial free consultation, she tells Alan what she has done and asks whether her actions were unlawful. Alan says Cathy has probably broken the law, but he is uncertain and it would cost Cathy $500 for the research necessary to find the answer. Cathy decides to take her chances. Later Cathy is prosecuted for the transaction. Cathy can prevent Alan from revealing what she told him about the transaction.

Ethics note: Although the attorney-client privilege controls the attorney's ability to reveal client confidences in court, in most instances, wholly apart from the rules of privilege, it would be unethical for an attorney to reveal client confidences, or to fail to invoke the privilege on behalf of the client when the occasion arises.

Rationale. The rationale for the attorney-client privilege is primarily utilitarian. The attorney-client relationship is important to the legal system and to society, and it cannot properly function unless clients feel free to be candid with their attorneys, telling them "the whole story," including those parts that might incriminate or otherwise prejudice the client.

Holder: As Example 10.5 illustrates, the client is the holder of the attorney-client privilege. If Cathy wishes to permit Alan to testify to their conversation, Alan cannot invoke the privilege to avoid testifying. A client/holder may be an individual, a corporation, or any other entity that is capable of employing a lawyer. Compare *Work Product Doctrine* (attorney also a holder).

Subject matter. The subject matter is whatever conversation the attorney and client had, so long as it was intended to be confidential and was for the purpose of seeking (or, in modern formulations, giving) professional legal advice. It matters not in Example 10.5 that Cathy had no pre-existing professional relationship with Alan when she came to see him, that she paid Alan nothing for the advice, or that she did not ultimately hire Alan or enter into any professional relationship with him.

Even if a professional relationship is established, certain facts are not generally within the privilege. Thus the fact of employment (that Cathy hired Alan as her attorney), the amount of the fee, the identity of the client, or facts about the client that, while communicated to the attorney, anyone could learn (for example, Cathy's appearance or address) are not usually privileged. There are exceptions, however, for unusual circumstances in which these normally innocuous facts would themselves reveal the substance of a confidential communication.

Example 10.6: Colin has not paid his income taxes or filed a return for several years. Colin's attorney Aaron tells him that he can pay his overdue taxes anonymously, so that if his earlier nonpayment comes to light, interest and penalties will have ceased to accrue at the time of payment. Colin pays his overdue taxes to the IRS anonymously, through Aaron. If Aaron is forced to reveal that Colin is his client, anonymity would be lost and the purpose of the provision for such payment defeated. In this instance the identity of Aaron's client will be privileged.

Tangible items.   Just as it is the communication that is privileged and not the fact communicated, if an item of tangible evidence (like a document) is transferred by the client to the attorney, it is no more privileged in the hands of the attorney than it was in the hands of the client; an attorney cannot be used to "launder" or conceal evidence. But again the document must be distinguished from the communication of it:

Example 10.7:   Cosmo is sued for knowingly misrepresenting the value of the painting he sold to Mary. Cosmo sends to Ari, his attorney, a copy of an appraisal of the painting that he had obtained prior to the transaction with Mary, asking Ari if it is of importance. The appraisal indicates that the painting is a worthless copy. Mary would like to prove both the existence of such an appraisal and Cosmo's knowledge of it. If subpoenaed from either Cosmo or Ari, the appraisal must be produced, regardless of whether it was communicated to Ari in connection with Ari's legal services. If, however, Ari is asked where he got the copy, the answer is privileged, since the fact of sending is itself a communication from Cosmo to Ari, one which in effect says, "I am in possession of this appraisal," or even "I consider this appraisal relevant."

A more difficult question arises if the item delivered to the attorney is tangible evidence of a crime, such as a murder weapon. Here there are overlapping issues of privilege and legal ethics. Generally the attorney would be expected to surrender the item voluntarily to the prosecution but need not reveal its source. (This rule usually is not, however, applied to incriminating documentary evidence.)

Representatives of attorney.   Communications to an agent or representative of the attorney, by the client or by the attorney on the client's behalf, are privileged like direct communications to the attorney. Thus statements to a doctor or accountant employed by the attorney to help prepare the client's case are protected. Some courts hold, however, that certain claims or defenses waive this derivative protection. For example, by raising the defense of insanity a criminal defendant may waive the privilege as to statements to a psychiatrist retained by the defense.

Corporate clients.   When the client is a corporation, the "holders" are the corporate officers, although it is not always clear whose communications to the attorney are privileged. Under the so-called **control group test,** only the communications of those participating in or controlling corporate decisions related to the attorney's advice are privileged. This test still prevails in some states, but it was rejected for federal courts by the Supreme Court in *Upjohn Co. v. United States*.[1] While *Upjohn* did not specifically set out a new test, it did list several factors the Court considered important in deciding whether an employee's communication to corporate counsel is privileged:

(1) Whether the corporation's management directed the employee to speak with counsel; (2) whether the communication's purpose was to obtain legal advice for the corporation; (3) whether the employee was aware of being interviewed for this purpose — of the legal implications of the communication; (4) whether the subject matter was within the scope of the employee's duties; and (5) whether the communication was considered and kept confidential by the corporation. Many states have now adopted some version of the *Upjohn* test. See, e.g., URE 502(a)(2).

Time limitations: The privilege attaches from the time the client first communicates with the attorney. It continues during and after the termination of the professional relationship, and usually it even survives the death of the client. Of course, after the client's death (or the dissolution of an entity) the privilege would have to be invoked by the client's personal representative or other appropriate successor.

Exceptions: The **crime or fraud exception,** probably the most commonly invoked, denies the privilege if the attorney's advice was sought to aid in the planning or commission of a crime or fraud. See URE 502(d)(1); CEC 956. (Some courts apply it as well to furtherance of a tort not involving fraud.) This must be carefully distinguished from seeking advice on the legal ramifications of a crime or fraud already committed, or as to whether planned actions would constitute a crime or fraud. Both of these come within the proper scope of the attorney-client relationship, as does advice on how the legal consequences of a crime or fraud, once committed, can be lawfully avoided.

Example 10.8:   Cameron has been arrested for robbing a bank. He tells his attorney Ada he committed the crime and asks if Ada can "get him off." After a careful review of the facts of Cameron's arrest, Ada concludes that, despite his guilt, Cameron may well be able to avoid prosecution on a technicality. All of the above consultation is protected by the attorney-client privilege and is not subject to the exception for furthering a crime or fraud.

Example 10.9:   Same facts as Example 10.8, except that Cameron tele-

1. 449 U.S. 383 (1981).

phones Ada, tells her what he has done, and asks Ada if she can help him to dispose of the "hot" money. Ada suggests a money launderer she knows, and adds that in any event she probably can get Cameron off on a technicality. None of the "consultation" is privileged, because Cameron was seeking not legal advice but assistance in the commission of the original crime and to make Ada an accessory after the fact.

Traditionally the improper advice must be sought or at least acquiesced in by the client; a few courts apply the exception even if the attorney initiated and the client did not acquiesce in the tainted advice.

Another major exception is for parties who are both claiming through a now-deceased client who was the holder of the privilege. See URE 902(d)(2); CEC 957. Note, however, that *both* parties must claim through the client, not just one.

Example 10.10: Tess's intestate heir Hilda contests Tess's will. In the contest between Hilda and the beneficiaries under the will, as both sides claim "through" Tess (one by will, the other by intestate succession), communications by Tess to her attorney are not privileged. Neither side can prevent testimony as to otherwise-admissible communications by Tess to her attorney.

Example 10.11: Tara's will leaves her estate to Ben. Clara, who was Tara's companion during Tara's last illness, files a contract claim against the estate, alleging that Tara promised her a bequest of $10,000 in consideration of her services. In this action, Clara would be considered a "stranger" who seeks to take *against* Tara's estate, rather than *through* Tara. Therefore the exception would not apply and Tara's personal representative would be entitled to invoke the privilege against revelation of Tara's communications to her attorney.

The distinction illustrated in Examples 10.10 and 10.11 has not been a popular one.

Notice how the exception being discussed dovetails with the hearsay exception for state of mind. Under the latter, statements of memory or belief are generally inadmissible to prove the fact remembered or believed, but statements by a testator relating to the execution or terms of a will are within the exception. Therefore, in a will contest like Example 10.10, not only would Tess's attorney be permitted to testify to Tess's confidential communications about her will, but those communications could be offered to prove the truth of the matters that they state.

A third important exception is for allegations of breach of duty by the attorney or the client. This usually arises in litigation involving both attorney and client, but in many jurisdictions it also covers litigation with third persons when such an issue arises. See URE 502(d)(3); CEC 958. The most common applications, of course, are an allegation of malpractice by the client (a suit for damages or a claim by a criminal defendant of incompetent representation) or a suit by the attorney against the client for nonpayment of fees.

The other common exceptions are for documents attested by the attorney (where the attorney has signed as a witness) and communications by joint clients to the attorney in a later action between the clients.

Waiver. The easiest way to waive this (or any) privilege is simply to fail to assert it when the opportunity arises. Other common forms of waiver include voluntary disclosure to a third person under nonprivileged circumstances and voluntary but inadvertent disclosure. The privilege can also be waived by taking such actions in a lawsuit as specifically raising the issue of "advice of counsel" as a part of a claim or defense. See *Waiver (In General)*.

Work Product Doctrine

The limited immunization from discovery or other disclosure of materials prepared by an attorney for litigation. It is not technically a privilege, for reasons indicated below; but its operation is very close to that of a privilege, and it often is applied in conjunction with the attorney-client privilege.

The modern work product doctrine is based on the Supreme Court's 1947 opinion in *Hickman v. Taylor.* It is largely embodied for federal courts in FRCP 26(b)(3). See also FRCrP 16(a)(2), 16(b)(2).

Essentials:
Holder: Both client and attorney.
Subject matter: Materials prepared in anticipation of litigation; mental impressions, theories, and plans of attorney.
Time limitations (subject matter):   Prepared when litigation pending or reasonably anticipated.
Time or forum limitations (exercise):   Usually same or subsequent proceeding; sometimes only same or related proceeding.
Principal exceptions: Substantial need, inability to obtain equivalent elsewhere; furtherance of crime or fraud.

Example 10.12:   Clay sues Doris for negligence following a collision between their cars. He consults attorney Alex, telling Alex that he might have been going over the speed limit at the time of the acci-

2. 329 U.S. 495 (1947).

dent. Alex takes verbatim notes of Clay's statements. He then interviews several eyewitnesses to the collision, noting any significant
statements and adding his own impressions of their reliability and
suitability as witnesses in court. He also takes a written, signed statement from each. During discovery, Doris' attorney requests copies
of Alex's notes and memoranda concerning the case. All would be
protected by the work-product doctrine (as qualified below). In addition, Alex's notes containing Clay's admission would also be protected by the attorney-client privilege.

Comparison to attorney-client privilege. It is important to distinguish
the work-product doctrine from the attorney-client privilege, especially
since they often arise in similar circumstances and may well overlap. The
principal differences, as more fully explained below, are illustrated by Table
10.1.

Holder: Unlike the attorney-client privilege, the work-product protection may be invoked by the client or by the attorney on the latter's own
behalf (although not contrary to the client's interests).

Subject matter: All materials prepared in anticipation of litigation are
protected. Those that represent or reveal the attorney's "mental processes,"
however, are distinguished from those that merely contain facts or data (see
below). Pre-existing documents or those prepared for other reasons, even if
they prove useful in the case, are not included. There does not, however,
have to be an actual case filed if litigation is reasonably certain to occur.

Time or forum limitations: So long as the material was prepared in
anticipation of litigation, it need not have been prepared during litigation.
Some courts limit the immunity to the litigation for which the material
was prepared. Most, however, extend it either to all subsequent litigation or
to any that is related to the original case.

Table 10.1

	Attorney-Client Privilege	Work Product Doctrine
Holder	Client	Client or attorney
Subject matter	Confidential communications to or from client	Any material prepared for litigation
Applicability	~~Absolute~~ *not*	~~Qualified~~ *limited*
Use	Discovery or trial	Usually discovery

Principal exceptions: The work product doctrine is one of qualified, or limited immunity. "Built into" the doctrine is the qualification that an opponent can reach attorney work product by demonstrating (as formulated in *Hickman v. Taylor* and FRCP 26(b)(3)): (1) a substantial need for the information; and (2) an inability to obtain the substantial equivalent of the material by other means.

Mental impressions. With respect to this qualification, however, there is a significant difference between work product representing an attorney's mental impressions and other materials. For the former, sometimes called **opinion work product,** a much more stringent test is applied, and some courts make this aspect of the immunity absolute. At the very least, according to FRCP 26 as interpreted by the Supreme Court in *Upjohn Co. v. United States,* "disclosure of mental impressions, conclusions, opinions, or legal theories" would require "a far stronger showing of necessity and unavailability by other means."

Thus in Example 10.12 above, while the written statements of the witnesses would be discoverable on an ordinary showing of need and inability otherwise to obtain the information, Alex's impressions and other subjective conclusions respecting the interviews would be either absolutely immune or require a much stronger showing of need and inability. The verbatim notes of Clay's statement might be treated as ordinary work product, despite its being a record of an oral interview; it seems to contain no mental impressions of the attorney. (It would, however, probably qualify under the attorney-client privilege since Clay was seeking legal advice.)

Crime or fraud. In addition to the inherent qualification of the work-product doctrine, an exception for material relating to furtherance of a crime or fraud is applied just as it is to the attorney-client privilege.

Waiver. As for the attorney-client privilege, voluntary disclosure waives the work product protection. A waiver for one purpose, however, is not necessarily a waiver for both, as the two are held independently of one another. For work product purposes, waiver is by disclosure to the opposing party, or by actions that make such disclosure likely, since it is only the opposing party from whom work product is being protected.

Waiver will also result from use of work product to refresh a witness's memory (see FRE 612), at least when used during testimony in court. Courts (like federal courts) that may require disclosure of writings used to refresh memory before trial disagree whether such use of attorney work product waives the immunity.

Marital Privileges (In General)

Evidentiary privileges based on the relationship of marriage. Common alternative designations are **husband-wife privilege** and **spousal privilege.**

There are two distinct marital privileges: one relating to testimony against a spouse, and the other protecting confidential marital communications. It is easy to confuse the elements of these two privileges, or to treat them as a single "marital privilege"; but although they may overlap in a given case, they are quite different in both rationale and operation, and some jurisdictions may recognize only one or the other.

Marital Testimonial Privilege

An evidentiary privilege that excludes testimony by one spouse against the other. See URE 504; CEC 970-73. Compare *Marital Communications Privilege.*

Essentials:

Holder: Usually witness spouse; sometimes party spouse.

Subject matter: Testimony contrary to party spouse's interest.

Time limitations (subject matter): Usually none; possibly marriage at time of alleged crime.

Time or forum limitations (exercise): During marriage; perhaps only criminal trials.

Principal exceptions: Proceedings between spouses, spouses as joint actors, crime or tort against witness spouse or minor child of either.

Example 10.13: George is prosecuted for robbing a bank, using a toy pistol. His wife Martha knows that George recently purchased a toy pistol, although the couple has no children. Martha cannot be compelled to testify (or, in some jurisdictions, can be prevented by George from testifying) to this fact.

In some jurisdictions a criminal defendant's spouse cannot even be called as a witness by the prosecution, obviating any need to invoke the privilege on the stand.

Rationale. The rationale is utilitarian and nonutilitarian. Marriage is a favored institution in our society, and marital harmony will be threatened or destroyed if a spouse like Martha is forced to testify against her husband; and the spectacle of forcing Martha to testify against George, or holding her in contempt if she refuses, is repugnant to us and would place the judicial system in a bad light.

Incompetency distinguished. Originally one was simply incompetent to testify for or against one's spouse. (Technically, the inability to testify *for* was incompetence, the inability to testify *against* more of a privilege.) In some jurisdictions the privilege is still designated as incompetency. In Example 10.13, if incompetent, Martha simply cannot testify, whether she wants to or not, and even if George wants her to. If a state characterizes a witness's disability as a matter of competency, rather than privilege, the rule applicable in federal court is determined under FRE 601 (competency), rather than FRE 501 (privilege). See generally *Incompetency*.

Comparison to Communications Privilege. For a chart comparing this privilege to the marital communications privilege, see the latter entry below.

<u>Holder</u>: Although earlier law often gave the privilege to the accused spouse or to both, under many modern formulations (including the Uniform Rules and in federal courts, following *Trammel v. United States*[3]) the privilege can be invoked only by the witness spouse. As the supposed basis for the privilege is the preservation of marital harmony, it is said that if the witness is willing to testify, there probably is little harmony left to preserve. Nor is permitting a willing spouse to testify as repugnant to our sensibilities.

<u>Subject matter</u>: The privilege covers only testimony that would be against the interests of the party spouse. Thus if in Example 10.13 Martha knows that George was with her shopping at the time of the robbery, she cannot refuse to testify in his favor to that effect.

<u>Time or forum limitations</u>: *Subject matter.* The testimony need not relate in any way to the spouses' marriage. Traditionally it also did not matter whether the witness and party spouses had been married at the time to which the testimony refers (for example, the time of the alleged crime). Because, however, this made it possible for a criminal defendant to "marry a witness into silence" after committing a crime, many jurisdictions now limit the privilege to testimony about a crime that occurred (or with which the defendant was charged) after the date of marriage. See, e.g., CEC 972(f).

Exercise. The witness and party must be married at the time of trial. If they are not, there is no marriage to damage by the testimony, and no repugnance in the public eye. To date, actual marriage is required; a modern "equivalent" will not do.

Criminal cases, party spouses. Most (but not all) jurisdictions limit the privilege to criminal cases. It also traditionally is limited to proceedings in which the nonwitness spouse is a party (usually a criminal defendant — see URE 504(b)); but it may in some jurisdictions be available for testimony

3. 445 U.S. 40 (1980).

against a spouse in any proceeding, even if the adversely affected spouse is not a party (see CEC 970).

Principal exceptions: The privilege is inapplicable in an action for a crime (or tort) committed against the witness spouse, or in an action between the spouses. Often it is also denied where a crime or tort has been alleged against a minor child of either spouse. There are many other exceptions that may exist in specific jurisdictions. See, e.g., CEC 972.

"Non-access" privilege.   A few courts apply the old rule that a husband or wife cannot testify to matters that would "bastardize" a child born after their marriage. This may or may not be limited to evidence of "non-access" of husband to wife and to the issue of legitimacy. It is of no effect in most modern jurisdictions.

Marital Communication Privilege

An evidentiary privilege that protects against the disclosure of confidential communications between spouses. See generally URE 504(a); CEC 980-87. Compare Marital Testimonial Privilege. This privilege is sometimes called the **spousal communication privilege** or the **marital confidences privilege.**

Essentials:

Holder: Usually communicating spouse; sometimes witness spouse or both.

Subject matter: Confidential communications, regardless of content. Some conduct may be included.

Time limitations (subject matter):   Communications made during marriage.

Time or forum limitations (exercise):   None; usually survives termination of marriage and death of holder.

Principal exceptions: Proceedings between spouses, spouses as joint actors, crime or tort against witness spouse or minor child of either.

Rationale: Like the testimonial privilege, it is utilitarian and nonutilitarian. Protecting marital communications fosters the marital relationship. Even if it did not, to force confidential, even intimate marital communications from the lips of a spouse would be repugnant to our sense of decency and propriety. And here the privacy rationale is most telling, given the constitutional protection given to marital privacy in other contexts.

Comparison to testimonial privilege.   It is very important to distinguish the two marital privileges, testimonial and communication. They operate quite independently of each other, although there is a great deal of overlap.

Thus the rules applicable to each must always be applied to the circumstances separately to determine whether one, the other, or both can be invoked.

Table 10.2 sets out the primary differences between the two privileges (using the majority position for each factor for convenience).

Example 10.14: George has robbed a bank. At home that evening, George tells his wife Martha what he has done. Later a mutual friend tells Martha where George stashed the stolen money. George is arrested and tried for robbery. At trial, under the *testimonial privilege*, Martha as holder may refuse to testify against George by revealing *either* the communication *or* the location of the money, provided she and George are still married at the time of trial. Under the *communication privilege*, since he and Martha were married at the time, George's statement probably will be presumed confidential and he, as the communicating spouse and holder, will be able to prevent Martha from revealing what he told her, but *not* what their friend told her. They need not still be married at the time of trial.

Holder: Modern approaches to this privilege generally make the communicating spouse the holder. See, e.g., URE 504. Since the theory is that confidential communications will be inhibited if they might later be subject to revelation, it is the spouse making the statement, not the one receiving it, who stands to be inhibited. Moreover, if on the stand the communicating spouse wishes to reveal the secret, the usual rationales of preserving marital harmony and avoiding repugnance would seem of little moment. Neverthe-

Table 10.2

	Testimonial privilege	*Communication privilege*
Holder	Witness spouse (or both)	Communicating spouse (or both)
Subject matter	Any testimony "against" spouse	Confidential communications
Time limitations (subject matter)	None (or married at time of crime)	During marriage
Time or forum limitations (exercise)	During marriage; criminal cases, spouse a party	None

212

less, some jurisdictions continue to vest the privilege in both spouses. See, e.g., CEC 980; but cf. CEC 987 (criminal defendant can force spouse to disclose communication to which defendant was party).

<u>Subject matter</u>: Only confidential communications made during marriage are included. Communications between spouses are generally assumed to be confidential, unless the subject matter or circumstances negate that assumption. But if there is a third person present, even a family member other than a child unable to understand, confidentiality is usually destroyed.

Unlike the attorney-client privilege, the usual rule is that eavesdroppers or others who come into possession of marital communications may testify to them, even if the communicating spouse attempted to keep them confidential. See URE 504. Nevertheless, some jurisdictions do protect against third-party disclosure (see, e.g., CEC 980). Even courts that permit interceptors to disclose confidential marital communications generally will draw the line at interception arranged or conspired in by the recipient spouse.

Civil cases. Unlike the marital testimonial privilege, the communication privilege usually applies in civil as well as criminal cases. Neither spouse need be a party to the case in which it is asserted.

Spousal conduct. Sometimes conduct of a spouse communicates information to the other spouse. If the conduct is an intended substitute for a verbal statement (such as nodding the head to indicate agreement), such **communicative conduct** is clearly privileged. If, however, it is intended as **noncommunicative conduct**, in many jurisdictions it is not privileged. In others virtually any conduct that the other spouse would not have observed, or even information that the other spouse would not have obtained, but for the marital relationship is privileged, at least if the acting spouse relied on the sanctity of the marital relationship. This includes clearly noncommunicative conduct and so goes well beyond the traditional form of the privilege.

Example 10.15: George has robbed a bank. He brings the stolen money (in bags marked "Bank Property") into the house. Saying nothing to his wife Martha as he enters the kitchen where she is preparing dinner, George puts the money into the kitchen cupboard. He then turns to Martha and gives her the "V for victory" sign. Martha is not surprised, because she knows from long association with George that he is lazy and in constant need of money.

At George's trial, courts that adhere to the standard and traditional meaning of "communication" would consider privileged the intentionally communicative conduct of the victory sign but deny George any privilege with respect to his noncommunicative conduct with the money. Courts that take an expansive view of spousal communication, however, would probably apply the privilege to the act of hiding the money, since it is unlikely George would have done it in front of Martha had he not trusted her to keep silent about it; and it is unlikely she would have observed it were she not his wife. Some would even apply it to testimony about George's laziness and need for money, to the extent at least that as George's wife Martha was in a unique position to observe those characteristics.

Time and forum limitations: *Subject matter.* The privilege applies only to communications made during marriage, in keeping with the privilege's rationale of fostering the marital relationship. As in the case of the testimonial privilege, "marriage" is generally defined narrowly, to include only legal marriage (although a legal "common law" marriage would qualify), and not equivalent nonmarital relationships. Thus if George and Martha in Example 10.15 had been living together in exactly the way spouses do for 15 years at the time of the crime, and even if they got married before trial, if they were not legally married at the time of the communications there is no privilege. There may, however, be an exception found if the communicating spouse was unaware of the marriage's illegality or voidability due to the other's bigamy or fraud.

Exercise. So long as the communication was made during marriage, it remains privileged thereafter whether or not the marriage survives. In Example 10.15, if the day after the crime Martha, in disgust with George, leaves him and they are divorced by the time of trial, the privilege remains. And even if George is dead and his estate sued by the bank for return of the money, generally his personal representative can invoke the privilege in his place.

Principal exceptions: There generally is no privilege in a proceeding in which one spouse has sued the other, or when one spouse is charged with a crime or tort against the person or property of the other or against a child of either. See URE 504(c). States may have a variety of other exceptions, for specific types of proceedings (such as bigamy — see CEC 985(c)) or communications (such as those that aid the commission of a crime or fraud — see CEC 981).

Physician-Patient Privilege

An evidentiary privilege that protects against the disclosure of confidential communications between doctor and patient. See URE 503; CEC 990-1007. See also Psychotherapist-Patient Privilege.

> Essentials:
> <u>Holder:</u>   Patient.
> <u>Subject matter:</u>   Confidential communications to physician, for purpose of treatment; possibly information acquired by observation or testing.
> <u>Time limitations (subject matter):</u>   None.
> <u>Time or forum limitations (exercise):</u>   None; usually survives death of patient.
> <u>Principal exceptions:</u>   Patient-litigant; particular types of proceedings (e.g., child abuse, will contests).

There was no physician-patient privilege at common law. Although it is widely criticized as unnecessary or useless, most jurisdictions now recognize it in some form. (URE 503 makes its adoption optional.) Even where recognized, it is one of the most limited of privileges, so riddled with exceptions as to be of little practical effect in most litigation. Because the pattern of coverage and exceptions varies so widely among the states, it is more dangerous to rely on generalities here than for most other privileges. (As usual, however, the most common rules are discussed unless otherwise indicated.)

This discussion is of the privilege for communications made to a physician only; there usually is a separate privilege (although it may be contained in the same rule) for communications to a psychiatrist or psychotherapist.

Federal courts.   As an example of the above variation, federal courts are divided as to whether to recognize a physician-patient privilege; some do, but several do not. In instances in which state law provides the rule of decision, however, state privilege law applies (FRE 501).

Rationale.   Originally the rationale for the physician-patient privilege was utilitarian: protection of the physician-patient relationship. Because, however, of a patient's strong motivation to tell a doctor the truth in seeking treatment (compare the hearsay exception for statements to physicians for diagnosis or treatment), this rationale seems weaker than for other privileges. Of late, weight has been placed on the protection of privacy and the sanctity of patient confidences as an additional rationale for the privilege.

Example 10.16:   Pat sees Doc for treatment of a venereal disease. Pat's former lover Larry later sues Pat for failing to tell Larry of her condition and transmitting the disease to him. Pat probably has a privilege to prevent Doc from testifying about her communications during her consultation with him, or from revealing his observations of her condition that he then made.

Holder: The patient, as the person who would be inhibited from full revelation to the doctor or embarrassed by public disclosure, is the holder of the physician-patient privilege. It can, however, be asserted on behalf of a patient who is unable to assert it personally. Thus in Example 10.16 Pat's guardian, if she has one, can invoke the privilege; and after Pat has died, her personal representative can assert the privilege in a suit against her estate. The physician is usually presumed to be authorized to assert the privilege on behalf of the patient. See URE 503(c); CEC 994(c); cf. CEC 995 (physician required to invoke where applicable).

Subject matter: Some statutes expressly apply only to communications as such (e.g., URE 503(b)); others include observations of the doctor, results of tests, and the like (e.g., CEC 992). Many of the former type have been interpreted as if more broadly worded. Observations are not covered, however, to the extent persons other than the physician could as easily have made them. In Example 10.16, the doctor's observation of a rash on Pat's face would not be included; a rash on her stomach would be.

The doctor's diagnosis or other statements to the patient related to treatment, and not just communications from patient to physician, should be privileged.

As is true of other communication privileges, the communication must be intended to be confidential to be privileged. Here, however, the presence of many third persons will usually be tolerated, so long as they are there to assist the patient or the doctor or are otherwise reasonably necessary to the process of diagnosis or treatment. Thus the presence of a patient's close family members or a doctor's nurse or technical assistant generally will not destroy confidentiality. Like the attorney-client privilege (and unlike marital privilege), there usually is protection against eavesdroppers, at least if the patient reasonably expected confidentiality.

Diagnosis or treatment. The privilege applies only to communications made for the purpose of, and relevant to, obtaining treatment of a disease or injury. Thus if the doctor was consulted only for the purpose of acquiring life insurance, or for obtaining expert testimony in court, there generally is no privilege.

Identity, fact of consultation. The identity of the patient or the fact that a doctor has been consulted are not usually considered confidential communications. If, however, these facts would reveal the nature of the communication respecting treatment, they may be privileged. In Example 10.16, if Doc is a specialist in venereal diseases, the fact and timing of Pat's consultation with him might reveal the very fact sought to be kept confidential — Pat's belief that she had such a disease — and it should be privileged.

Time or forum limitations: The privilege applies from the time the physician-patient relationship is established.

Generally the privilege survives the death of the patient and can be invoked by a personal representative.

Principal exceptions: There are so many and varied exceptions to the physician-patient privilege that it is often said that the exceptions swallow the privilege, making it risky to depend upon.

The most common exception, and that which makes the privilege inoperative when patients would most like to invoke it, is the **patient-litigant exception.** See, e.g., URE 503(c)(3); CEC 996. With varying strictness, this exception denies a privilege with respect to any claim or defense in which the medical condition for which the physician was consulted is placed in issue. This includes (and in some jurisdictions is limited to) cases in which the patient sues or defends based on specific personal injuries. It does not include, however, a general defense or denial when the opposing party is the one who has raised the issue of the patient's medical condition.

Example 10.17: As in Example 10.16, Pat has consulted Doc for treatment of venereal disease. If Pat sues Larry for infecting her with the disease, she cannot invoke the privilege with respect to what she may have told Doc (or any other physician, for that matter) about it. But if subsequent lover Lon sues Pat for transmitting the disease to him, her mere denial of the allegation would not affect the privilege.

Other specific proceedings in which the privilege may not apply include will contests, actions between the physician and patient, matters involving child abuse or child custody, and either certain serious or all criminal proceedings.

Some statutes include exceptions similar to those for attorney-client privilege, such as consultations in aid of a crime or tort or when both parties claim through a deceased patient. See, e.g., CEC 997, 1000.

Finally, when a statute requires a physician to report certain observations to governmental authorities (such as signs of child abuse or gunshot wounds), the privilege will not prevent or excuse the making of the report. Nevertheless, in some states the privilege would remain with respect to any other disclosures of that information.

Waiver. Many of the exceptions just discussed can be viewed alternatively as instances of waiver of an existing privilege. Thus even if particular communications meet all of the requirements for privilege, if the patient/ holder then puts the relevant medical condition in issue in a subsequent lawsuit, that action waives the privilege that would otherwise exist, and that still exists to the extent of matters not related to the issue raised.

Testimony by the patient about the privileged communication (especially on direct) waives the privilege; in some courts testimony only about the condition is also a waiver.

Psychotherapist-Patient Privilege

An evidentiary privilege that protects against the disclosure of confidential communications between psychotherapist and patient. See URE 503; CEC 1010-27. See also Physician-Patient Privilege.

<u>Essentials</u>:

<u>Holder</u>: Patient.

<u>Subject matter</u>: Confidential communications to psychotherapist; possibly information acquired by observation or testing.

<u>Time limitations (subject matter)</u>: None.

<u>Time or forum limitations (exercise)</u>: None; usually survives death of patient.

<u>Principal exceptions</u>: Patient-litigant, particular types of proceedings (e.g., civil commitment, child custody).

This privilege is more accepted and widespread than the older physician-patient privilege, existing in some form in every state. Most of its characteristics are the same as the physician-patient privilege, and often the two privileges are contained in the same rule (e.g., URE 503). Therefore, only those aspects of the privilege that differ from the physician-patient privilege will be discussed here; for other aspects, see *Physician-Patient Privilege*.

Federal courts recognize this privilege, the Supreme Court having approved its adoption as a development of the common law under **FRE 501**.

Rationale. Although the utilitarian rationale of fostering a favored relationship applies here as it does to the physician-patient privilege, it is widely believed that total candor is much more necessary to the psychotherapist-patient relationship than it is to that of physician and patient. Furthermore, the consequences to society of a lack of privilege would be more serious, because (again unlike the case of persons with physical illnesses) those most in need of psychological help would be reluctant to seek it, and if untreated they would pose a serious threat to society. This has led not only to greater acceptance of the psychotherapist-patient privilege, but also to its often broader provisions.

Relationships covered. Because psychological therapy and assistance is provided by so many classes of professionals, the privilege may be granted broadly to all of these relationships. For example, URE 503 includes both medical doctors and licensed psychologists; CEC 1010 includes everything from these to qualified registered nurses, marriage and child counselors, clinical social workers, and the assistants, interns, and trainees who support them. (The latter assistants would usually be included anyway to the extent they are assisting the principal practitioner.) The federal privilege includes licensed social workers, as do most state versions. *Caveat:* If a state has a separate statute for medical doctors and psychotherapists, it is possible that by definition psychiatrists will fit within only the former, with the anomalous result that a relationship with a medically-trained and licensed therapist will enjoy less protection than that with a therapist who lacks a medical degree.

Exceptions and waiver. This privilege is more likely to cover criminal cases, because of the danger that those who have committed or are afraid they might commit criminal acts will refuse treatment, with the obvious result. There would generally be an exception for civil commitment proceedings, and in many courts for child custody hearings. A criminal defendant's insanity plea generally waives the privilege; if not, the defendant's subsequent introduction of evidence of insanity will do so. Otherwise, the exceptions tend to be the same as or similar to those for the physician-patient privilege.

A few states balance the patient's interest against the need for the evidence in each case. Most states, and the federal courts, do not.

Clergy-Penitent Privilege

An evidentiary privilege that protects against the disclosure of confidential communications to a member of the clergy or similar religious functionary, in that person's professional capacity as a spiritual advisor. See URE 505; CEC 1030-34. The privilege is also variously known as the **priest-penitent privilege** (as at common law) and the **religious privilege** (as under the Uniform Rules).

The privilege at common law was first accepted in Ireland, to protect the confessional of the Catholic Church, and it remained quite narrow for some time. Modern rules are much broader, however, and generally protect confidential communications within any recognized religious tradition.

Essentials:

Holder: Usually penitent; sometimes also or only clergy.

Subject matter: Confidential (may be limited to "penitential") communications to clergy.

Time limitations (subject matter):   None.

Time or forum limitations (exercise):   None; usually survives death of penitent.

Principal exceptions: None specifically attached to this privilege; waiver possible.

Rationale: The common rationale for the clergy-penitent privilege is utilitarian — one must be free to speak candidly to one's priest, minister, rabbi, or equivalent religious functionary, and clergy must be protected against being forced to divulge penitents' confidences. Religion is an institution our society desires to foster, or at least not to hinder.

England has not adopted such a privilege, apparently because it is felt there that no court would ever order a religious communication to be revealed, and if it did the cleric would never reveal it. American authorities have put less trust in the courts in this respect; to the extent, however, that it could be argued that no privilege is needed, the societal repugnance at forcing or attempting to force a penitent or cleric to reveal such secrets sufficiently justifies its existence.

Holder: The penitent (or "communicant") generally is a holder of the privilege, although the cleric can invoke the privilege on the penitent's behalf. See URE 505(c). Many statutes also permit clergy to invoke the privilege independently of the penitent (see, e.g., CEC 1034), and more rarely the cleric may be deemed the sole holder.

Subject matter: Some statutes limit the privilege to penitential communications or even, more explicitly, to confessions. Others refer generally to communications. Whatever its designation, it may be limited to communications in the nature of confessions and the seeking of spiritual counsel, or it may be interpreted broadly to include any communications that properly constitute a part of the clergyman's function within the church.

In keeping with the above, the communication must be for or within the purposes covered by the statute. It is not enough that one speaks to a cleric in private, for example to seek assistance as a friend rather than as a spiritual advisor; nor is it sufficient to seek marital advice if the privilege is limited to spiritual counseling.

The statute may require or imply that, under the tenets of the subject religion, the cleric be obligated to keep the communication secret.

The privilege is generally available to prevent eavesdroppers and other interceptors of the communication from revealing it.

Who qualifies as clergy. Although the clergy-penitent privilege was originally intended chiefly for the Catholic confessional and was designated "priest-penitent" privilege, modern statutes use general language and are clear in their inclusion of all (at least traditional) religions. Many specifically mention not only priests but ministers, rabbis, and even Christian Science practitioners. Clearly, exclusion of any arguably legitimate religion or denomination would be both poor politics and poor constitutional law.

Time or forum limitations: The clergy-penitent privilege attaches whenever the proper type of communication is made.

The privilege may be invoked although the penitent is no longer a member of the religious faith in question, and it usually survives the death of the penitent. A few statutes limit it to civil cases.

Principal exceptions: There may be no exceptions specifically attached to the clergy-penitent privilege, and certainly not the litany of exceptions that accompany most communication privileges. Given the nature of the communications that would come within the privilege, none may be needed; and if the "confessional" or equivalent is to remain inviolate, it must not be subject to too many official breaches.

Waiver, however, is possible as it is with other communication privileges. When there are joint holders of the privilege (cleric and penitent), a waiver by one probably waives the privilege as to the other as well. See CEC 912.

Governmental Privileges

Evidentiary privileges that protect against the disclosure of certain official information or secrets of state. See URE 508; CEC 1040.

There are, in fact, several different privileges that the government can invoke to protect information that it deems necessary or advisable to keep secret, all of which are discussed below. They may be set out separately in a statute or they may be included in one general statement of privilege, and some may be available while others are not. Those specific privileges are: **state secrets** (or **military and diplomatic secrets**) **privilege**; **executive privilege**; **agency policy deliberations privilege**; and the privilege for **law enforcement investigatory files.** The latter two may be included in a more generalized **official information** or **governmental information** privilege. Discussed in a separate entry are the so-called informer's privilege and the grand jury privilege.

Essentials:

Holder: The government.

Subject matter: various, from state secrets to agency deliberations.

Time limitations (subject matter):   None.

Time or forum limitations (exercise):   For some, none; others may end when the relevant subject matter ends.

Principal exceptions: Where privilege is qualified, sufficient showing of need for the evidence.

The privilege for military and diplomatic secrets was definitively discussed by the Supreme Court in *United States v. Reynolds*;[4] similar illumina-

4. 345 U.S. 1 (1953).

tion of executive privilege is found in the Court's decision in *United States v. Nixon*.[5]

State privileges may or may not follow the format of federal ones. For example, URE 508 adopts no specific governmental privileges, but only those created by federal statutes that the state is required under the Constitution to recognize, together of course with any created by the state's own constitution or statutes. CEC 1040, on the other hand, creates a specific privilege for "official information."

Various state and federal statutes, ranging from the Interstate Commerce Act to "hit and run" statutes, require a person to make a report of a condition or event. Such statutes may at the same time create a **privilege for required reports.** On the other hand, if a required report is public information, it may not be privileged. E.g., CEC 1026.

Rationale: The rationale for governmental privileges is strongly utilitarian. Revelation of the communications involved here could compromise national security, impair presidential decisionmaking, and impede the operations of governmental agencies and officials. Since, however, there is no perceived repugnance to forcing governmental officials to reveal their secrets and no issue of personal privacy, most of these privileges are qualified only and give way to a stronger, competing need for the information in litigation.

To some extent required reports privileges may be intended not just to protect confidentiality and encourage such reports, but to anticipate a claim of self-incrimination privilege on the part of the person required to report.

FOIA. Governmental privilege in federal courts is mostly common law. The **Freedom of Information Act** (FOIA), however, which grants the public access to most government documents, contains certain exceptions, information not available to the public. Information available to the public is, of course, also available to litigants (thus "not privileged"). Information excepted from public access will generally also be unavailable (and thus "privileged") in court; but this is not necessarily true, as some information to which the general public need not have access may still be available to the litigant who can show a specific need for it. The privileges for agency policy deliberations and law enforcement investigative files, discussed below, are specifically recognized as exemptions from access by the FOIA.

In addition, specific federal statutes may deem certain information classified or otherwise unavailable, providing a basis for a claim of privilege.

Distinguished from other privileges. In several ways, governmental privileges are different from most other privileges. First, they are not limited to communications as such, although they do involve confidential information. Second, some of them are qualified, not absolute. Third, if they are

5. 418 U.S. 683 (1974).

successfully invoked, the court may be empowered to "compensate" the other party for the loss of evidence by various means, including dismissal. Finally, at least presidential privilege has been held to be constitutionally based.

Holder: The government is the holder of all of the privileges discussed here, with the exception of the required reports privilege. If the government does not invoke the privilege, a private litigant cannot do so on either the government's or the litigant's own behalf. It must be invoked by the proper governmental official, in the case of state secrets privilege by the head of the affected department.

Subject matter: The subject matter of governmental privileges is quite varied. Military and diplomatic secrets, and secrets of state generally, are clearly protected. Presidential privilege is for the confidential advice and deliberations between the president and his advisors, essentially a communications privilege. The agency policy deliberations privilege covers just that: communications among governmental officials related to the formulation of policy, including the evaluation of alternative courses of action and preliminary proposals, whether or not they are eventually adopted. The privilege for law enforcement investigative files is self-explanatory.

Time or forum limitations: There are few time limitations relating to when the communication in question was made. The agency policy deliberations privilege applies only to communications made before the policy in question was finally adopted.

Most of these privileges last only as long as they are needed; and since most are qualified only, a court weighing need against cost will give no weight to a need that has lapsed. A military secret privilege cannot be exercised if there is no longer a danger from its disclosure, although how and by whom that danger is assessed is open to some question. Agency policy deliberations are privileged even after the policy is adopted or the communicating official has died. Law enforcement files, however, generally are not privileged once the matter investigated is concluded, although there may be exceptions if the court finds a continuing need for secrecy.

Principal exceptions: In a sense, exceptions are built into most governmental privileges, because they are only *qualified*, that is, subject to abrogation if a party can demonstrate a need that outweighs the policy favoring secrecy. The only unqualified privilege is that for military and diplomatic secrets. As discussed below, the court can weigh a litigant's need for the information in determining how deeply to delve into the validity of the government's claim of privilege; but once it decides there is indeed a proper occasion for invoking the privilege, it is absolute and no showing of need will overcome it. All other privileges discussed here are qualified.

Although executive privilege is qualified, confidential presidential communications are "presumptively privileged" (*Nixon*). They will yield, however, to a "demonstrated, specific need in a pending criminal trial." A lesser showing of necessity should suffice for the agency privileges.

Effect of invoking privilege. Unlike most privileges, governmental privileges are not only mostly qualified, but even to the extent they are absolute in the sense that the court cannot order disclosure, the court may be empowered or even enjoined to compensate the disappointed litigant for the loss of the privileged evidence. This compensation may take any appropriate form, from striking a witness's testimony to dismissing the case. See URE 508(c); CEC 1042. In federal court, at least, the government will be put to this choice only when it is the plaintiff or moving party in a civil action or the prosecution in a criminal case; the government cannot both prosecute a defendant and invoke a privilege to deprive the defendant of material evidence (*Reynolds*). State statutes, however, may apply sanctions more broadly. Thus URE 503(c) requires an appropriate finding or order against the government whenever a privilege is sustained and a party is deprived of material evidence.

Procedure. The rules for passing upon the diplomatic and military secrets privilege were set out in *Reynolds*. It must be invoked by the relevant department head, who has personally considered the matter. If the court determines "from all the circumstances" that there is a "reasonable danger" disclosure will jeopardize national security, the court may not insist upon examination *in camera* in order to rule on the privilege. Furthermore, the degree of need for the information by the litigants determines how deeply the court must probe into the claim of privilege; if there is little need, a bare formal claim of privilege will suffice. The Court implied (but did not state) that if a court is not satisfied "from all the circumstances" that the claim is valid, it may then require limited disclosure, to the court alone, *in camera*.

A claim of executive privilege is treated differently, as stated in *Nixon*. It apparently must be invoked by the President. *In camera* inspection is permitted, with the burden on the party seeking the information to demonstrate sufficient need to overcome the President's presumptive privilege.

State statutes will vary: for example, CEC 915 expressly permits *in camera* disclosure in ruling upon the official information or informer's privileges.

CIPA. To combat the specter of so-called **graymail,** when a criminal defendant claims a need to disclose classified information in the hope that the government will be forced to dismiss the prosecution rather than take a chance on disclosure, Congress passed the **Classified Information Procedures Act** (CIPA). Under this statute, the question of the right to disclosure, together with any sanctions that would attach to a government refusal, can be decided *in camera* after advance notice.

Informer's Privilege

An evidentiary privilege that protects against disclosure of the identity of a government informer. See, e.g., URE 509; CEC 1041. Informer's privilege is a form of governmental privilege. It would more accurately be called the "privilege for the identity of informers," although this is a bit awkward.

Essentials:

Holder: The government (but waivable by informer).

Subject matter: Identity of informer.

Time limitations (subject matter): None.

Time or forum limitations (exercise): None.

Principal exceptions: Qualified privilege; need for disclosure weighed against policy for secrecy.

Holder: "Informer's privilege" is a misnomer, but it is commonly used. The term "informer" refers to the subject matter of the privilege, not to its holder, which in almost all instances is the government, not the informer. See URE 509(a).

Subject matter: Usually only the identity of the informer is privileged. Some decisions have included also the content of the informer's communication; but this seems justifiable only where the content would reveal the informer's identity.

An **informer** is one who has furnished information about a possible violation of the law, to (or for transmittal to) a law enforcement officer or someone else charged with enforcing the law. The Uniform Rule also includes the staff and members of legislative investigatory committees.

Principal exceptions: *Qualified privilege.* The informer's privilege is a qualified one. It will give way to a court's determination that a party's need is greater than the policy for secrecy. This is especially true in criminal cases, of course. If the court orders disclosure and the government declines, the court will dismiss the case (or apply a lesser sanction, if appropriate).

Under the Supreme Court's decisions in *McCray v. Illinois*[6] and *Roviaro v. United States*,[7] the privilege will usually be upheld if the issue is merely probable cause for a search or arrest warrant; but it will often have to give way to a defendant's rights when the issue of guilt is at stake and the inform-

---

6. 386 U.S. 300 (1967).
7. 353 U.S. 53 (1957).

er's identity is material to the defense. Many courts routinely (though not invariably) require an *in camera* disclosure, with appropriate protection for the informer, before ruling on the privilege.

Prior disclosure. If the informer's identity has already been disclosed by the informer or a holder to those who (in the quaint but revealing phrase often used) "would have cause to resent the communication," there is no privilege. Nor can the government generally invoke the privilege against the wishes of the informer, who thus can in effect waive it though not a holder. See CEC 1041(c). In addition, testimony by the informer for the government may waive the privilege. See URE 509(c)(1)-(2).

Surveillance sites. In many jurisdictions there is a new privilege related to that for the identity of informers: protection of the **location of police surveillance sites.** It serves much the same purpose for law enforcement as the more established informer's privilege.

Grand Jury Privilege

A rule of secrecy of grand jury testimony and deliberations.
Grand jury secrecy is codified in FRCrP 6(e) and equivalent state statutes. Individual statutes vary and should be consulted for detailed analysis.

Rationale: Historically, grand jury proceedings have been considered secret, for several reasons: to encourage free and open deliberations and testimony, to prevent those not indicted from being unnecessarily exposed to public ridicule, and to prevent those who are to be indicted from learning of it prematurely and either fleeing or seeking to influence the jurors.

The privilege attaches to both the testimony of witnesses before the grand jury and the deliberations of grand jurors. It is the former that is most often invoked, is most controversial, and has been most clearly codified.

Grand jury privilege assures the secrecy of grand jurors and others involved in the process such as government attorneys. Witnesses themselves, however, cannot be either prevented from revealing their own testimony or forced to do so.

Exceptions to secrecy are generally for disclosure to government attorneys for criminal prosecution based on the jury's investigation. Private civil litigants and, in most cases but perhaps to a lesser degree, government attorneys bringing civil or administrative proceedings must show particularized need for the information, such as the use of a witness's prior statements before the grand jury to impeach present testimony.

Criminal defendants are generally entitled to see their own grand jury testimony, and at least in federal courts under the Jencks Act they also can see the grand jury testimony of other government witnesses who already have given direct testimony at trial.

Privilege Against Self-Incrimination

A constitutional or statutory right not to give testimonial evidence that would tend to subject one to criminal liability.

The privilege against self-incrimination derives from the Fifth Amendment to the Constitution, and it is made applicable to the states by the Fourteenth Amendment. Various state statutes and constitutions contain a similar privilege, and while a state's provisions, as interpreted by its courts, cannot be less stringent (that is, provide less protection) than the federal constitution, they can be and sometimes are more stringent, providing more protection. In most instances the states follow the federal model and Supreme Court interpretations of it. In this discussion, unless otherwise indicated, the privilege explained will be that under the Fifth Amendment; state equivalents are usually similar but should be checked in specific instances.

There are several types of constitutionally-based exclusionary rules, such as those relating to illegally-obtained evidence and certain confessions. The only one discussed here is the privilege against self-incrimination, and that discussion is only a brief outline of the topic. This is partly because it is impracticable in a work of this nature to attempt more than an overview of such an extensive subject. It is also because in recent years the subject of self-incrimination, together with the other constitutional rules referred to, has been treated primarily in courses in constitutional law or criminal procedure. In consequence, most evidence casebooks now omit reference to the privilege, and most evidence courses cover it briefly or not at all. This work, given the same choices, covers it briefly.

The privilege against self-incrimination protects both a witness in court and a criminal accused, whether a witness or not. The rules differ somewhat between these two classes. The most obvious difference is that a criminal accused need not even take the stand to invoke the privilege, but can decline to be called as a witness at all.

The holder of the privilege is the person seeking to avoid self-incrimination. Only natural persons, and not corporations or other entities, have such a privilege.

Definition of incrimination. **Self-incrimination** refers only to criminal liability as such, and not to any of its collateral disabilities such as social ostracism. (Certain quasi-criminal proceedings, such as forfeiture, may also be covered.) If there is no risk of criminal liability, there is no privilege.

The risk of incrimination must be "real and appreciable," and not "imaginary and unsubstantial," although incrimination usually need not entail a risk of actual prosecution as a practical matter.

Testimonial incrimination only. The privilege is limited to **testimonial self-incrimination,** which generally means compelling one to make an *in-*

tentional assertion or expression of one's knowledge or belief of factual information. The compelled action may be verbal expression or some physical activity, such as the production of documents. Most physical activity, however, especially when it merely has the effect of passively revealing information about the subject's physical characteristics, is not considered testimonial.

Example 10.18:   Derek is suspected of killing Vincent. He is compelled to confess to the crime, to give a blood sample to be compared to blood left at the scene, and to appear in a lineup with three other men to be identified by a witness. Only the confession is testimonial and a violation of Derek's privilege against self-incrimination.

Documents and other tangible items.   Compelled production of pre-existing objects, including documents, is not generally within the privilege, at least with respect to the item produced. The act of production, however, may itself be a testimonial assertion of fact that is protected, if it would be self-incriminatory. (*Fisher v. United States.*[8])

Example 10.19:   Doris is ordered to produce "all memoranda and notes written by Doris relating to the theft from XYZ Co. on December 5." The notes and memoranda themselves are not protected, although they may contain incriminating (i.e., self-incriminating) features or statements, because their incriminating aspects were pre-existing and not compelled. The very act of production, however, is at least a statement by Doris that she believes they are what was asked for and that she wrote them, thereby authenticating them in a future proceeding.

Note the similarity to the distinction regarding attorney-client privilege, between an unprivileged pre-existing document or object transferred by the client to the attorney and the privileged "communicative act" of transferring it.

Corporate agents who produce documents in that capacity are considered to be acting for the corporation only, and the act of production cannot be used against the agent personally.

Compulsion necessary.   Testimonial self-incrimination must be *compelled* to be within the privilege. **Compulsion** generally exists when a witness's right to refuse to give the information has been denied. That is, there must be a valid assertion of the privilege which is rejected, except when the requirement would be unreasonable because the subject is under custodial interrogation (see *Miranda v. Arizona*[9]) or otherwise lacks truly free choice.

8. 425 U.S. 391 (1976).
9. 384 U.S. 436 (1966).

Compulsion may also be through some penalty imposed for exercising the privilege. A common example is the drawing of adverse inferences from a criminal accused's failure to testify (see *Griffin v. California*[10]), but most other penalties and disadvantages would be equally prohibited.

Generally if a defendant does not choose to testify, neither the present nor any prior invocations of the privilege to remain silent can be used adversely. If, however, the defendant voluntarily testifies at trial, any prior invocation (affirmative assertion) of the privilege, in or out of court, can be used to impeach.

If requested, the court must instruct the jury not to draw adverse inferences from the defendant's failure to testify.

Invoking the privilege. A criminal accused invokes the privilege against self-incrimination merely by declining to take the stand. A non-accused witness, however, or a person not presently in court, usually must invoke the privilege specifically in response to each question or request (unless the invocation itself is incriminating). The court must then determine whether there is a sufficient risk that a response would be self-incriminatory. Here the standards are somewhat unclear and courts tend to have considerable discretion, typically exercising it in favor of the claim of privilege. Courts will try to avoid forcing the claimant to make an incriminatory disclosure in order to prove it would be incriminatory; but sometimes an *in camera* disclosure to the judge will be necessary.

Waiver. A failure to invoke the privilege waives it. An ordinary witness waives the privilege as to facts (and related details) that the witness has voluntarily revealed prior to taking the stand. A criminal accused who chooses to testify at all generally has waived the privilege at least with respect to cross-examination on related matters, although some courts tie the scope of the waiver to the jurisdiction's rules on the proper scope of cross-examination (see Chapter 8). In any event, the privilege usually is not waived as to questions relevant only to credibility. See **FRE 608(b)**, URE 608(b).

A waiver is for the remainder of that proceeding, although it is sometimes unclear what constitutes a "proceeding." Usually a waiver does not extend to a different stage (grand jury investigation, guilt stage, sentencing hearing, and so forth) of the same overall proceeding.

Exceptions. The so-called **required records exception** removes any Fifth Amendment privilege for refusal to produce certain records (or other tangible items) that are required to be kept pursuant to a government regulatory scheme. So long as the records are of a type that are ordinarily kept by persons engaged in such a regulated activity, and the records have some

10. 380 U.S. 609 (1965).

"public aspects" or relation to the public interest, they must be produced, and their custodian can be punished for failure to produce them.

There is also no privilege if there is no risk of incrimination; if the risk is removed, the privilege disappears. Thus the granting of **immunity from prosecution** may eliminate the claimant's right to invoke the privilege. **Use immunity** refers to a promise not to use the compelled testimony itself against the witness in a criminal prosecution; nor generally can any evidence be used that was derived from the immunized testimony (**derivative use immunity**). **Transactional immunity** is a broader protection, against prosecution for any transactions about which the witness testifies under compulsion. Federal law generally requires only use (and derivative use) immunity to be granted (*Kastigar v. United States*[11]); state law varies and may require transactional immunity. Where use immunity is sufficient, issues arise as to whether particular evidence is "tainted" by the immunized testimony — that is, whether the proffered evidence is truly independent of, and would have been available even in the absence of, the immunized testimony.

Miscellaneous Privileges

There are potentially as many privileges as there are classes of individuals who believe that the confidentiality of their communications should be protected, or types of testimony that society might consider it repugnant to require. Moreover, whenever a relationship is arguably analogous to that which enjoys an existing privilege (for example, accountants to attorneys, social workers to psychotherapists), there is a good chance that this similarity will be used as a basis for urging adoption of the new privilege, with mixed success. Most of these potential privileges have been proposed, formally or informally, over the years, and there are always new professions, classifications, and relationships created that lead to new assertions of privilege.

It would be impractical to attempt to list all of those privileges that have found sufficient favor to be recognized by some court or legislature, absolutely or qualifiedly, much less to attempt to discuss their detailed attributes. Following, however, is a brief description of some of the more notable of these "minor" privileges.

Many states and lower federal courts have recognized a **journalist's privilege,** sometimes called a **shield law,** protecting against the forced disclosure of a journalist's sources of information, by analogy to the informer's privilege. And like the informer's privilege, its holder is usually the "informee," the journalist, not the source. The journalist's privilege is qualified, yielding to a sufficient showing of need, especially by criminal defendants.

11. 406 U.S. 441 (1972).

It may be state constitutionally based, but it has no federal constitutional foundation (*Branzburg v. Hayes*[12]).

Several states recognize an **accountant's privilege.** It is analogous to attorney-client privilege, and it generally has the same or similar features. Note that even without a separate privilege, an accountant can easily be in the position of an expert employed by an attorney, and certain communications may thus come within the attorney-client privilege.

Gaining recognition in many states are certain **victim-counselor privileges.** Perhaps most common are those for confidential communications between sexual assault victims or domestic violence victims and their respective counselors. See, e.g., CEC 1035-1036.2; 1037-1037.7. The Uniform Rules have no such privileges.

Other popular privileges cover such diverse subjects as trade secrets, political votes, and certain teacher-pupil communications. As indicated, the list is potentially endless. Ours ends here.

---

12. 408 U.S. 665 (1972).

11

Burdens of Proof and Presumptions

A. Burdens of Proof
   Burdens of Proof (In General)
      Affirmative Defense
   Burden of Production
      Burden of Producing Evidence
      Burden of Evidence
      Burden of Going Forward
      Legally Sufficient Case
      "Getting to the Jury"
      Equipoise
   Directed Verdict
      Nonsuit
      Peremptory Ruling
      Peremptory Nonsuit
      Judgment as a Matter of Law
      Conditional Judgment
      Conditional Peremptory Ruling
   Burden of Persuasion
   Allocation of Burdens of Proof
   Standards of Proof
      Civil Standard
      Preponderance of the Evidence
      Balance of Probabilities
      Enhanced Civil Standard
      Clear and Convincing Evidence
      Criminal Standard of Proof
      Beyond a Reasonable Doubt
   Prima Facie Case
      Prima Facie Evidence
B. Presumptions
   Presumption (In General)
      Rebuttable Presumption
      Prima Facie Presumption
      Basic Fact
      Presumed Fact

Presumption of Fact
Presumption of Law
Permissive Presumption
Permissive Inference
Res Ipsa Loquitur
Conclusive Presumption
Irrebuttable Presumption
Rebuttal of Presumptions
Thayer (or Bursting Bubble) Rule
Morgan Rule
Tactical Presumptions
Conflicting Presumptions
Presumptions in Criminal Cases (In General)
Permissive Presumption (Criminal Cases)
Rational Connection
Mandatory Presumption (Criminal Cases)

Introduction and Overview of Chapter

This chapter covers a subject — or really two related subjects — often neglected in evidence and other procedural courses: presumptions and burdens of proof. They would fit nicely into a civil procedure course, but they also belong in a well-rounded course in evidence; for while they do not concern particular types of evidence, they do affect the presentation of evidence and its effect on the case.

The first part of the chapter discusses the burdens of production and persuasion — who has them, how they are satisfied, and the result if they are not. The second part of the chapter covers presumptions. It distinguishes them from inferences, their less-weighty cousins; illustrates the reasons for them and circumstances under which they arise; and then explains the ongoing controversy over their operation and effect.

Both subjects are illustrated by a series of diagrams that, if followed through the chapter, should help to take the mystery, and the frequent confusion, out of the study of burdens of proof and presumptions.

A.   BURDENS OF PROOF

Burdens of Proof (In General)

The generic name for the two types of burden that must be satisfied by one or the other party: the burden of producing evidence and the burden of persuasion. Also, the traditional name for the burden of persuasion.

As the above definition indicates, "burden of proof" is a slightly confusing phrase, because it is commonly used in two different ways. Traditionally, and still to some extent today (see, e.g., CEC 500), it denotes the ultimate burden of persuading the trier of fact in one's favor, what today is more commonly called the "burden of persuasion." It is and was also used, however, to mean the overall concept of evidentiary burdens, including both the burden of production and the burden of persuasion. As such the concept is more properly designated in the plural, "burdens of proof," although for convenience the singular will often be employed. It is used here in its generic sense only, and the individual burdens will be treated in separate entries.

One also may speak of a "burden of pleading." Rules of pleading require one or the other party to plead a particular issue in order to make it a part of the case. Although this chapter will not be concerned with pleading burdens as such, we will see that the placement of such a burden can serve as a guide to the allocation of the burdens of proof at trial. See *Allocations of Burdens of Proof.*

✱The burden of production is always a matter for the judge; the burden of persuasion is always for the trier of fact.✱Although the principles of burdens of proof are theoretically the same whether the case is tried to a judge or a jury, many aspects of their operation are not of the same practical importance when the judge and jury are the same person. Therefore, except where specifically indicated otherwise, the discussion in this chapter will assume that each case is being tried to a jury.

Note that each burden, whether of production or persuasion, applies not to an entire case, but only to *individual issues or elements of a case.* If there is more than one issue in a case, the burden respecting one may be on plaintiff, that respecting another on defendant. Thus, in the usual negligence case, the plaintiff has the burdens of proof on the issue of the defendant's negligence, but the defendant has the burdens of proof on such affirmative defenses as contributory negligence. In fact, the defendant generally has the burdens of production and persuasion (as well as pleading) on any **affirmative defense,** a defense that does not deny the plaintiff's prima facie case but asserts some new matter that permits the defendant to prevail in spite of it.

For ease of illustration, most of the examples in this chapter assume that the plaintiff has the burdens, and most assume that if the plaintiff fails to satisfy them, the defendant prevails. While this is true whenever the issue involved is crucial to the plaintiff's case, it is not necessarily true for all issues. Sometimes a party that fails to satisfy a burden of production or persuasion on one issue can still prevail by satisfying it on another: If the plaintiff fails to prove intent, proof of negligence may save the case; if the defendant fails to establish contributory negligence, proof that the statute of limitations has expired will succeed just as well (if not better).

Burden of Production

The requirement that a party produce a sufficient amount of evidence on an issue to permit a reasonable jury to find in the party's favor, thus avoiding a directed verdict on that issue. This burden is also known as the **burden of producing evidence,** the **burden of evidence,** or the **burden of going forward** (with the evidence).

Caveat: Some, especially older, definitions of the burden of production place it on any party who is in danger of losing, whether by a directed verdict or by a jury verdict. Similarly, it may be defined as the duty of a party to make or meet a prima facie case. These definitions can be confusing, especially as they theoretically could place the burden on both parties at once. In any event, these are not the usual modern definition of burden of production, and they should be avoided.

Example 11.1:   Phillipa sues Daryl for negligently injuring her. After the jury is selected, Aaron, Phillipa's attorney, rises and addresses the court: "Your honor, my client respectfully rests her case." Phillipa will lose the case, even if Daryl does nothing at all, because Phillipa had the burden of producing evidence. She did not produce any, and the court will direct a verdict against her and in favor of Daryl.

While the above scenario is unlikely to occur, it starkly illustrates the effect of the burden of production. If the plaintiff has it (and a plaintiff usually does — see *Allocation of Burdens of Proof*), she must present some evidence to have any chance of succeeding. If she does not, she will automatically lose, as the judge will grant a directed verdict (or enter a judgment) for her opponent.

Example 11.2:   Same facts as Example 11.1, except that sensing that something is amiss, Phillipa's attorney changes his mind and presents some evidence of Daryl's negligence (perhaps an eyewitness account of the incident). *Daryl's* attorney now rises and "rests his case" — that is, declines to put on evidence and asks for a directed verdict in Daryl's favor. Whether a directed verdict is granted now depends on whether or not Phillipa has presented sufficient evidence to avoid a nonsuit, that is, sufficient evidence to satisfy her burden of production. If she has, the case will continue, and if Daryl really rests with no evidence, it will now be decided by the jury. If she has not, Daryl will win just as if Phillipa had produced no evidence at all, as in Example 11.1.

Note that while Daryl can ask for a directed verdict at the close of plaintiff Phillipa's case, Phillipa cannot. Daryl must be given a chance to put on evidence, no matter how strong Phillipa's case seems to be.

Caveat: Directed verdict not mandatory. When the evidence theoretically would justify a directed verdict, this does not mean the court necessarily *will* direct a verdict for the plaintiff or defendant, but only that it *could* do so. Judges often are reluctant to direct a verdict for the party having the burden of persuasion. This is especially so when the strength of the evidence rests largely on witnesses' credibility, which is traditionally a matter for the jury to determine. One alternative, if the judge truly believes a party is entitled to prevail as a matter of law, is to deny a directed verdict, in the expectation that the jury will find for that party. If it does not, the judge belatedly takes the case from the jury by entering a judgment notwithstanding the verdict (JNOV). See *Directed Verdict.*

Quantum of evidence. How much evidence need a plaintiff like Phillipa in the above examples introduce to avoid a directed verdict? While the answer can be made very complicated by various formulas, the short answer is *enough evidence to persuade the judge that a reasonable jury could find in Phillipa's favor.* Such a quantum of evidence constitutes what may be termed a **legally sufficient case.** (This is sometimes called making a prima facie case, but because that term is used in different and sometimes inconsistent ways, it will be avoided in this explanation.) What Phillipa must do to avoid a nonsuit, in other words, is to present sufficient evidence to "**get to the jury.**"

The process so far can be illustrated by the following diagram:

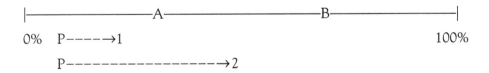

In this diagram, the solid line represents evidence that might be introduced by a party (here Phillipa) on an issue (here negligence), from none at all (0%) to the amount that would make the issue absolutely certain (100%). Of course, certainty is rare, so the end point is largely theoretical and for reference only.

Point A on the line represents that amount of evidence that would (in the judge's opinion) permit a reasonable jury to find in Phillipa's favor. Thus, if Phillipa presents an amount of evidence reaching only position 1, she will suffer a directed verdict or nonsuit, just as if she had presented none at all. But if her evidence reaches position 2, taking her case past point A, she will have satisfied her burden of production and will get to the jury on the issue of negligence. (Point B, about which you probably can guess, will be explained shortly.)

Effect of satisfying burden. Once a party with the burden of production has produced enough evidence to avoid a directed verdict, that party no longer has the burden of production, at least on that issue. But where it now resides requires some further illustration.

Example 11.3: In Phillipa's suit against Daryl (see Examples 11.1 and 11.2), Phillipa has now satisfied her burden of production by presenting evidence that the judge considers sufficient to permit a reasonable jury to find in her favor. Daryl's request for a nonsuit against Phillipa is therefore denied. Daryl declines to put on any evidence (continues to "rest his case"). Phillipa's attorney now rises and asks for a directed verdict in Phillipa's favor. Whether it is granted depends on whether Phillipa has presented enough evidence not only to *permit* a reasonable jury to find in her favor, but to *require* it to find for her.

The diagram now is as follows:

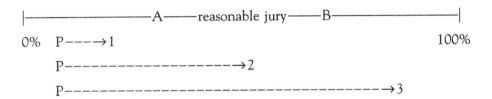

Point "B" represents the amount of evidence that so predominates in Phillipa's favor that no reasonable jury could find against her. If Phillipa has presented an amount of evidence reaching position 2, as indicated earlier the jury can reasonably find for her, but it also can reasonably find against her. She has gotten to the jury, but the jury still must decide the case. If, however, Phillipa has presented (in the judge's opinion) an amount of evidence reaching position 3, she has gotten to and *past* the jury, and (if no other evidence is presented) the judge will take the case away from the jury and direct a verdict in her favor.

Clearly, the burden of production is always a matter for the judge's determination. The areas up to point A and beyond point B represent circumstances in which the *judge* will decide the case; whereas in the area between points A and B the *jury* will decide the case. Where the evidence "resides" in the judge's mind determines whether the jury gets the case; if it does, then where it resides in the jury's mind determines who wins the case. Obviously, an ability to read minds would be an invaluable asset to a trial lawyer.

Shifting burdens. Once Phillipa has produced her evidence, where is the burden of production? That depends on the amount of evidence she has produced. If she has produced only an amount reaching position 1 and (in the judge's mind) she has not reached point A, the burden of production is still on her and she loses. If she has produced an amount of evidence reaching position 3 and has gone beyond point B, the burden of production has shifted to Daryl. This is because if Daryl does not produce sufficient evidence of his own, he is in danger of a directed verdict against him. And according to the definition of "burden of production" given above, the burden is on whichever party is in danger of a directed verdict upon failure to produce a certain amount of evidence, in this instance Daryl.

There is, however, one other possibility, and it is a very important one: If Phillipa has produced an amount of evidence reaching position 2 and has reached past point A, into the area between A and B, but she has not reached point B, then *the burden is on no one at all*, because no one is in danger of suffering a directed verdict for failure to produce further evidence. This last point is extremely important because it is the usual situation. Parties with the burden of production, if they satisfy it at all, will far more often produce just enough evidence to get to the jury (between points A and B) than enough to get past the jury and to a directed verdict (past point B). It is, in fact, relatively rare for the evidence to get past point B in the absence of a presumption (see below).

To illustrate (BPE represents the burden of producing evidence):

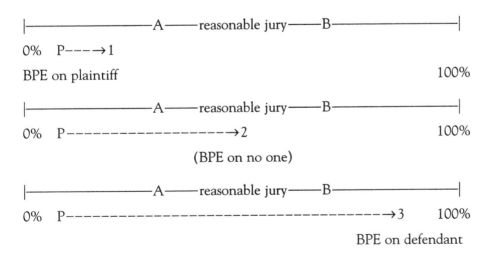

Opponent's options. If Phillipa has produced enough evidence to put the case in the "reasonable jury" area between points A and B, Phillipa's opponent Daryl may, of course, put on his own evidence. But Daryl might prevail even if he does nothing at all. As discussed elsewhere (see *Burden of Persuasion*), Phillipa has the ultimate burden of persuading the jury of her position. When the two sides have rested, the jury will decide whether it is sufficiently convinced by Phillipa's evidence to find in her favor. If not, it will find for Daryl. It must be convinced by a preponderance of the evidence (see *Standards of Proof*), which on our diagram means it must believe the evidence for Phillipa has gone beyond "50%" (position 1 below). If it believes the evidence favors Daryl or is equally balanced at 50% (sometimes called "in **equipoise**," position 2 below), because Phillipa has the burden of persuasion, Daryl will win.

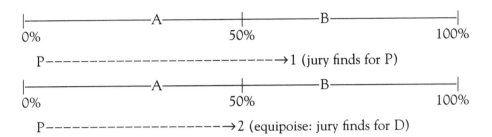

(Note that the 50% position is theoretical only. It is not necessarily true that proving a statistical probability of better than 50% assures a party victory. See the "blue bus" case in Chapter 4, Example 4.7.)

Opponent's response to avoid directed verdict.   If, however, Phillipa's evidence is strong enough (in the judge's mind) to push her position past point B, thereby shifting the burden of production to Daryl, Daryl must respond or risk a directed verdict against him. If he does respond, he, like Phillipa, must present sufficient evidence (in the judge's mind) to get to the jury, that is, into the area between points A and B. If he does that, he will avoid a directed verdict and could prevail if (in the jury's mind) the balance of the evidence is no longer in Phillipa's favor. Note that because Daryl does not have the ultimate burden of persuasion, he, unlike Phillipa, need not bring the evidence back (in the jury's mind) beyond the 50% mark, but need only bring it *to* that mark. If the jury decides that the evidence is in equipoise, Daryl wins.

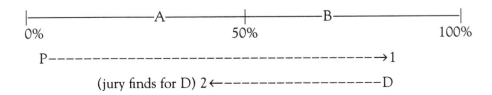

240

Remember that once Daryl has presented enough evidence to avoid a directed verdict and leave the decision for the jury, no one has the burden of producing evidence.

Shifting the burden back.   Suppose, however, that Daryl puts on sufficient evidence in rebuttal of Phillipa's case that he doesn't simply leave the case in the "reasonable jury" area between points A and B, but he pushes it back (in the judge's mind) all the way past point A. Now it is Phillipa who is again in danger of a directed verdict, and who therefore has the burden of production, which has shifted back to her. She must again produce sufficient evidence (in the judge's mind) to avoid a directed verdict:

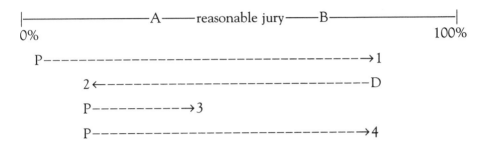

Here Phillipa has either pushed the evidence back into the "jury" area (position 3), or has managed to push it all the way back past point B (position 4). In the latter event, the burden of production has again shifted back to Daryl.

In theory then, the burden of production can shift back and forth throughout the trial, like the ball in a tennis match. The parties will not always know where it is in the judge's or jury's mind, for it is only at those points at which a directed verdict (or equivalent) can be sought that the court will tell them where it thinks the evidence resides. Deciding when to rest one's case is thus an important (and sometimes risky) matter of trial tactics.

The judge and jury may change their opinion of the case with every witness or even from one statement of a witness to another. As a practical matter, however, with one exception it is rare for the burden of production, in the sense of where the evidence stands when a party could seek a directed verdict, to shift back and forth many times. After the plaintiff's case in chief, if the burden has shifted to the defendant, it will shift back only if the defendant can push the evidence all the way back past point A, a difficult task. Even if that is done, it will shift back again only if the plaintiff then assembles a new body of evidence that pushes the case back past point B again, an even more difficult task. At some point, either the court will not permit any further evidence to be presented, or the parties will run out of the devastating kind of evidence that can destroy an opponent's case and justify a directed verdict in the offering party's favor.

The exception to the above statement occurs when there are presumptions operating. Because presumptions by themselves shift the burden of production, they can have the effect of causing the burden to shift back and forth quite strikingly. See *Presumptions*.

Finally, while the burden of production can and does shift back and forth throughout a trial, at least under one major theory the burden of persuasion never shifts. Once it has been placed on plaintiff or defendant, it stays there through the entire trial, until it is "used" by the jury in making its ultimate assessment of the evidence. See *Burden of Persuasion*.

Directed Verdict

A judge's order entering judgment or directing that the jury bring in a particular verdict. In the case of a defendant's motion against a plaintiff, the order may be termed a **nonsuit,** but the meaning is the same. The terms **peremptory ruling** or **peremptory nonsuit** (as well as peremptory finding or instruction) are synonymous, merely indicating that the ruling of the court for plaintiff or defendant is final. A modern equivalent term is **judgment as a matter of law,** which is accurate but a bit awkward. The terminology may depend on whether the judge is ruling on the entire case or only one nondispositive issue. "Directed verdict" and "nonsuit" are still most often encountered and are used in this chapter.

A directed verdict takes the case away from the jury, permitting the judge to make the final decision.

Example 11.4: Pierre sues Doreen for negligence. At the close of Pierre's case, Doreen moves for a directed verdict in her favor (a nonsuit of the plaintiff). If Doreen's motion is successful, the jury will be directed to find in Doreen's favor, and Pierre will be deprived of an opportunity to convince the jury that it should find in his favor. Pierre will have failed to get to the jury.

If a directed verdict takes the case away from the jury, a party with the burden of producing evidence gets to the jury by avoiding a directed verdict. Thus the measure of satisfying the burden of production is generally phrased in terms of *avoiding the risk of a directed verdict*. See generally *Burden of Producing Evidence*.

When a directed verdict is granted. A court may order a directed verdict when it is convinced that a reasonable jury could not find in one party's favor, even if viewed in a light most favorable to that party. It may, but it need not, make such an order since it may prefer to let the jury make the ultimate decision in the case. (It then might grant a judgment notwithstanding the verdict if the jury is so unreasonable as to find for the wrong party.) Also, the court almost always will defer to the jury on questions of the credibility of witnesses (compare Example 11.20).

Standard for grant or denial. There is considerable literature, and confusion, respecting the proper standard for granting or denying a directed verdict. What most formulas come down to, however, is simply that to avoid a directed verdict the court must be convinced that a reasonable jury, applying the standard of proof appropriate to the case, could find in favor of the party opposing the motion. In Example 11.4, Doreen's motion should fail if a reasonable jury could, in the judge's view, find negligence by Doreen by a preponderance of the evidence. Were it a criminal case, by the currently accepted view the evidence would have to permit reasonable persons to find in the prosecution's favor beyond a reasonable doubt.

If there is conflicting evidence (and especially if there are questions of the credibility of witnesses) with respect to certain facts, the court may issue only a **conditional judgment,** sometimes called a **conditional peremptory ruling**: *If* the jury is persuaded of certain facts, then it must find for the party. This is commonly the case when a basic fact from which another fact might be presumed is disputed or depends on assessments of credibility. See *Presumptions.*

Burden of Persuasion

The requirement that a party ultimately persuade the trier of fact with respect to a particular issue, and according to the appropriate standard or quantum of proof. The burden of persuasion is also sometimes called the burden of proof (see, e.g., CEC 115); but in modern usage the latter term is generally used, if at all, to designate both the burdens of production and persuasion. See *Burdens of Proof.*

Example 11.5: Pedro sues Diana in a jury trial for breach of contract. Pedro has the initial burden of production on the elements of his case, such as offer and acceptance. Assuming Pedro has met this burden, and Diana has met her burden of production on any affirmative defenses she may have, the case goes to the jury. This being a civil case, in order for Pedro to win the jury must be convinced from the evidence, as to each necessary element of Pedro's case, that Diana more probably than not was in breach of contract. If it decides that it is more probable that there was no breach, *or if it believes the evidence leaves the issue equally balanced* between Pedro's and Diana's positions, then Pedro will lose.

Note carefully the italicized phrase, as it is the essence of the civil burden of persuasion. To "persuade" the jury means more than to muster as good a case as one's opponent: it means to present a *better* case; to establish it by a *preponderance* of the evidence, not an equal amount. Thus, the party who has the burden of persuasion always must persuade the trier of fact at least that it has the better case; and in some instances (such as criminal cases) it must do even more (see *Standards of Proof*).

The burden of persuasion, unlike the burden of production, is always a matter for the trier of fact, whether judge or jury. It comes into play directly only when the trier of fact is ready to decide an issue. Until then it lies dormant, ready to guide the jury and, in civil cases, to "break any ties" between the parties. (Some would say it is not even allocated until the end of the trial, and therefore it cannot be said to shift back and forth. This is a nice metaphysical point that has no practical effect for our purposes.) In civil cases, where the standard of proof is a preponderance of the evidence, a trier does not need much guidance when it is clearly convinced of one party's case or the other. Therefore it is only when the trier cannot decide between the two sides — when they are in equipoise — that the burden of persuasion comes directly into play at all.

The party that has been allocated the ultimate burden of persuasion on an issue will generally (though not always) have the initial burden of producing evidence on that issue as well. Since in equipoise the party with the ultimate burden of persuasion loses, it follows that the party with the burden of persuasion must present at least some evidence to get the case "off center" and into a positive position. Note that the reverse of this proposition is also true. If the initial burden of production has been allocated to a party, the same party probably has the burden of persuasion on that issue.

Allocation of Burdens of Proof

The process of determining which party will have the obligation either to produce evidence or ultimately to persuade the trier of fact on an issue or an element of a case.

There are many theories of how burdens of proof are allocated, and in some instances it remains a mystery. Equally baffling may be determining who in fact has been allocated the burden on a particular issue. There are, however, some generally accepted theories of how burdens are allocated, and how to tell how they have been allocated.

It should first be said that, with relatively rare exceptions, at least initially the burdens of production and persuasion are allocated to the same party. Therefore the following discussion will not distinguish between the two burdens of proof.

1. How Burdens are Allocated

Sometimes burdens of proof are allocated mechanically (such as according to the relative position of statutory language) and arbitrarily (as when that statutory language was not meant to have such an effect). But at least where the allocation can be seen to have some rational basis, the following are the generally accepted rational bases:

— *a. Fairness and efficiency.* Probably the most common reason for allocating the burden of proof is fairness between the parties. Thus the burden is almost always allocated to the plaintiff (or the prosecution in a criminal case), because the plaintiff is asking the court to change the status quo, to take some action in the plaintiff's favor (and to the defendant's detriment). It seems only fair to require, therefore, that the plaintiff justify, at least initially, such a request. If the plaintiff presents no affirmative justification and does not ultimately convince the court of some reason to act, the court in turn is justified in doing nothing. This is also a matter of efficiency, since it limits access to the courts' considerable mechanisms of action to those who are prepared and able to give it reason to act.

Fairness also explains other bases for allocation, in particular the theory that the party with the best access to, or control over, the evidence, or who would find it easiest to produce, should have the burden of producing it. This is true as far as it goes, but almost every tort or criminal case illustrates that it is easily subordinated to other policies. Although the defendant is often likely to have better access to evidence of what happened than does the plaintiff or prosecution, we generally allocate the burden of proof to the latter.

b. Policy. Sometimes the law favors or disfavors a particular claim or defense. If so, it may enforce its view through the allocation of burdens.

Example 11.6: Pearl sues Damon for defamation, for saying she had cheated at cards. Damon contends that his statement was true, and that truth is an absolute defense to defamation. The assertion of the truth of a defamatory statement is a disfavored defense, and until recently, responsibility for its proof was always placed on the defendant. Thus while Pearl would have the burden of proving most elements of the defamation, such as the defamatory meaning and publication to a third person, Damon would be allocated the burden of proving that Pearl in fact cheated. Now, however, for other policy reasons of a constitutional nature (protecting free speech), it is the plaintiff who must prove falsity in cases governed by the First Amendment. Thus, if Pearl is a public figure or official, she probably will have to prove she did not cheat. As indicated below (see "proving a negative"), this shift may make Pearl's task more difficult than was Damon's.

Other policies may be more general. For example, the desire to preserve a defendant's presumption of innocence requires that the burden as to few (if any) elements of a criminal case be placed on the defendant. See *Presumptions in Criminal Cases*.

c. Probability. A third frequent basis for allocation is probability, that is, which party's proposition is the more likely to be true? All things being even and the issue in doubt, we err on what our experience tells us is probably the right side.

Example 11.7: Dentist Perry sues Delia for nonpayment of his bill for services. Delia contends that she already paid the bill. Payment will be an affirmative defense that Delia must plead and prove; that is, the burden of proof of payment is on Delia. This can be explained in several ways. While most bills are paid, most bills upon which suit is brought have not been paid; therefore, the risk of losing the case (of nonpersuasion) is on Delia, for according to the probabilities she most likely did not pay. It can also be said that once the admitted obligation arose, it is more likely that it continued than that it was changed by Delia's payment, although this argument is much stronger for more unusual changes like accord and satisfaction. Finally, this example fits the (somewhat discredited) theory that one should not have the burden of proving a negative; it is far easier for Delia to prove that she paid, with a receipt or cancelled check, than for Perry to prove that she did not, a "nontransaction" for which no "nonreceipts" are issued.

Note that although in the case of payment the burden is usually allocated according to the probabilities for litigated contracts rather than for contracts in general, in some instances the probability used will be that for general, unlitigated circumstances. There is no apparent basis for this difference.

d. Discredited bases. There are at least two supposed bases for allocation of the burden of proof that recent commentators have rejected. As shown below, outright rejection of both may be a bit hasty.

Proving a negative. Examples 11.6 and 11.7, the defamation and payment cases, illustrate a supposed basis for allocation that is misleading and often misunderstood. It is said that a party should not be given the burden of proving the negative of a proposition. Often it is more difficult to prove

246

something did not happen or exist than to prove that it did. (How does Pearl prove she did not cheat at cards, even if she did not? It is probably much easier for Damon to prove that she did cheat, if indeed she did and she was caught at it.) Nevertheless, it is almost always possible to frame a proposition in either a positive or negative way ("Pearl cheated" is the same as "Pearl did not play fairly"), and so most commentators dismiss this "rule" of allocation as unhelpful or misleading.

___ *Essential element.*   Another common statement is that the respective parties must prove the essential elements of their claim or defense. This test has even been officially codified (see, e.g., CEC 500). The problem, as many have pointed out, is that while this statement is true, it does not tell us what are those "essential elements." (Is falsity an essential element of a defamation claim, or is truth an essential element of one's defense?) In this way, it begs the question. Nevertheless, once we learn the essential elements, under this maxim the burdens of proof will follow.

2.   How to Tell How Burdens are Allocated

It is one thing to propose theories of allocation and quite another to determine how (under any theory) a particular allocation has been made. In Example 11.7, how do we know, other than by finding a precedent, who must prove payment or nonpayment? While there are no foolproof rules, there are some good starting points.

___ *Statutory allocation.*   The easiest way to determine who has the burden of proof is to find a statute that expressly allocates it on specific issues. Sometimes a substantive statute does so; sometimes the allocation is found in the rules of evidence; but in most cases there is no such legislative guidance and one must resort to imprecise generalities, such as those which follow.

___ *Proving follows pleading.*   In most instances, if one knows the burden of pleading, the burden of proof will be the same. Thus, if under state law Delia must plead payment in order for it to be an issue in the case, most likely (but not necessarily) she also has the burden of proving it. Of course, if one does not know the burden of pleading, this rule is of no help.

"Mechanical" rules.   There are some allocation rules based on the wording of a statute or an agreement, what have been called "mechanical" rules. Generally, the plaintiff must prove the elements found in the enacting clause of a statute, even an exception that is found there; otherwise, an

exception must be proved by the defendant (that is, the party relying on it).

Example 11.8:   The hamlet of Pleasantville sues Dalton under a statute that states, "Fences in residential neighborhoods may not exceed six feet in height." Dalton's fence is seven feet in height. Under the usual formula, Pleasantville, as the one relying on the statute, will have the burden of proving not only the height of Dalton's fence, but also that Dalton lives in a residential neighborhood. If, however, the statute had read, "Fences may not exceed six feet in height; provided, however, that in nonresidential neighborhoods fences may be up to seven feet in height," the burden of proving he was in a nonresidential neighborhood, the exception to the stated rule, would be on Dalton.

Obviously, this method of determining allocation is quite arbitrary, unless we assume that the legislature, in deciding between the two forms of expression, consciously chose this one in order to implement one of the bases for allocation (policy, probability, fairness) set out earlier. Legislatures seldom do so.

Contracts also may offer a "mechanical" allocation of burdens. If in Example 11.8 Dalton had agreed in writing "not to build a fence higher than six feet," then under a mechanical test the burden would be on Pleasantville to prove the fence was higher; but if he had agreed "not to build a fence, except that a fence lower than six feet shall be permitted," proof that the fence was lower would lie with Dalton.

In a way, these mechanical methods of recognizing allocation also become a reason for allocation. That is, if there was no conscious allocation made by the legislature, then the only reason we allocate the burden to Pleasantville is simply that the statute, as constructed, tells us to. Any retrospective attribution of a more rational basis is pure fiction.

Criminal cases.   In general, it is unconstitutional to allocate to a criminal defendant any element of the charged crime. Under current Supreme Court decisions, determining what is an element of the crime and what is an affirmative defense is largely mechanical. If the statute creating the offense makes certain facts necessary for a conviction, they are elements of the crime; if a conviction can be had in the absence of a fact (or that fact's presence or absence is not inconsistent with the existence of all of the elements of the crime), the defendant can be allocated the burden of proof of that fact. The only qualification is that the offense, as then constituted, must not itself violate the constitution for permitting conviction in the absence of some constitutionally necessary element.

Standards of Proof

The quantum, or relative amount, of evidence required for a party with the burden of persuasion to prevail.

There are three general standards of proof: the *civil standard*, the *enhanced civil standard*, and the *criminal standard*.

Example 11.9: Philomena brings a lawsuit against Dwight. At the end of the case the principal issue is submitted to the jury. The jury believes that the evidence, on balance, slightly favors Philomena's position (that is, it is slightly more likely that the facts are as Philomena contends than as Dwight contends). Whether Philomena or Dwight prevails depends on the nature of the lawsuit. If it is an ordinary case of negligence, Philomena will win; if it is a special case requiring an enhanced standard, or if it is a criminal case, Philomena will lose.

The **civil standard** is simply that Philomena, as the party with the burden, must persuade the jury that her case (that is, her position as to the facts) is more likely true than not; if the jury is persuaded against Philomena's facts or is equally persuaded either way, Philomena loses. This standard usually is expressed as requiring Philomena either to prevail by a **preponderance of the evidence** — the evidence for her position must preponderate over the evidence against it — or to prevail on the **balance of probabilities.** (The latter phrase may be rejected by courts that believe verdicts should be expressed in terms of factual certainties, rather than "mere probabilities.") Although this is not a mechanical process or an exact science, it can be illustrated by the same type of diagram as is used to illustrate burdens of proof and presumptions:

0%   50%   100%

Here the left side of the scale represents no evidence of negligence, the right side absolute certainty of negligence. The midpoint, 50%, finds the jury in doubt, because the evidence seems to leave the case equally balanced (in equipoise) between Philomena and Dwight. To prevail on the civil standard, Philomena's evidence must (in the jury's mind) at least cross — even barely — that midpoint.

The **enhanced civil standard** applies whenever a court or legislature decides that more than the usual amount of proof should be required of a party to prevail on an issue. This may be because the issue is quasi-criminal and therefore it requires a standard between civil and criminal. Deportation and civil commitment proceedings are examples. The standard may also be applied because the legislature is distrustful of the evidence in a certain type of case and wants to make it more difficult for the party relying on it to prevail, unless the trier of fact is *really* convinced. An example is an attempt to contradict the apparently clear intent of a testator through extrinsic evidence. And where certain propositions are favored, perhaps with the aid of a presumption, their rebuttal may be disfavored by enhancing the standard of proof.

The enhanced civil standard is usually expressed as **clear and convincing evidence,** more impressively as clear, cogent, and convincing evidence, or less alliteratively as clear, convincing, and satisfactory evidence, and there are several other variations on this theme as well. On our theoretical scale of evidence, it would fall somewhere between 50% and 100%, although just where one cannot say.

The enhanced civil standard is sufficiently imprecise and difficult to measure that its chief value may be as a device to remind the court or jury to "be extra-careful of the evidence in this case." On the other hand, its very imprecision gives the judge broadened discretion to take the case from the jury on the grounds of failure to meet the higher standard.

The **criminal standard of proof** is, of course, "**beyond a reasonable doubt.**" Although a great deal can be and has been said about what this formula means, in truth it means just what it says: The trier of fact must entertain no doubt of the defendant's guilt that a reasonable person would consider significant. Thus, the standard does not require absolute certainty; it just requires as close to certainty as a reasonable person can expect to come.

As a matter of constitutional law, the prosecution must prove beyond a reasonable doubt every necessary element of the crime charged (*In re Winship*[1]).

Prima Facie Case

Evidence that is sufficient "at first sight" to support a verdict in a party's favor; or, evidence that is sufficient "at first sight" to support a directed verdict in the party's favor, or to invoke a presumption. The term **prima facie evidence** has the same meaning.

In this or any context, "prima facie" generally has the connotation of something that has a certain surface appearance ("at first sight" or "on its face") but is subject to further consideration and possible change. (See, e.g., *Prima Facie Presumption*.)

"Prima facie" is a term that courts love to use whenever they refer to a party having demonstrated a "sufficient case"; but they are not always clear

---

1. 397 U.S. 358 (1970).

or consistent as to the type of sufficient case they mean. The first of the above definitions, essentially "a good case *for the jury*," is the more usual and useful way to use the phrase, but one must always be cautious about whether this is the meaning intended.

Used in its first and usual sense, prima facie means sufficient evidence to satisfy the burden of producing evidence, that is, to get to the jury. Thus, in this chapter's diagrams illustrating burdens of proof and presumptions, a plaintiff who presents enough evidence to pass point A on the scale has presented prima facie evidence or a prima facie case. A better term, if one is needed, for this quantum of evidence is *legally sufficient case*.

When used in its second and less usual sense, the phrase means that one party has managed to shift the burden of production to the opposing party, either by presenting evidence that by itself warrants such a shift or by proving a basic fact and thereby invoking a presumption. On the diagram, the party has gotten past points A and B, to position 2.

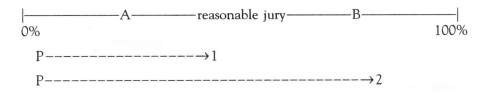

This work uses prima facie in its first and most common sense.

B. PRESUMPTIONS

Presumption (In General)

An evidentiary rule that requires the finding of one fact from the known or proven existence of some other fact, unless sufficient evidence is introduced to rebut the existence of the presumed fact.

The term "requires" in the above definition is crucial, because presumptions are regularized and mandatory processes: *Whenever* fact A is established, fact B *must* be presumed, unless and until properly rebutted. In other words, a presumption automatically shifts the burden of producing evidence with respect to a presumed fact to the opposing party. See **FRE 301.** In some jurisdictions, it even shifts the ultimate burden of persuasion to the opposing party (e.g., URE 301(a)). California has both rules, for different presumptions. CEC 603-04, 605. For purposes of the present discussion, it is assumed that, as under the FRE, a presumption merely shifts the burden of production. The effect of it shifting the burden of persuasion and the difference between these theories is discussed under *Rebuttal of Presumptions*.

In criminal cases there is some different terminology used and presumptions require a different analysis. They are thus treated separately — see *Presumptions in Criminal Cases*. This discussion assumes a civil case.

The fact that the ordinary presumption can be overcome by contrary evidence makes it a **rebuttable presumption.** The less-common term **prima facie presumption** is synonymous.

> *Example 11.10:*   Pete sues Dottie for nonpayment of rent. Dottie contends that she mailed the cash to Pete, but Pete denies receiving it. Dottie presents proof that she put the money into the mail. In many states if Dottie proves the fact of proper mailing, the fact of receipt by Pete (that is, delivery in due course to the addressee) will be presumed. As the presumption is rebuttable, it would be up to Pete then to produce evidence that the money was not received, or the judge will direct a verdict against him on that crucial issue.

The fact which, if proven, requires the finding of another fact — the fact of mailing in Example 11.10 — is called the **basic fact.** The fact required to be found — the fact of receipt — is called, naturally enough, the **presumed fact.**

The initial effect of a presumption on the issue of receipt would thus be diagrammed as follows, with position 1 being the effect of proof of mailing without the aid of the presumption, and position 2 being the effect of the same evidence with the presumption:

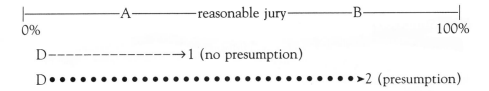

In this example it is assumed that proof of the basic fact of mailing is itself sufficient evidence to permit the jury to infer receipt, and so satisfies Dottie's burden of production. Note, however, that even if proof of the basic fact would not have satisfied Dottie's burden of production (would have left the evidence short of point A), the presumption would still have pushed it past point B and shifted the burden to Pete. It is obvious that the presumption is a powerful weapon in the evidentiary arsenal. Just how powerful depends on the effect of rebuttal evidence, discussed elsewhere. See *Rebuttal of Presumptions*.

252

Other meanings of "presumption."   At least in civil cases, there is only one true presumption, as just defined. There are, however, numerous other rules or types of evidence that have been given the name "presumption."

Inferences masquerading as "permissive presumptions."   At one extreme is the so-called **presumption of fact** (as opposed to a **presumption of law,** a true presumption as defined above) or **permissive presumption,** which is really nothing but a **permissive inference.**

Example 11.11:   Penny sues Daniel for negligent driving. Penny presents evidence that Daniel's car struck Penny in a crosswalk, the weather was clear, and there were no other cars around at the time. Penny did not see Daniel's car before she was hit, so there is no direct evidence presented of how Daniel was driving or why the car struck Penny. Upon Daniel's motion for a nonsuit, the court rules that under the circumstances, Penny has satisfied her burden of production; the jury may (but need not) infer that Daniel was driving negligently when his car struck Penny. Even if the court purports to be invoking a "presumption of fact" to derive negligence from these circumstances, all it has really done is to rule that the inference of negligence is permissible, but not mandatory, from Penny's circumstantial evidence. There is no true presumption.

Caveat: When dealing with criminal cases, the terms "mandatory presumption" and "permissive presumption" are in current use, with the approximate meanings indicated above. See *Presumptions in Criminal Cases.*

Res ipsa loquitur distinguished.   One source of confusion is the tort doctrine of **res ipsa loquitur.** Properly used, it is just a regularized form of permissive inference from circumstantial evidence, given a fancy Latin name. If a plaintiff cannot produce direct evidence of how an injury occurred, but the circumstantial facts "speak for themselves" that the defendant was most likely negligent, then under res ipsa loquitur the plaintiff satisfies the burden of production and gets to the jury.

Some courts, however, assign to the Latin phrase a more significant meaning than it was originally intended to have: that it creates a presumption of negligence. The burden of production is shifted to the defendant and the plaintiff is entitled to a directed verdict in the absence of rebutting evidence. A few courts, in some circumstances, even invoke the doctrine to shift the burden of persuasion to the defendant. This diverse usage is confusing, and it must be carefully watched for in reading cases.

Example 11.12:   Same facts as Example 11.11, except that the court decides that pedestrians are not usually struck in crosswalks in clear weather unless the driver was negligent, and therefore the facts fit the doctrine of res ipsa loquitur. The result should be the same; Penny has simply satisfied her burden of production. If, however, the court gives to res ipsa loquitur the effect of a presumption, it may direct a verdict in Penny's favor in the absence of sufficient rebutting evidence by Daniel, such as evidence that Daniel's tire blew out and caused his car to skid into the crosswalk.

Rules of law masquerading as "conclusive presumptions." At the other extreme is what is often called a **conclusive presumption,** or **irrebuttable presumption.** This usage is more common than permissive presumption (see, e.g., CEC 601, 620) and not really misleading, so long as one keeps in mind that what it means is not so much "presumption" as "conclusion" — fact A is not just *presumed* from fact B, it is finally *concluded.*

Because a conclusive presumption does not permit any rebuttal by the opposing party, it has properly and more accurately been characterized as a rule of law. That is, it is another way of stating some matter of policy or expediency that has been finally and conclusively declared.

Example 11.13: Same facts as Example 11.11 (Penny struck by Daniel's car in a crosswalk), except that Daniel is only six years old (but very precocious). A state statute provides that "a person under the age of seven is conclusively presumed incapable of committing a tort." Thus Daniel would automatically be found not to have been negligent, and Penny's case fails. The legislature has decided that, as a matter of law, young children should not be held liable for their torts, regardless of the provable capacities and actions of any individual child. This is, then, simply a legal definition of who may be sued in tort. It may, but certainly need not, be expressed in the form of a conclusive presumption.

Presumptions masquerading as something else. Many presumptions are not actually designated as such. A statute may simply say that, if fact A has occurred, the law will proceed as if fact B were true. For example, if two people die simultaneously, for certain purposes and in the absence of evidence to the contrary, the property of each is disposed of as if that person survived the other. See Example 11.18. This is as much a presumption (rebuttable or conclusive) as if it were so designated.

Basis of presumptions. The previous examples illustrate also *why* presumptions are created, which is essentially for the same reasons as burdens of proof are allocated. Fact B may, for example, be presumed from fact A because of the probability of fact B existing whenever fact A is present; because there is a strong policy favoring fact B; and/or because it is fair or procedurally expedient to consider fact B established by fact A.

Example 11.14:   Same facts as Example 11.11, except that the car that
struck Penny was driven by Daniel but is owned by Oscar. Penny
sues Oscar, alleging that Daniel was driving with Oscar's permission.
In this jurisdiction, once ownership is established, there is a presumption of permission to drive. This presumption probably is based
upon a combination of the above factors: the probability that a
driver has borrowed a car with permission rather than stolen it; the
policy of making owners (with "deep pockets" and the ability to
insure and to keep their cars out of incompetent hands) liable for
accidents involving their vehicles; and the fairness and expediency
of putting the burden of production on Oscar, who has easier access
than does Penny to evidence of how Daniel came to be driving the
car.

Most presumptions have a combination of rationales, but most derive
at least in part from probability, although a few — like the presumption
of survival in simultaneous death statutes — are based more on policy or
expediency than on probability. This heavy reliance on probability will
prove significant in the discussion of the competing theories of the effect of
presumptions. See *Rebuttal of Presumptions.*

Similarly, in Example 11.12 a policy of protecting pedestrians who are
legally crossing (or perhaps of disadvantaging jaywalkers) might explain the
presumption of negligence, as well as the probability that, when a pedestrian
in a crosswalk is struck, the driver was negligent and the fairness of making
Daniel explain what happened to make him hit Penny. And in Example
11.13 a policy against holding young children legally responsible for their
actions would lead to a presumption against negligence, and a particularly
strong policy might lead to a "conclusive" presumption — a rule of law.

Rebuttal of Presumptions

*The presentation of evidence, by a party against whom a presumption operates,
of the nonexistence of the presumed fact, which if sufficient satisfies the party's
burden of production and may totally destroy the effect of the presumption.*

Presumptions are fairly straightforward devices, and there is little disagreement over their basic operation, that is, everyone agrees that a presumption imposes on the opposing party the burden of producing evidence.
There are few controversies in the law, however, to match that which developed and is ongoing over the effect on a presumption of rebuttal evidence
presented by that opposing party.

Example 11.15:   Polly sues Damon, alleging nonpayment of a debt. Damon claims to have mailed a cash payment to Polly, but Polly denies
receiving it. Damon has the burden of production as to payment

(see Example 11.7). Damon presents evidence that the payment was mailed to Polly, from which, if believed, a reasonable jury could infer that she received it. At this point Damon has satisfied his burden of production, although the evidence probably is not so compelling as to shift the burden to Polly. Therefore the jury will decide the issue of payment from this and any other evidence in the case.

Example 11.16: Same facts as Example 11.15, except there is a *presumption* in the jurisdiction that an item placed in the mail and properly addressed with the necessary postage has been received in the ordinary course of the mail (see Example 11.10). If Damon now proves proper mailing (the basic fact), the fact of receipt will be presumed, and the burden of production will shift to Polly. If Polly does nothing, she will lose on this issue as a matter of law.

Note that this is an example of a burden of proof being placed on the defendant, and of a presumption that favors the defendant's position. The analysis is the same, of course, as for burdens and presumptions favoring the plaintiff.

The effect of the presumption so far can be illustrated as follows:

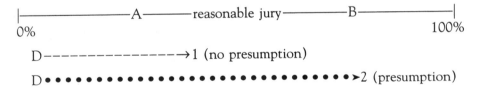

Example 11.17: Same facts as Example 11.16 (presumption of receipt), except that Polly now presents evidence to rebut the presumption, specifically her records of each item of mail received by her business each day. If this evidence meets the test of sufficiency (see below), it will at least satisfy Polly's burden of production. Its further effect on the presumption, however, will depend on the theory of presumptions applied in the jurisdiction. At the very least, as indicated, Polly will get to the jury on the issue of payment, but the presumption will have shifted the burden of persuasion to her. At the most, Polly's counterevidence will not only get her to the jury, but it will cause the presumption to disappear, leaving not a trace.

Disputing the basic fact. Note that the rebuttal discussed here is evidence disputing the presumed fact. It is also possible to dispute the basic fact that gives rise to the presumption. If only the basic fact is disputed, the court will give the jury a conditional instruction, to find the presumed fact if, but only if, it is persuaded of the existence of the basic fact. The effect of the presumption is not changed, however; it always operates only upon proof of the basic fact, and if that fact is proven, it will require a finding of the presumed fact.

How much evidence.   There is disagreement over just how much evidence Polly must produce in order to rebut Damon's presumption, except all now agree that a "scintilla" of evidence will not suffice. For present purposes, the amount can be equated to that which is necessary to avoid a directed verdict in any other circumstance: sufficient evidence to permit a reasonable jury to find against the presumed fact. This includes even seemingly weak evidence, if its weight depends on the credibility of witnesses. See *Directed Verdict.*

The competing theories.   Although there are numerous positions taken on the effect of a presumption and of its rebuttal, the two major approaches (and the only ones to concern us here) are those designated the Thayer (or Thayer-Wigmore) rule and the Morgan rule, named for their principal advocates of an earlier generation. The best way to understand the divergent positions currently taken by the federal and various state courts is to examine the reasons they have taken those positions. In greatly simplified (but necessarily somewhat lengthy) form, the competing arguments proceed as follows.

Under the **Thayer** (or **bursting bubble**) **rule,** once sufficient evidence has been presented by the opposing party, the presumption disappears, like a burst bubble, leaving no trace or effect behind. The case is in the posture it was, or would have been, in the absence of any presumption, and the burden of persuasion is unaffected. See **FRE 301.** Assuming Damon's evidence of mailing would have taken his case to the jury regardless of the presumption (see Example 11.15), Damon must convince the jury of payment on the balance of probabilities, and if the case is left evenly balanced in the jury's mind, Damon loses.

But under the **Morgan rule,** although the presumption itself disappears (is rebutted), it leaves behind a "residual" effect. This effect varies, but most commonly the presumption shifts the burden of persuasion to the opposing party. See URE 301. Thus, even though Polly has presented sufficient evidence to carry her burden of production on the issue of payment (a burden initially shifted to her by the presumption in Damon's favor), she now must convince the trier of fact on the balance of probabilities that she did not receive payment. If at the close of the case the evidence on this issue (in the jury's mind) is evenly balanced, Polly will lose. To illustrate:

Thayer rule:

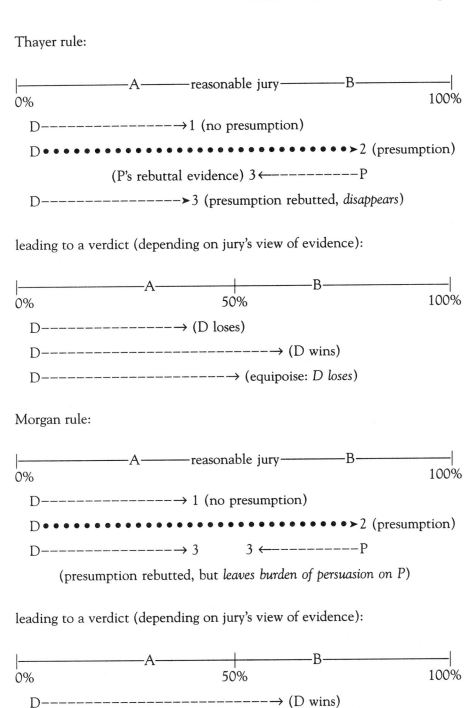

```
|——————————A———reasonable jury———————B———————|
0%                                                    100%

    D----------------→1 (no presumption)

    D•••••••••••••••••••••••••••➤2 (presumption)

            (P's rebuttal evidence) 3←----------P

    D----------------➤3 (presumption rebutted, disappears)
```

leading to a verdict (depending on jury's view of evidence):

```
|——————————A————————+————————B———————————|
0%                      50%                          100%

    D----------------→ (D loses)

    D------------------------------→ (D wins)

    D-------------------------→ (equipoise: D loses)
```

Morgan rule:

```
|——————————A———reasonable jury———————B———————|
0%                                                    100%

    D----------------→ 1 (no presumption)

    D•••••••••••••••••••••••••••➤2 (presumption)

    D----------------→ 3        3 ←----------P
```

    (presumption rebutted, but *leaves burden of persuasion on P*)

leading to a verdict (depending on jury's view of evidence):

```
|——————————A————————+————————B———————————|
0%                      50%                          100%

    D-------------------------------→ (D wins)

    D-------------------→ (D loses)

    D-------------------------→ (equipoise: D wins)
```

Reasons for difference. The basic reason for the ongoing dispute over the effect on presumptions of rebutting evidence is simply that presumptions do not appear out of thin air, but they are created for reasons (see *Presumptions (In General)*). If, it is contended, these reasons were good enough to warrant creation of the presumption in the first place, surely they are good enough to justify some continuing effect of the presumption even after counterevidence has been offered. If the presumption completely disappears simply because the opposing party has managed to come up with some (perhaps barely sufficient) evidence, it has not been given its due weight.

The answer to this assertion is, at best, "Well, yes and no." The following examples illustrate why.

Example 11.18:   Harold and Maude, husband and wife, were both killed when their small boat capsized during a storm. There were no witnesses to the tragedy. Pamela, a claimant through Harold's estate, wishes to prove that between Harold and Maude, Harold was the "survivor," that is, that Maude died before Harold. Her opponent is Derek, the executor of Harold's estate. Pamela has the initial burden of production on this issue. If, as is likely, Pamela has evidence of the accident's occurrence and the death of both Harold and Maude, but no evidence of who died first, Pamela will lose on the issue of survivorship. Ignoring (for our purposes) the essentially nonexistent possibility that the two died at the same precise millisecond in time, at best the chances are even that either Harold or Maude was the (momentary) survivor. Therefore Pamela cannot get to the jury and will lose by nonsuit.

```
|─────────────────A──── reasonable jury ──── B──────────────|
0%    P─────→ 1 (P loses)                                100%
```

But compare:

Example 11.19:   Same facts as Example 11.18, except that a common statutory presumption provides that if Harold and Maude die simultaneously, for purposes of succession to Harold's property and in the absence of evidence to the contrary, Harold will be presumed to have survived Maude. This is strictly a matter of policy and expediency, since as indicated there is no actual probability that either survived the other. It is expedient because there is usually no evidence to show who died an instant or a minute before the other, and it is good policy because there are tax and social disadvantages to leaving property to a person already deceased and unable to enjoy it. With the aid of this presumption, Pamela meets her burden of production. And because there is unlikely to be any rebuttal evidence available, Pamela prevails.

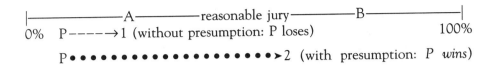

But suppose the case is slightly different:

Example 11.20: Same facts as Example 11.19, except that Derek, the opposing party, takes the stand and claims to have been in a nearby boat fishing and to have heard Maude cry for help a minute after he saw Harold go under. On cross-examination Derek cannot satisfactorily explain why he did not try to help Harold and Maude, why he did not report the incident to the police, how he could hear Maude call during such a fierce storm, or what he was doing out there in the first place. Further, he is shown to be a convicted felon and to have lied under oath on numerous previous occasions. Nevertheless, he refuses to recant, and the evidence stands for what it is worth. The court is convinced that Derek is lying, and it is sure the jury would agree; yet the matter of credibility is generally left to the jury, even when the court thinks it is clear, barring physical impossibility or outright self-contradiction. Therefore the presumption is considered "rebutted" by Derek. The effect, under the Thayer rule, is not that the issue goes to the jury, but that Pamela loses her case. Because the presumption now disappears completely, the case is left as it was at the outset: Pamela has insufficient evidence to carry her burden of production (much less her burden of persuasion) on the issue of survival.

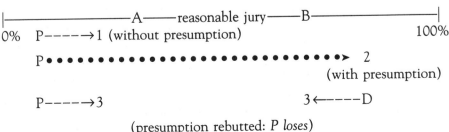

What bothers the Morgan theorists is that despite all of the sound reasons for creating the presumption of survival, Derek's attempted rebuttal by barely credible, self-serving evidence destroys it, with the result that Pamela, whose position was initially favored by the presumption, loses. Moreover, although the testimony of Derek would almost certainly be rejected by the jury, the jury will never have the chance to reject it, because Pamela has not enough evidence to get past a nonsuit.

Giving presumptions more weight. The solution to this dilemma, or at least the solution most often advocated, is to give a presumption greater effect than merely to shift the burden of production to its opponent. If a presumption also places on the opposing party the ultimate burden of persuasion, parties like Pamela will not be left without any benefit from the disappearing presumption when parties like Derek present barely-credible evidence. With the ultimate burden of persuasion on Derek to *disprove* that Harold survived, unless Derek comes up with fairly strong rebuttal evidence, Pamela wins.

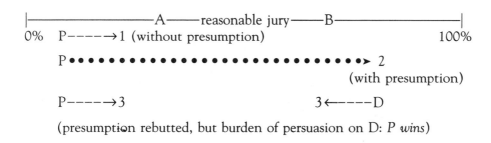

(presumption rebutted, but burden of persuasion on D: *P wins*)

But wait! The problem here exists in large part because Pamela's initial evidence (that Harold and Maude died in a common disaster) is not strong enough by itself to get Pamela to the jury on the issue of Harold's survival. Compare Example 11.16, which concerned the presumption that an item properly mailed by Damon was in due course received by Polly. Recall that for this presumption, the basic fact of mailing is itself logically probative of receipt, and the presumption is primarily based on probability, not policy. Even if the presumption of receipt is rebutted by Polly's barely-credible, self-serving testimony that she did not receive Damon's money, Damon will not likely lose. This is because even if the presumption disappears and the burden of persuasion remains on Damon, Damon's evidence, unlike Pamela's in Example 11.20, will at least get him to the jury. If, as is probable, the jury disbelieves Polly's testimony, it will find in Damon's favor. True, Damon got no help from the presumption; but because of the strong probability behind it, he needed none. The case would be diagrammed:

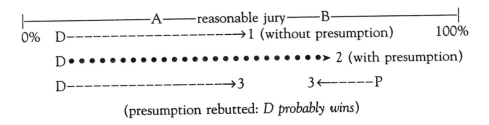

(presumption rebutted: *D probably wins*)

Of course, there is always the "in between" case, in which the basic fact provides just enough evidence to get to the jury, but not enough to prevail without "help" from the presumption. Similarly, the rebuttal evidence may be strong and credible, making it more likely that the jury will be convinced by it. In either case, one could still argue that the presumption ought to provide further assistance to the favored party. On the other hand, if the policy behind the presumption is not a particularly important one, then regardless of the strength of the rebuttal evidence perhaps the presumption should have no greater effect than Thayer's theory gives it.

Just how great is the Thayer-Morgan problem, then, depends to a great degree on the extent to which presumptions are based on probability (like mailing/receipt) or on pure policy considerations (like simultaneous death statutes), and on the strength of either the probability or the policy. As indicated earlier, most presumptions are based partly or mostly on probability; as such, they aid litigants who are nonetheless capable of at least getting to the jury without their help. A few are based solely on a strong policy, and these do need help if they are to be fully effective.

The Uniform Rules, as currently revised, take a straight Morganian approach, as did the original draft of the Federal Rules. All presumptions are declared to impose the burden of persuasion on the opposing party. See URE 301.

The Federal Rules, as finally promulgated, take what appears to be a Thayerian approach: **FRE 301** imposes the burden of production on the opposing party, but it expressly "does not shift" the burden of persuasion from the party upon whom "it was originally cast." It does not, however, necessarily forbid some of the alternatives that lie in between the two extremes, discussed below. In addition, FRE 301 does not apply if (as is often true) a federal statute creates a presumption with a different effect; and **FRE 302** applies state law as to presumptions affecting "an element of a claim or defense as to which state law provides the rule of decision." (Compare FRE 501, 601.) This means most state presumptions will apply in federal diversity (and a few other) cases. There is some controversy over whether it is a good idea for FRE 302 to distinguish so-called **"tactical presumptions"** (in the Advisory Committee's phrase) from those relating to a substantive "element of a claim or defense," and it is unclear even that federal courts make any real attempt to do so. (Compare the use of the term in criminal cases — see *Permissive Presumption (Criminal Cases)*). Certain presumptions, like those involving an automobile owner's permission to drive (see Example 11.14) or res ipsa loquitur (see Example 11.12) commonly and clearly concern an element of a claim or defense. Distinguishing some others can be difficult.

URE 302 is the state equivalent of FRE 302 — essentially its mirror image. If federal law supplies the rule of decision as to an element of a claim or defense, it also governs the effect of a presumption.

Compromises and alternatives. There is no shortage of proposals for compromise between the Thayer and Morgan approaches to presumptions. A few will be sketched here. None is perfect, and each has only a limited following.

Expressly differentiating presumptions. It can be argued that at most what is needed is a rule that adjusts the effects of a presumption according to the need to give it greater than "Thayerian" weight. California attempts to do this by expressly dividing presumptions into those that affect only the burden of production and those that also affect the burden of persuasion. Briefly, the former are those that implement no public policy other than to facilitate the determination of the present case, such as recognition of probabilities; the latter implement some other public policy, such as the validity of marriages. There is a list of examples of each type of presumption (as well as of conclusive presumptions). See CEC 601-70. Needless to say in this highly controversial area, the California approach has its admirers and detractors, as well as those who like the idea but quibble with the details.

Informal and ad hoc alternatives. Although many if not the majority of courts today purport to apply the Thayer, bursting bubble rule to presumptions, they may deviate from that rule in certain situations. Where there is a particularly strong social policy behind a presumption, a court may compromise by requiring that rebuttal evidence meet a stronger than usual standard, such as "clear and convincing" or "uncontradicted, unimpeached" evidence. They also may comment to the jury about the existence of the presumption, to alert it to the strong policy behind the bubble prior to its bursting. In cases of very strong policies, primarily the presumption of legitimacy from birth to a married woman, Thayerian courts may even impose the burden of persuasion on the party opposing the presumption, despite a general rule against this Morganian move. And some federal courts seem simply to ignore Rule 301 and shift the burden of persuasion whenever they think it appropriate.

The norm, then, is a certain amount of flexibility under the Federal

Rules and similar regimes. A jurisdiction's treatment of any particular presumption should therefore be researched and never taken for granted.

Conflicting Presumptions

Presumptions that appear to dictate conflicting outcomes on the same issue.

Example 11.21: John and Marsha were married in 1990. John has died and Marsha claims the proceeds of his retirement plan, for which she must prove she was legally married to John at his death. Son Lyle also claims the proceeds and proves that John was previously married, to Susan, in 1950. Under a common presumption, an apparently valid marriage is presumed to be in fact valid; but another common presumption provides that a marriage (or any condition) once shown to exist is presumed to continue to exist. Marsha invokes the first presumption; Lyle invokes the second. They lead to opposite results. Some way must be found to reconcile them. A way generally is found, favoring the second marriage. Either a court invokes a third presumption, that when a person has been married twice, it is presumed that the first marriage was dissolved and the second is valid; or it simply invokes the one considered to have a weightier policy behind it, in this case the presumption of a valid marriage.

An alternative to the two resolutions illustrated by Example 11.21 is that pure Thayerian principles can be applied and both presumptions can disappear. At least where significant social policies are behind one or both of the presumptions, this solution is not favored.

Presumptions in Criminal Cases (In General)

Rules applicable in criminal cases that either permit or require the finding of one fact from the proof of another.

Unlike presumptions in civil cases, those in criminal cases are divided into two types, (1) mandatory presumptions and (2) permissive presumptions. For constitutional reasons, most presumptions in criminal cases are permissive only, which means in essence that they are merely inferences. These two types of presumption are discussed in separate entries below.

When considering criminal case presumptions, one must always keep an eye on the constitutional pronouncements of the Supreme Court. Of particular importance are *In re Winship*[2] and *County Court of Ulster County v. Allen.*[3] The FRE do not address presumptions in criminal cases.

2. 397 U.S. 358 (1970).
3. 442 U.S. 140 (1979).

The discussion that follows applies only to presumptions against a criminal defendant. Presumptions against the prosecution would receive the same treatment as those in civil cases.

Permissive Presumption (Criminal Cases)

The name for a permissive inference in a criminal case, which allows but does not require the trier of fact to find one fact from the proof of another.

As discussed elsewhere in this chapter, in civil cases a presumption at least shifts the burden of production to the opposing party, who is then in danger of a directed verdict in the absence of rebutting evidence. In some jurisdictions a presumption also places or shifts the burden of persuasion. In most instances it would be unconstitutional to shift either burden to a criminal defendant. See *Mandatory Presumption (Criminal Cases)*. Nevertheless, in criminal cases the Supreme Court in *Ulster County v. Allen* chose to employ the term "permissive presumption." It should be understood to mean nothing more than a regularized form of permissive inference, like the usual effect of res ipsa loquitur in a civil case.

Example 11.22: Dena is on trial for illegal possession of an unregistered firearm. The prosecution proves that when Dena was arrested, such a firearm was found in the car she was driving. A state statute provides that the finding of a firearm in a vehicle is presumptive of its possession by anyone in that vehicle. If this statute is construed to create only a permissive presumption, the judge will instruct the jury that, upon the finding of the basic fact of presence of the firearm in the car, it *may but need not find (infer)* that the defendant was in possession of that firearm. Any indication that the jury *must* find possession from presence would make this a mandatory presumption and raise significant constitutional issues (see *Mandatory Presumption (Criminal Cases)*).

What occurs in Example 11.22 would simply be called a permissive inference in a civil case. It satisfies the prosecution's burden of production on that issue, but it does not shift the burden of production to the defendant.

Rational connection, "in context" rules. If the presumption in a criminal case is permissive only, it is constitutional if there is a **rational connection** between the basic fact and the presumed fact, and if the latter more probably than not follows from the former. In determining this, the presumption is considered in its context, taking into account the state of all the evidence. Thus, in Example 11.22, if one can say that there is a rational connection between presence and possession, and that given the fact of presence and the evidence adduced in the case the fact of possession is more likely than not, the permissive presumption is constitutionally valid. See *Ulster County v. Allen* (presumption of possession valid). Compare URE 303(b), which is almost identical with the rule approved by the Supreme Court for federal courts but rejected by Congress. It applies a reasonable doubt standard to all but "tactical presumptions," those (such as the presumption of receipt from mailing) that do not establish guilt, are not an element of the offense, and do not negative a defense.

Standard for basic fact. If the presumption is permissive, usually the basic fact need only be proved by a preponderance of the evidence. An exception would be a presumption as the sole basis for guilt. Since guilt must be found beyond a reasonable doubt, the basic fact in such a case would also have a reasonable doubt standard.

Jury instructions. The instructions to the jury should not even hint that a permissive presumption is mandatory or shifts the burden of persuasion to the defendant. Ideally, the instruction avoids the term "presumption" and anything that has the same connotation, in favor of clearly stating that the jury may draw but is not bound by the suggested inference. Indeed, some state law does not permit even the latter type of instruction, rejecting it as an improper comment on the evidence.

Mandatory Presumption (Criminal Cases)

A true presumption in a criminal case, which shifts the burden of production or persuasion to the defendant.

A so-called "mandatory" presumption is simply the ordinary rebuttable presumption encountered in civil cases (which by definition is always mandatory). A constitutionally valid mandatory presumption would be rare. The law regarding mandatory presumptions is still in doubt. At the very least, it appears that the basic fact must support the presumed fact beyond a reasonable doubt, and it must do so on its face, without regard to the evidence in the case.

Example 11.23: Drasella is convicted of knowingly possessing illegally manufactured drugs X and Y. Knowledge of illegality was presumed from her admitted possession of the drugs. Drug X has no legal uses and is commonly known to be manufactured only illegally, whereas drug Y has both legitimate and illegitimate uses and is sometimes manufactured legally. If the court finds that "on its face" — without considering the evidence in this case — the fact that a person is found with drug X supports a jury's inference beyond a reasonable doubt that the person was aware of its illegal manufacture, the mandatory presumption is valid. But if the same cannot be said of drug

Y, at least without knowing such facts of the case as where Drasella got the drug, from whom, and so forth, only a permissive presumption would be appropriate with respect to that drug.

There are, however, several aspects of mandatory presumptions that remain uncertain and much debated, primarily because many issues have been addressed only in dictum in *Allen* (which concerned a permissive presumption) and other cases and some pronouncements seem inconsistent with others. For example, some commentators doubt that any mandatory presumption that shifted the burden of persuasion as well as the burden of production would be constitutional, whereas others believe that even shifting the latter burden would be impermissible; on the other hand, *Allen* suggested that a presumption shifting to the defendant an "extremely low" burden that could be satisfied by "any" evidence might have to satisfy only the permissive presumption standards. Also, although *Allen* states that a mandatory presumption's basic fact need only be "sufficient to support an inference of guilt beyond a reasonable doubt," some cases and commentators suggest that the constitution requires a much more certain connection between the basic and presumed facts.

States may, of course, follow different approaches so long as they are within Supreme Court guidelines. Compare URE 303(b) (jury may not be directed to find a presumed fact against defendant); CEC 607 (reasonable doubt standard).

12 Judicial Notice

Introduction and Overview of Chapter

Judicial notice is not evidence at all, but rather a substitute for evidence. As such, it often is omitted from evidence courses or relegated to a few comments at the end of the term. Nevertheless, judicial notice is an important part of the adjudicative process, and the very fact that it substitutes for evidence means that one must be aware of just when the rules of evidence apply and when they do not.

This chapter begins by defining judicial notice and so-called "jury notice," which is neither evidence nor judicial notice but is a necessary part of the process of understanding and evaluating either. It then sets out the two major types of fact that can be judicially noticed, adjudicative and legislative. Separately discussed are judicial notice of law and in criminal trials, both of which follow their own peculiar patterns.

Judicial Notice

The establishment of a matter of fact by the court, without the need for formal proof.

Example 12.1: Marilyn is charged with selling liquor in her store at the corner of Sixth and Alder Streets last November 23rd and 24th, in violation of a statute that prohibits the sale "within two blocks of any school" of "any alcoholic beverage" on a day "when school is in session." The court takes judicial notice of the facts that there is a high school on the corner of Sixth and Alder Streets, and that last November 24th was Thanksgiving. These are both *adjudicative facts*, which pertain to the specific parties and issues before the court. The first is commonly known in the community and the second, whether or not commonly known, is capable of certain verification, and both are beyond reasonable dispute.

In interpreting the statute as including a high school within the definition of "school," the court takes note of the legislative history of the statute, showing an intent to include all levels of schools and to lessen the exposure of minors to alcohol. It also notes the commonly known fact that high school students are mostly minors and would be at least as likely as grammar school students to be adversely affected by a nearby source of alcohol. The court is thus taking judicial notice of *legislative facts*, those that aid the court in making or evaluating law. Adjudicative and legislative facts are discussed separately below.

Judicial notice is not a form of evidence, but it is a substitute for evidence. It is a "shortcut" to proof, providing a means by which the court can establish certain facts necessary to its or the jury's decision efficiently and without the expenditure of time and effort that formal proof entails. It can do this because either the facts involved are beyond reasonable dispute, as is generally true of noticed adjudicative facts, or the facts are a part of the lawmaking process and therefore peculiarly within the judge's control, as is true of legislative facts.

Jury Notice

That general background information that everyone is expected to bring to the fact-finding process. The facts to which jury notice refers are sometimes called simply **basic facts.**

Example 12.2:   Laurel sues Chris on a contract calling for Chris to "deliver to Laurel at the Jones Building, no less than ten tons of no. 1 grade ripe tomatoes, by November 15, 1995." It is stipulated that Chris delivered five tons of oranges on December 1, 1995. The jury will not be instructed about, but will be assumed to know, at least the following: the meaning of the English words in the contract; the difference between tomatoes and oranges; and that December 1 is after November 15. All of these are matters of jury notice. The jury will not, however, be expected to know the definition or implication of a tomato's being graded "no. 1," and for this (if it becomes an issue) the parties will have to supply evidence, as for any other fact.

Although "jury notice" is a common term for the type of background information just described, it is not so much a defined process as an informal recognition that jurors are not "blank slates." They come to the adjudicative process with pre-existing knowledge of the world and their society, and if they did not, they could not do their job as jurors. Jury notice is included here mostly to contrast it with the more formal process of judicial notice.

Generally facts subject to jury notice are taken for granted; neither parties nor the court will mention them or take any formal steps to establish them. Most evidence codes, including the Federal Rules, ignore them. Only if there is some question as to a fact or its commonality (such as the use of an obscure slang expression) will there be a need to invoke either judicial notice or formal evidentiary proof.

Of course, despite the terminology, judges sitting without a jury are presumed to have the same store of knowledge and information as jurors.

Sometimes a distinction is drawn between *communicative facts* (knowledge of language and its variants) and *evaluative facts* (knowledge of the world in which we live, the "ordinary affairs of life," necessary to understand and evaluate the facts in a case — tomatoes, oranges, and months).

There is necessarily an overlap between facts subject to formal judicial notice and those that are within jury notice. If the fact is commonly known, usually judicial notice will be invoked only if the fact is particularly at issue in the case and not just a matter of general background information. Thus if there really were a dispute over whether the fruit Chris delivered were tomatoes or oranges, the court might take judicial notice of the fact that ripe tomatoes are red in color and shiny, or it might require proof in the form of expert testimony as to the horticultural scope of the term "tomato."

Jury notice is also usually (but not necessarily) much more general than judicial notice. That water is wet, that paper burns, that certain injuries are painful, or in Example 12.2 that words have particular meaning or tomatoes have a certain appearance are matters basic to everyday living; whereas the location of the Jones Building, while probably common knowledge in the community and therefore subject to judicial notice, is not.

Jury notice, like judicial notice, must be carefully distinguished from facts uniquely known to a particular juror. These are not properly the subject of either type of notice, and they may even disqualify the juror (or judge) from sitting in the case. Juror notice encompasses that which "everyone" knows, and not that which any particular juror just happens to know.

Example 12.3:   Same facts as Example 12.2, except that juror John is a former tomato farmer who knows the meaning of the "no. 1" grade. John should have been excused on voir dire if the attorneys did not want to have a juror with pre-existing knowledge or expertise regarding the lawsuit. If he was not, it would nevertheless be improper for John to share his expertise with the other jurors, as this would go beyond the evidence offered by the parties. By the same token, it would be equally improper for juror Janet to visit the library and read about tomato grading while still sitting in the case.

Here also there is an overlap, between what a judge or juror knows as an individual and what they know in common with most others in the community. It sometimes is difficult for an individual judge or juror to determine whether facts they take for granted are equally well known to the general community.

Adjudicative Facts

Facts noticed that <u>concern only the matter litigated</u>, and that would otherwise have to be proved by the introduction of evidence by the parties. See **FRE 201**; URE 201.

Adjudicative facts are just the normal facts in issue in a lawsuit, which it has been said concern "who did what, where, when, how, and with what motive or intent." They are generally contrasted with legislative facts, which are used by a court or legislature as the basis for making or evaluating law.

Example 12.4:   Pat sues David for negligence following an automobile accident. The accident occurred as Pat was crossing Pine Street at 8 p.m. on Friday, January 3. Pat alleges that David was going the wrong way on a one-way street and that he was not using his headlights, although it was after sunset, the time after which drivers are required by law to use them. The contested issues are: (1) Was David driving the car that struck Pat? (2) In what direction was the car going? (3) Was the street one-way in the other direction? (4) Was it after sunset? (5) If so, were David's headlights on? and (6) Was David negligent? Facts 1, 2 and 5 are ordinary "historical" facts subject to the usual methods of proof, by submission of evidence of eyewitnesses, admissions, and so forth. Fact 6 is a mixed question of fact and law that can be answered only after and on the basis of the establishment of facts 1 through 5. Facts 3 and 4, although they could be proven by the same usual methods, are likely subjects of judicial notice, as adjudicative facts.

There are two types of adjudicative facts subject to judicial notice: matters of common knowledge in the community and matters of verifiable certainty. Both must be beyond reasonable dispute, so that the court can dispense with the usual need for proof and take the shortcut of judicial notice.

Common knowledge means that, in essence, "everyone knows" the noticed fact. **FRE 201(b)(1)** refers to facts "generally known within the territorial jurisdiction of the trial court." There need not, however, be universal knowledge; it will suffice that the average person in the community would know a fact, that practically everyone knows it, or even that most well-informed members of the community would know it. The community referred to is that in which the trial is being held.

In Example 12.4, fact 3, whether Pine Street is one-way and in which direction, is the only candidate for this type of judicial notice, provided it is sufficiently well-known and beyond reasonable dispute among the average well-informed citizens of the community. It would not do that, for example, Pine Street was an obscure alley known only to a few people who live on or near it, even if the judge or jurors just happened to live there. Likewise, in Example 12.1 the location of the high school would be common local knowledge.

Verifiable certainty means that the fact can be verified by easy reference to unimpeachable sources, in the language of **FRE 201(b)(2)** "capable of accurate and ready determination by resort to sources whose accuracy cannot reasonably be questioned." Common examples are scientific tables, historical and geographical references, and dictionaries. In Example 12.4, the exact time the sun set that day is a fact capable of verification by unimpeachable sources. The same is true of the date of Thanksgiving in Example 12.1. (Whether or not school is in session on Thanksgiving in that community might be both a verifiable certainty and sufficiently commonly known to be noticed under the previous heading.)

Binding on jury. There has, over the years, been some disagreement as to whether, once judicial notice is taken, a jury must accept it, or whether they can find that the facts are otherwise. Because judicial notice is generally taken only of (adjudicative) facts that are indisputable, it follows that once it is taken, neither the parties nor the jury should be allowed to dispute those facts. Thus, most courts instruct a jury that facts judicially noticed must be accepted as true, at least in civil cases. See **FRE 201(g).** (With respect to criminal cases, see below.) Those few jurisdictions that take notice of *almost* indisputable facts may permit juries to reject noticed facts, in effect relegating judicial notice to the status of a rebuttable presumption.

Presentation of Evidence. Judicial notice, once taken, is binding on the parties as well as the jury. They are not permitted to dispute a fact, as by the presentation of evidence or argument to the jury, once the fact has been judicially noticed. This does not mean that parties have no opportunity to contest either the taking or the tenor of notice; the problem is one of timing. As noted below, parties will usually be given an opportunity to argue for or against the taking of notice and the content of any notice taken, but that argument is to the judge, not to the jury. Once notice is taken and the opportunity to change the judge's mind has passed, the parties as well as the jury (or judge) are bound by the noticed facts.

Procedure. A court generally may take judicial notice either on its own motion or when requested by a party. If requested and supplied with appropriate source material, the court may be *required* to take notice, as under **FRE 201(d).** Under the Federal Rules, parties are not entitled to prior notification or any formal hearing before judicial notice is taken, although when notice is by request of a party this should serve as notification to the opposing parties. Some states do require prior notice and opportunity to be heard. See CEC 455.

Although there is no provision for prior notification, once judicial notice is taken, **FRE 201(e)** requires that upon timely request parties be given an opportunity to be heard as to the "propriety" of taking notice and the "tenor" of the notice taken. As under FRE 104(a), the rules of evidence do not apply to such a hearing.

The court may use any source it considers reliable in deciding whether to take judicial notice. Of course, the parties are free to supply the judge with whatever information they believe supports their position.

Timing. Judicial notice can be taken at virtually any juncture in a trial, from pre-trial proceedings to appeal. See **FRE 201(f).** An appellate court usually can take notice of whatever could have been noticed by the trial court, whether or not the trial court did so. It also, of course, can review the propriety of the notice that was taken below. Parties can request notice at any stage of the proceedings, although a failure to request it at trial may cause it to be untimely on appeal.

Criminal Trials. There are several respects in which judicial notice may be treated differently in criminal and civil trials. Most stem from constitutional considerations, in particular an accused's Sixth Amendment right to trial by jury, or simply a concern for fairness.

The primary difference between civil and criminal judicial notice is that the latter may not be considered binding on the jury, despite its being nominally "indisputable." This is the position of the Federal Rules (**FRE 201(g)**) and of some states. Many states, however, and the Uniform Rules (URE 201(g)) do not draw this distinction, making both civil and criminal notice binding. Some states take a middle position, permitting a jury to reject only those noticed facts that favor the prosecution.

Federal courts usually will decline to permit post-trial notice of adjudicative facts in jury trials of criminal cases.

Judicial notice of law. Traditionally a court would take judicial notice of domestic law, that is, the law of its own jurisdiction, but not of foreign law, which had to be proven as a fact. Today most state courts, under the **Uniform Judicial Notice of Foreign Law Act** or a variant of it, will notice the case law and statutes of their own state and of sister states, as well as federal law. Federal courts will notice federal law and that of all states. Taking notice may be mandatory or permissive, with many states making notice of domestic law mandatory and sister-state law permissive or subject to a requirement of reasonable notification by the party desiring it. See, e.g., CEC 451-53. If sister-state law is not or cannot be noticed, it must be pleaded and proved, and failing this courts generally presume it is identical to domestic law. A lesser level of notice might also apply to municipal ordinances and administrative regulations.

As for the law of foreign nations, this was traditionally the least likely noticed, and it still is treated as a fact to be proved in most states. Some states, however, do take notice of foreign law, as do federal courts under FRCP 44.1 and FRCrP 26.1. As in the case of sister-state law, if foreign law is not proved as a fact, the court may presume it is the same as domestic law, at least if the foreign country has a common-law system or the rule invoked has a common-law counterpart.

Legislative Facts

Facts noticed for the purpose of aiding the court in making or evaluating law.

Example 12.5: Nancy is injured by a drill press manufactured by Mass Production Co. (MPC). She cannot prove MPC was negligent in manufacturing the press, but she argues that strict liability principles should apply and MPC should be liable if Nancy can prove that the drill press had a manufacturing defect. This is a case of first impression in the state. After the trial court denies Nancy's claim, she appeals to the state's court of appeals. In deciding to permit a strict liability claim, the appellate court takes judicial notice of the legislative facts that (1) products injure many people every year; (2) it often is difficult or impossible for injured consumers to prove negligent manufacture, even if it exists; (3) this difficulty is largely due to the methods of production and marketing used by manufacturers; and (4) manufacturers are in a better position than consumers to bear the cost of such injuries and to spread it among all consumers through insurance and pricing.

Legislative facts are distinguished from adjudicative facts, which aid the trier of fact in adjudicating the matter in issue, and which relate to that specific matter. If in Example 12.5 the court had decided to adopt strict liability only for "inherently dangerous" products, it (or the trial court on remand) might further have taken judicial notice of the adjudicative fact that a drill press of the size and description of that which injured Nancy is indeed inherently dangerous. If so, the court would have been noticing a fact not to aid its lawmaking function, but to help it apply that law to the specific facts of the case before it.

Note that in Example 12.5 it was the appellate court that took judicial notice of the legislative facts. This is the most common situation, since appellate courts are more often in a position to "make law" than are trial courts, and they are also more likely to refer expressly to their having taken such notice.

Evaluating law. Legislative facts are used by courts not only to make law, but also to interpret or evaluate law made by the legislature. Thus in Example 12.1, the court took judicial notice of the effect of selling alcohol near a high school and of a statute's legislative history in interpreting the legislature's use of the term "school."

Disputability. Unlike adjudicative facts, legislative facts need not be indisputable for judicial notice of them to be taken.

Example 12.6: Same facts as Example 12.5, raising the issue of strict products liability, except a dissenting judge argues that, in his view, consumers are much better bearers of the cost of non-negligent injuries than are manufacturers, who would not be able to raise prices sufficiently to cover the cost of lawsuits under a strict liability regime. He further contends that manufacturers will have much more difficulty insuring against such lawsuits than the majority would have us believe. These "facts," of course, are totally contrary to those on which the majority opinion rested. Both sides probably would concede that reasonable persons could hold either view. Which version of these disputed legislative facts is noticed depends ultimately not on its certainty but on the number of votes it has.

This ability to notice disputable legislative facts is vital to the lawmaking process, because it allows the law to grow and to change even if the facts underlying it are still unsettled or are subject to reasonable differences of interpretation. Thus, another court might agree with the dissent in our case, still another adopt a third version of the facts, and so the law evolves. Even the same court may change its mind about legislative facts, or find that they have indeed changed over time. One of the best examples of this process is the Supreme Court's decisions in *Hawkins v. United States*[1] and

1. 358 U.S. 74 (1958).

United States v. Trammel.[2] In *Hawkins,* the Court found that making both spouses holders of a privilege to prevent adverse spousal testimony best served to preserve marital harmony; but 22 years later the Court decided that only the testifying spouse should hold the privilege, because if one spouse was willing to testify against the other, there was little left of the marriage to preserve. One of the justices in *Trammel* pointed out that he had said as much 22 years earlier, concurring in *Hawkins.* Obviously either the nature of marriage had changed, or the Court's view of that legislative fact had changed, or both.

A court can use any available source for legislative facts. It may or may not seek party input as to the social, political, or practical implications of its decision. The most famous example of such a submission is a **Brandeis brief,** named for the extensive compilation of statistical, empirical, and sociological data respecting working hours for women that was submitted to the Supreme Court by (later-Justice) Louis Brandeis in *Muller v. Oregon.*[3]

The Federal Rules contain no rules or guidelines respecting judicial notice of legislative facts. FRE 201 is expressly limited to notice of adjudicative facts. Federal courts are thus left to take whatever steps they deem appropriate in noticing legislative facts.

2. 445 U.S. 40 (1980).
3. 208 U.S. 412 (1908).

Master Word List

Federal Rules of
Evidence List